"*Global Food Security: What Matters?* is a timely textbook on a topic that remains of utmost importance. University students and scholars gain tools and knowledge toward an understanding of how food security and food systems are related, with essential country case studies that are truly global in scope."

— **Dr Shenggen Fan**, *Director General, IFPRI (International Food Policy Research Institute), Washington, USA*

"Zhang-Yue Zhou's *Global Food Security: What Matters?* is an amazingly complete and comprehensive reference textbook on the subject of food security in the world today. It covers every aspect and dimension of the subject from history, concepts, and experience to challenges, policy, and institutions in an easy-to-understand way. What makes the book outstanding is also the clear conceptual presentation of policy choices and their consequences and impacts, with numerous real-country examples from across the world. I very strongly recommend this book as a complete international text and reference book on food security, as well as the related food policies and economics."

— **Vasant P. Gandhi, PhD (Stanford)**, *NABARD Chair Professor, Centre for Management in Agriculture, Indian Institute of Management, Ahmedabad, India*

"The issue of secure food supply across the world is often presented and explained in parts. The author has done an immense service by tackling the issue of global food security in a whole system, multi-disciplinary way, taking careful note of all the dimensions and influences involved in determining the access to daily food, or lack of it, of people all around the world. Solutions to parts are not solutions to wholes: this multi-dimensional problem of food security can only be understood, explained, and solved using the comprehensive perspective presented in this extremely useful work.

Global Food Security: What Matters? is a masterly primer with a whole-of-system, global perspective. It is a comprehensive work providing readers with a useful and useable understanding of the detail and principles – all that matters – about the scientific, economic, and institutional factors that determine the current state and future of world food supply and demand.

This succinct, well-written book leads readers through the meaning, detail, determinants, and solutions to problems of the current state of global food security. Readers are introduced, almost by stealth, to understanding the key economic principles at play. The importance of institutions and politics to causing problems of food security, and solving them, is prominent, while detailed carefully chosen case studies make the book an invaluable pedagogical source."

— **Dr Bill Malcolm**, *Associate Professor, Department of Agriculture and Food Systems, University of Melbourne, Australia*

"Food security is a hot topic at public policy debates in many countries due to its importance in national security, agricultural and rural development, general welfare of the population, poverty alleviation, and more. As such, it has stimulated interest across different population groups. This book certainly meets the needs of a large audience, especially that of non-professionals.

It provides a comprehensive and quite complete review of the evolution of the concept of food security, a set of widely accepted measurements of food security, and a detailed comparative analysis of the status of food security across the globe, as well as major reasons behind the disparity of food security among nations and regions. The contents of the book will help readers understand fundamental information regarding food security, and the book also provides very useful information for those who are interested in further study in the field."

— **Dr Funing Zhong**, *Distinguished Professor, College of Economics and Management, Nanjing Agricultural University, China*

Global Food Security

This book looks at food security from a socio-economic perspective. It offers a detailed and systematic examination of food security from its historical backgrounds, concepts and measurements, to the determinants and approaches to achieve food security. The book also introduces the key challenges and root causes of food insecurity.

Through country-specific cases, the book highlights instances of both successful and disastrous national food security management and their outcomes. The invaluable learning experiences of these countries shed light on food security practices, and the straightforward demand-supply framework effectively guides readers in understanding food security issues.

This is an essential resource for anyone who is keen to learn more about food security, particularly researchers and university students who are new to the field. The book endeavours to help us reflect on the current phenomenon and strategise better for the future.

Zhang-Yue Zhou is a Professor at the College of Business, Law, and Governance at James Cook University, Australia. He is Founding Director of the Asian Agribusiness Research Centre at the University of Sydney and the Centre for AusAsia Business Studies at James Cook University. His recent publications include *Food Insecurity in Asia: Why Institutions Matter* and *Achieving Food Security in China: The Challenges Ahead*.

Routledge Textbooks in Environmental and Agricultural Economics

Economics and Management of the Food Industry
Jeffrey H. Dorfman

Rural Wealth Creation
Edited by John L. Pender, Thomas G. Johnson, Bruce A. Weber and J. Matthew Fannin

Economics of Agricultural Development
World Food Systems and Resource Third Edition
George W. Norton, Jeffrey Alwang and William A. Masters

Agricultural Policy in the United States
Evolution and Economics
James L. Novak, James Pease and Larry Sanders

Agribusiness Management 5th Edition
Freddie L. Barnard, Jay T. Akridge, Frank J. Dooley, John C. Foltz and Elizabeth A. Yeager

Principles of Agricultural Economics
Second Edition
Andrew Barkley and Paul W. Barkley

An Introduction to Climate Change Economics and Policy
Second Edition
Felix R. FitzRoy and Elissaios Papyrakis

Environmental Economics
Shunsuke Managi and Koichi Kuriyama

Energy Economics
Peter M. Schwarz

US Agricultural and Food Policies
Economic Choices and Consequences
Gerald D. Toland, Jr., William Nganje, and Raphael Onyeaghala

Global Food Security
What Matters?
Zhang-Yue Zhou

For more information about this series, please visit www.routledge.com/Routledge-Textbooks-in-Environmental-and-Agricultural-Economics/book-series/TEAE

Global Food Security

What Matters?

Zhang-Yue Zhou

Routledge
Taylor & Francis Group

LONDON AND NEW YORK

First published 2020
by Routledge
2 Park Square, Milton Park, Abingdon, Oxon OX14 4RN

and by Routledge
52 Vanderbilt Avenue, New York, NY 10017

Routledge is an imprint of the Taylor & Francis Group, an informa business

British Library Cataloguing-in-Publication Data
A catalogue record for this book is available from the British Library

Library of Congress Cataloging-in-Publication Data
Names: Zhou, Zhang-Yue, author.
Title: Global food security : what matters? / Zhang-Yue Zhou.
Description: First Edition. | New York : Routledge, 2019. | Series: Routledge textbooks in environmental and
agricultural economics | Includes bibliographical references and index.
Identifiers: LCCN 2019032998 (print) | LCCN 2019032999 (ebook) | ISBN 9781138222748 (hardback) | ISBN
9781138222793 (paperback) | ISBN 9781315406947 (ebook)
Subjects: LCSH: Food security. | Food supply. | Food industry and trade.
Classification: LCC HD9000.5 .Z46 2019 (print) | LCC HD9000.5 (ebook) | DDC 338.1/9--dc23
LC record available at https://lccn.loc.gov/2019032998
LC ebook record available at https://lccn.loc.gov/2019032999

ISBN: 978-1-138-22274-8 (hbk)
ISBN: 978-1-138-22279-3 (pbk)
ISBN: 978-1-315-40694-7 (ebk)

Typeset in Sabon
by Swales & Willis, Exeter, Devon, UK

To my wife, Jihong

Contents

Contents

Figures

Tables

Tables

Boxes

Preface

As an introduction to food security, this book is written for both undergraduate and postgraduate students who have little prior exposure to the concept of food security but are keen to grasp its fundamentals. The book follows an intuitive framework that is based on food demand and supply and how they can be balanced in order to improve a country's food security.

Demand and supply are economic concepts. However, it is not essential for one to have prior knowledge of economics to use this book. Elementary economic concepts, where necessary, are explained in plain language in the text. Some useful discussions or proofs are presented in appendixes for those with economic knowledge to explore. As such, this book is reader-friendly for others who are interested in food security, e.g., government officials who administer food security or researchers who have just stepped into this important field. It can also serve as a useful resource for short training courses/workshops to help participants to get familiar with some fundamentals of food security.

What is food security? "Food security exists when all people, at all times, have physical and economic access to sufficient, safe and nutritious food that meets their dietary needs and food preferences for an active and healthy life", according to the Rome Declaration on World Food Security adopted at the 1996 World Food Summit. Food is a matter of life and death. It has an immediate appeal to deep-rooted human feelings. One key feature of food is that it has to be obtained within much stricter time constraints than many other necessities of life.

Since 1996, pledges have been made at various world food summits to achieving food security for all. So, what is the status of food security today? According to the latest statistics by the United Nations, the proportion of the global population that is food insecure is still over 10% in the late 2010s. This means out of every ten persons on the planet, one person is undernourished. Globally, the total number of the undernourished is over 800 million!

Ironically, the amount of food produced in recent decades has been more than enough to feed all the people on the planet. The UN data show that, at the global level, the supply of calories has been adequate and improving. The current calorie supply represents a major improvement compared to that of the early 1990s.

Hence, it is not that we human beings cannot produce enough but it is that sufficient food is not made available to, and cannot be accessed by, all those in need. As such, there is a strong need to understand what affects the demand for and the supply of food and how demand and supply can be adequately balanced at various levels, from global, through national, regional, and household levels, to individual levels. This text helps the reader to understand and focus on how to balance food demand and supply at the global and national levels.

There are six parts to this text. Part 1 introduces the reader to the concept of food security and the frameworks used to evaluate food security. It also provides an overview of the current status of global food security. The overview prompts the necessity to grasp food security fundamentals as presented in the rest of the text. Parts 2 and 3 address major factors that affect the demand for and the supply of food. Understanding how such factors work helps devise measures to balance food demand and supply as dealt with in Part 4. Part 4 first discusses many measures used at the national level to balance food demand and supply. It then highlights the efforts at the international level to facilitate national governments to manage their food demand and supply balance. Part 5 shows country experiences in their quest for food security and examines the causes for food security differences between countries. The final part, Part 6, brings all the threads together and points out that ultimately the quality of a country's institutions determines its level of food security. It goes further to say that, of all institutions, the strength of governmental institutions is most important to success or failure in achieving a country's food security.

The text can be used for one-semester courses at both the undergraduate and postgraduate levels. For undergraduate students, instructors may find the contents of the text are adequate. For students at postgraduate levels, instructors may encourage them to also tackle those "Discussion Questions" for which some research will be needed. For classes that have undertaken prior studies in economics, some materials from chapter appendixes, especially the appendix in Chapter 9, can be discussed, and students are challenged to analyse the impacts and consequences of some policy measures used by their governments in food security management.

Zhang-Yue Zhou
Townsville, Australia
28 June 2019

Acknowledgements

I record my sincere thanks to the following colleagues and students, friends, and Routledge staff for all the generous support they gave me during the preparation of this manuscript.

- My colleagues and PhD students at James Cook University for discussing and clarifying various ideas on numerous occasions: (Jane) Tingzhen Chen, Haipeng Jin, Van Le, (Lidia) Jing Li, Luke Neal, Dao Nguyen, Chung Phan, Sizhong Sun, Riccardo Welters, (Carter) Ding Xu, Samira Zare. Haipeng Jin and Chung Phan provided assistance to collect data, produce tables, and draw graphs. Sizhong Sun helped to simulate the relationships between income elasticities and income level. Riccardo Welters read parts of the manuscript and had discussions with me on concepts and terms on many occasions.
- Academics and industry practitioners who read and commented on parts of the manuscript, provided data and information, or answered my questions: Vasant Gandhi (NABARD Chair Professor and Chairman of the Centre for Management in Agriculture, Indian Institute of Management in Ahmedabad), Brad Gilmour (Distinguished Fellow, Asia Pacific Foundation of Canada), Yi Hu (Principal Research Officer, Advanced Analytical Centre, James Cook University, Australia), Morris Namoga (Managing Director, NQS Direct Limited, Solomon Islands), Joo-Ho Song (Senior Economist, GS&J Institute, South Korea), Tichaona Pfumayaramba (Agricultural Economist, Queensland Department of Agriculture and Fisheries, Townsville), Weiming Tian (Professor of China Agricultural University in Beijing), Ziping Wu (Principal Agricultural Economist, Agri-Food and Biosciences Institute, Belfast).
- My "personal editor", John Mullen (Distinguished Fellow, Australasian Agricultural and Resource Economics Society), for kindly reading and editing my manuscript, with his over four decades of expertise in food and agricultural research. Dr Mullen has been the first reader of my book manuscripts for the past several years. He has been very patient with my style of writing, given me hints of perspectives to improve my manuscript, which otherwise I would have not had a chance to contemplate, and offered me – in Mullen's forthright manner – many valuable and constructive comments and suggestions to improve my writing. Dr Mullen has helped to make my books more readable.
- To write this book, while my earlier research has been beneficial, I have also benefited enormously from a project on Asia's food security. The project, for which I was the leader, was funded by the Asian Development Bank and accomplished in 2016 by a team of experts from countries in Asia and other continents. Country research on India (Vasant Gandhi, NABARD Chair Professor and Chairman of the Centre for Management in Agriculture, Indian Institute of Management in Ahmedabad), Israel (Miri Endeweld, Head of the Economic Research Department in the Research and Planning Administration of the

National Insurance Institute of Israel, and Jacques Silber, Professor Emeritus of Economics at Bar-Ilan University, Israel), Japan (Akihiko Hirasawa, General Manager/Senior Chief Economist, Norinchukin Research Institute), and North and South Korea (Joo-Ho Song, Senior Economist, GS&J Institute, South Korea, and Taejin Kwon, Director, Center for North Korean and Northeast Asian Studies at GS&J Institute, South Korea) was extremely valuable in enriching the case studies of this book. The acquaintances established through this international collaboration also enabled me to carry out field investigations for the writing of this book in Israel and Japan in 2017. Dr Miri Endeweld helped me to meet individuals from both government departments and non-governmental organisations who work on food security related matters in Israel. Dr Akihiko Hirasawa arranged a very carefully thought-through visit program for me, which allowed me to meet farmers in Japan's food-producing regions, village leaders, food traders, food processors, researchers in universities and research institutions, and officials of various government departments at various levels. Professor Jacques Silber showed me major agricultural areas in Northern Israel and a kibbutz – an Israeli-style agricultural cooperative.

- My university, James Cook University, under its Special Studies Program (SSP), granted me a six-month period of leave to work on the book in the first half of 2017. The funding support through the SSP also enabled me to conduct field work in several countries that are included as country cases in this book; that is, China, Israel, Japan, and the Netherlands.
- Staff at Routledge for their professional and skilful support in bringing this text to publication. Yongling Lam, Book Editor for Business Management and Economics, encouraged me and had faith in me writing this text. Samantha Phua, Senior Editorial Assistant, provided assistance all the way through during the preparation of the book manuscript. It is absolutely a great pleasure to work with both Yongling Lam and Samantha Phua.

Abbreviations

ADB	the Asian Development Bank
ADER	average dietary energy requirements
ADESA	average dietary energy supply adequacy
APTERR	the ASEAN Plus Three Emergency Rice Reserve
ASEAN	Association of Southeast Asian Nations
ASTI	Agricultural Science and Technology Indicators
b	billion
CGIAR	Consultative Group on International Agricultural Research
CPI	Corruption Perception Index
DES	dietary energy supply
DWL	deadweight loss
ECOWAS	the Economic Community of West African States
EIU	the Economist Intelligence Unit
EU	the European Union
FAO	Food and Agriculture Organization
GDP	gross domestic product
GFSI	Global Food Security Index
GHI	Global Hunger Index
GOI	the Government of India
IDR	import dependence ratio
IEF	the Index of Economic Freedom
IFPRI	International Food Policy Research Institute
IMF	International Monetary Fund
k	1000
kt	1000 tonnes
kcal	kilocalories
m	million
mt	million tonnes
NGO	non-governmental organisation
PDS	the Public Distribution System, India
PPP	purchasing power parity
PoU	prevalence of undernourishment
R&D	research and development
RDI	recommended daily intake
SAARC	South Asian Association for Regional Cooperation
SAG	share of agricultural GDP

Abbreviations

SOFI	*Status of Food Insecurity*
SSR	self-sufficiency ratio
t	tonne
TARWR	total actual renewable water resources
UK	the United Kingdom
UN	the United Nations
US	the United States
WFP	World Food Programme
WHO	World Health Organization
WTO	World Trade Organization

Food security and related variables (2017 unless otherwise indicated)

Country	Global Food Security Index (GFSI) Score	Corruption Perception Index (CPI) Score	Democracy Index (DI) Score	The Index of Economic Freedom (IEF) Score	TARWR per inhabitant (2011) m³	Total land area (2016) 1000 km²	Arable land out of total land (2015) %	Per capita arable land ha	Total population Million persons	Population density Persons per km²	Per capita (GDP) (PPP) $, current international Score	GINI index Score	Poverty headcount ratio at $1.90 a day %	The year of data for GINI index and poverty headcount ratio
Algeria	51.5	33.0	35.6	46.5	324	2381.7	3.1	0.19	41.3	17	15260	27.6	0.5	2011
Angola	33.2	19.0	36.2	48.5	7544	1246.7	3.9	0.18	29.8	24	6644	42.7	30.1	2008
Argentina	67.3	39.0	69.6	50.4	19968	2736.7	14.3	0.90	44.3	16	20785	41.4	0.7	2014
Australia	83.3	77.0	90.9	81.0	21764	7682.3	6.0	1.93	24.6	3	48460	34.7	0.5	2010
Austria	81.6	75.0	84.2	72.3	9236	82.5	16.3	0.16	8.8	107	52398	30.5	0.7	2015
Azerbaijan	57.8	31.0	26.5	63.6	3727	82.7	23.4	0.20	9.9	119	17398	16.6	0.0	2005
Bahrain	68.6	36.0	27.1	68.5	88	0.8	2.1	0.00	1.5	1936	47527			
Bangladesh	39.7	28.0	54.3	55.0	8153	130.2	59.6	0.05	164.7	1265	3869	32.1	19.6	2010
Belarus	63.0	44.0	31.3	58.6	6068	202.9	28.0	0.60	9.5	47	18837	26.7	0.0	2015
Belgium	79.8	75.0	77.8	67.8	1702	30.3	27.4	0.07	11.4	376	47840	27.7	0.0	2015
Benin	39.6	39.0	56.1	59.2	2900	112.8	23.9	0.26	11.2	99	2272	47.8	49.6	2015
Bolivia	51.3	33.0	54.9	47.7	61707	1083.3	4.1	0.42	11.1	10	7560	46.7	6.4	2015
Botswana	59.4	61.0	78.1	70.1	6027	566.7	0.7	0.18	2.3	4	16988	60.5	18.2	2009
Brazil	67.7	37.0	68.6	52.9	41865	8358.1	9.6	0.39	209.3	25	15484	51.3	3.4	2015
Bulgaria	62.9	43.0	70.3	67.9	2861	108.6	32.3	0.49	7.1	65	20948	37.4	1.5	2014
Burkina Faso	33.1	42.0	47.5	59.6	737	273.6	21.9	0.33	19.2	70	1862	35.3	43.7	2014

(continued)

Country	Global Food Security Index (GFSI) Score	Corruption Perception Index (CPI) Score	Democracy Index (DI) Score	The Index of Economic Freedom (IEF) Score	TARWR per inhabitant (2011) m³	Total land area (2016) 1000 km²	Arable land % of total land (2015) %	Per capita arable land (2015) ha	Total population Million persons	Population density Persons per km²	Per capita (GDP)(PPP) $, current international	GINI index Score	Poverty headcount ratio at $1.90 a day %	The year of data for GINI index and poverty headcount ratio
Burundi	25.1	22.0	23.3	53.2	1462	25.7	46.7	0.12	10.9	423	734	38.6	71.7	2013
Cambodia	43.3	21.0	36.3	59.5	33282	176.5	21.5	0.24	16.0	91	4009	46.6	23.8	2014
Cameroon	41.6	25.0	36.1	51.8	14254	472.7	13.1	0.27	24.1	51	3715	34.0	0.5	2013
Canada	82.2	82.0	91.5	78.5	84483	9093.5	4.8	1.22	36.7	4	46705	43.3	38.4	2011
Chad	28.3	20.0	15.0	49.0	3731	1259.2	3.9	0.35	14.9	12	1941	47.7	1.3	2015
Chile	74.7	67.0	78.4	76.5	53387	743.5	1.8	0.07	18.1	24	24635	42.2	0.7	2015
China	63.7	41.0	31.0	57.4	2060	9388.2	12.7	0.09	1386.4	148	16807	51.1	4.5	2015
Colombia	60.1	37.0	66.7	69.7	45432	1109.5	1.5	0.04	49.1	44	14473	42.1	77.1	2015
Congo, Dem Rep	25.5	21.0	16.1	56.4	18935	2267.1	3.1	0.09	81.3	36	887	48.4	1.5	2012
Costa Rica	69.3	59.0	78.8	65.0	23778	51.1	4.5	0.05	4.9	96	17073	41.5	28.2	2015
Cote d'Ivoire	42.5	36.0	39.3	63.0	4026	318.0	9.1	0.13	24.3	76	3936	25.9	0.0	2015
Czech Republic	75.8	57.0	76.2	73.3	1248	77.2	40.6	0.30	10.6	137	36327	28.2	0.2	2015
Denmark	80.3	88.0	92.2	75.1	1077	42.3	56.0	0.41	5.8	137	51364	44.7	1.9	2015
Dominican Rep	54.8	29.0	66.6	62.9	2088	48.3	16.6	0.08	10.8	223	16030	46.0	3.4	2015
Ecuador	55.2	32.0	60.2	49.3	28938	248.4	4.3	0.07	16.6	67	11587	31.8	1.3	2015
Egypt	56.6	32.0	33.6	52.6	694	995.5	2.9	0.03	97.6	98	11584	40.6	1.9	2015
El Salvador	53.1	33.0	64.3	64.1	4052	20.7	36.2	0.12	6.4	308	8006	39.1	26.7	2015
Ethiopia	33.3	35.0	34.2	52.7	1440	1000.0	15.1	0.15	105.0	105	1899	36.7	1.4	2013
Fiji		58.5	63.4	32892	18.3	9.0	0.18	0.9	50	9555	27.1	0.0	2015
Finland	81.0	85.0	90.3	74.0	20427	303.9	7.4	0.41	5.5	18	44866			

Country	Global Food Security Index (GFSI) Score	Corruption Perception Index (CPI) Score	Democracy Index (DI) Score	The Index of Economic Freedom (IEF) Score	TARWR per inhabitant (2011) m³	Total land area (2016) 1000 km²	Arable land out of total land (2015) %	Per capita arable land (2015) ha	Total (2015) population Million persons	Population density Persons per km²	Per capita (GDP) (PPP) $, current international	GINI index Score	Poverty headcount ratio at $1.90 a day %	The year of data for GINI index and poverty headcount ratio
France	82.3	70.0	78.0	63.3	3343	547.6	33.7	0.28	67.1	123	42850	32.7	0.0	2015
Germany	82.5	81.0	86.1	73.8	1874	348.9	34.0	0.15	82.7	237	50639	31.7	0.0	2015
Ghana	47.9	40.0	66.9	56.2	2131	227.5	20.7	0.17	28.8	127	4492	42.4	12.0	2012
Greece	71.9	48.0	72.9	55.0	6519	128.9	17.3	0.21	10.8	83	27602	36.0	1.5	2015
Guatemala	49.6	28.0	58.6	63.0	7542	107.2	8.7	0.06	16.9	158	8150	48.3	8.7	2014
Guinea	34.0	27.0	31.4	47.6	22109	245.7	12.6	0.26	12.7	52	2242	33.7	35.3	2012
Haiti	29.1	22.0	40.3	49.6	1386	27.6	38.8	0.10	11.0	398	1815	41.1	23.5	2012
Honduras	48.6	29.0	57.2	58.8	12370	111.9	9.1	0.11	9.3	83	4986	49.6	16.2	2015
Hungary	72.2	45.0	66.4	65.8	10435	90.5	48.7	0.45	9.8	108	28108	30.4	0.5	2015
India	48.9	40.0	72.3	52.6	1539	2973.2	52.6	0.12	1339.2	450	7059	35.1	21.2	2011
Indonesia	51.3	37.0	63.9	61.9	9332	1811.6	13.0	0.09	264.0	146	12284	39.5	7.2	2015
Ireland	85.6	74.0	91.5	76.7	11489	68.9	14.9	0.22	4.8	70	75648	31.8	0.2	2015
Israel	79.2	62.0	77.9	69.7	235	21.6	13.7	0.04	8.7	403	38262	41.4	0.5	2012
Italy	75.9	50.0	79.8	62.5	3147	294.1	22.4	0.11	60.6	206	39427	35.4	2.0	2015
Japan	79.5	73.0	78.8	69.6	3399	364.6	11.5	0.03	126.8	348	43279	32.1	0.2	2008
Jordan	58.3	48.0	38.7	66.7	148	88.8	2.6	0.02	9.7	109	9153	33.7	0.1	2010
Kazakhstan	56.0	31.0	30.6	69.0	6633	2699.7	10.9	1.68	18.0	7	26435	26.9	0.0	2015
Kenya	42.2	28.0	51.1	53.5	738	569.1	10.2	0.12	49.7	87	3285	40.8	36.8	2015
Korea, North		17.0	10.8	4.9	3155	120.4	19.5	0.09	25.5	212				
Korea, South	74.7	54.0	80.0	74.3	1440	97.5	15.0	0.03	51.5	528	38335	31.6	0.2	2012
Kuwait	74.6	39.0	38.5	65.1	7	17.8	0.4	0.00	4.1	232	71943			
Lao P.D.R.	33.1	29.0	23.7	54.0	53038	230.8	6.6	0.23	6.9	30	7023	36.4	22.7	2012

(continued)

Country	Global Food Security Index (GFSI) Score	Corruption Perception Index (CPI) Score	Democracy Index (DI) Score	The Index of Economic Freedom (IEF) Score	TARWR per inhabitant (2011) m^3	Total land area (2016) 1000 km^2	Arable land out of total land (2015) %	Per capita arable land (2015) ha	Total population Million persons	Population density Persons per km^2	Per capita (GDP) (PPP) $, current international	GINI index Score	Poverty headcount ratio at $1.90 a day %	The year of data for GINI index and poverty headcount ratio
Madagascar	27.2	24.0	51.1	57.4	15810	581.8	6.0	0.14	25.6	44	1555	42.6	77.6	2012
Malawi	31.3	31.0	54.9	52.2	1123	94.3	40.3	0.22	18.6	198	1202	45.5	71.4	2010
Malaysia	66.2	47.0	65.4	73.8	20098	328.6	2.9	0.03	31.6	96	29449	41.0	0.0	2015
Mali	39.4	31.0	56.4	58.6	6313	1220.2	5.3	0.37	18.5	15	2214	33.0	49.7	2009
Mexico	65.8	29.0	64.1	63.6	3983	1944.0	11.8	0.18	129.2	66	18273	45.8	4.1	2014
Morocco	52.8	40.0	48.7	61.5	899	446.3	18.2	0.23	35.7	80	8217	39.5	1.0	2013
Mozambique	33.7	25.0	40.2	49.9	9072	786.4	7.2	0.20	29.7	38	1248	54.0	62.9	2014
Myanmar	44.8	30.0	38.3		24164	653.1	16.7	0.21	53.4	82	6161	38.1	6.4	2015
Nepal	44.5	31.0	51.8	55.1	6895	143.4	14.7	0.07	29.3	204	2697	32.8	15.0	2010
Netherlands	82.8	82.0	88.9	75.8	5461	33.7	30.7	0.06	17.1	509	52503	28.2	0.0	2015
New Zealand	81.0	89.0	92.6	83.7	74066	263.3	2.2	0.13	4.8	18	41109			2014
Nicaragua	50.0	26.0	46.6	59.2	33492	120.3	12.5	0.25	6.2	52	5842	46.2	3.2	2014
Niger	29.5	33.0	44.4	50.8	2094	1266.7	13.3	0.84	21.5	17	1017	34.3	44.5	2014
Nigeria	38.4	27.0	44.4	57.1	1762	910.8	37.3	0.19	190.9	210	5875	43.0	53.5	2009
Norway	81.4	85.0	98.7	74.0	77563	365.2	2.2	0.16	5.3	14	61414	27.5	0.2	2015
Oman	73.9	44.0	30.4	62.1	492	309.5	0.1	0.01	4.6	15	41675			
Pakistan	47.8	32.0	42.6	52.8	1396	770.9	39.5	0.16	197.0	256	5527	33.5	4.0	2015
Panama	62.5	37.0	70.8	66.3	41445	74.3	7.6	0.14	4.1	55	24469	50.8	2.0	2015
Paraguay	56.5	29.0	63.1	62.4	51157	397.3	12.1	0.72	6.8	17	13082	47.6	1.9	2015
Peru	59.2	37.0	64.9	68.9	65068	1280.0	3.2	0.13	32.2	25	13434	43.5	3.6	2015
Philippines	47.3	34.0	67.1	65.6	5050	298.2	18.7	0.05	104.9	352	8343			2015
Poland	74.1	60.0	66.7	68.3	1608	306.2	35.6	0.29	38.0	124	29122			2015

Country	Global Food Security Index (GFSI) Score	Corruption Perception Index (CPI) Score	Democracy Index (DI) Score	The Index of Economic Freedom (IEF) Score	TARWR per inhabitant (2011) m³	Total land area (2016) 1000 km²	Arable land out of total land (2015) %	Per capita arable land (2015) ha	Total population Million persons	Population density Persons per km²	Per capita (GDP) (PPP) $, current international	GINI index Score	Poverty headcount ratio at $1.90 a day %	The year of data for GINI index and poverty headcount ratio
Portugal	79.0	63.0	78.4	62.6	6427	91.6	12.4	0.11	10.3	112	31673	35.5	0.5	2015
Qatar	73.3	63.0	31.9	73.1	31	11.6	1.1	0.01	2.6	227	128374	35.9	5.7	2015
Romania	67.7	48.0	64.4	69.7	9885	230.1	38.1	0.44	19.6	85	26657	37.7	0.0	2015
Russia	66.2	29.0	31.7	57.1	31561	16376.9	7.5	0.85	144.5	9	25533	45.1	56.0	2013
Rwanda	39.8	55.0	31.9	67.6	868	24.7	46.7	0.10	12.2	495	2039	40.3	38.0	2011
Saudi Arabia	71.0	49.0	19.3	64.4	85	2149.7	1.6	0.11	32.9	15	53779			
Senegal	44.2	45.0	61.5	55.9	3039	192.5	16.6	0.21	15.9	82	3450	40.3	38.0	2011
Serbia	60.6	41.0	64.1	58.9	16460	87.5	29.6	0.37	7.0	80	15429			
Sierra Leone	28.7	30.0	46.6	52.6	26680	72.2	21.9	0.22	7.6	105	1527	34.0	52.2	2011
Singapore	84.0	84.0	63.2	88.6	116	0.7	0.8	0.00	5.6	7916	93905			
Slovakia	70.0	50.0	71.6		9156	48.1	28.8	0.25	5.4	113	31616	26.5	0.7	2015
South Africa	64.0	43.0	72.4	62.3	1019	1213.1	10.3	0.23	56.7	47	13498	63.0	18.9	2014
Spain	78.1	57.0	80.8	63.6	2400	500.2	24.7	0.27	46.6	93	37998	36.2	1.0	2015
Sri Lanka	53.0	38.0	64.8	57.4	2509	62.7	20.7	0.06	21.4	342	12835	39.2	1.9	2012
Sudan	34.8	16.0	21.5	48.8	1445	2376.0	8.3	0.39	40.5	23	4904	35.4	14.9	2009
Sweden	81.7	84.0	93.9	74.9	18430	407.3	6.3	0.26	10.1	25	50208	29.2	0.5	2015
Switzerland	81.6	85.0	90.3	81.5	6946	39.5	10.1	0.05	8.5	214	64712	32.3	0.0	2015
Syria	33.3	14.0	14.3		809	183.6	25.4	0.25	18.3	99		35.8	1.7	2004
Tajikistan	35.9	21.0	19.3	58.2	3140	138.8	5.3	0.09	8.9	64	3195	34.0	4.8	2015
Tanzania	35.4	36.0	54.7	58.6	2083	885.8	15.2	0.25	57.3	65	2946	37.8	49.1	2011
Thailand	58.3	37.0	46.3	66.2	6309	510.9	32.9	0.24	69.0	135	17872	36.0	0.0	2015
Togo	37.2	32.0	30.5	53.2	2388	54.4	48.7	0.36	7.8	143	1660	43.1	49.2	2015

(continued)

Country	Global Food Security Index (GFSI) Score	Corruption Perception Index (CPI) Score	Democracy Index (DI) Score	The Index of Economic Freedom (IEF) Score	TARWR per inhabitant (2011) m³	Total land area (2016) 1000 km²	Arable land out of total land (2015) %	Per capita arable land (2015) ha	Total population Million persons	Population density Persons per km²	Per capita (GDP) (PPP) $, current international	GINI index Score	Poverty headcount ratio at $1.90 a day %	The year of data for GINI index and poverty headcount ratio
Tunisia	58.8	42.0	63.2	55.7	434	155.4	18.7	0.26	11.5	74	11911	35.8	2.0	2010
Turkey	61.1	40.0	48.8	65.2	2873	769.6	26.8	0.26	80.7	105	26519	42.9	0.3	2015
Uganda	43.3	26.0	50.9	60.9	1913	200.5	34.4	0.17	42.9	214	1864	41.0	35.9	2012
Ukraine	54.1	30.0	56.9	48.1	3089	579.3	56.2	0.72	44.8	77	8667	25.5	0.1	2015
UAE	70.9	71.0	26.9	76.9	19	83.6	0.4	0.00	9.4	112	73878			
United Kingdom	84.2	82.0	85.3	76.4	2346	241.9	24.8	0.09	66.0	273	43269	33.2	0.2	2015
United States	84.6	75.0	79.8	75.1	9802	9147.4	16.6	0.47	325.7	36	59532	41.0	1.0	2013
Uruguay	69.7	70.0	81.2	69.7	41124	175.0	13.8	0.70	3.5	20	22562	40.2	0.1	2015
Uzbekistan	47.5	22.0	19.5	52.3	1760	425.4	10.3	0.14	32.4	76	6865	35.3	62.1	2003
Venezuela	50.2	18.0	38.7	27.0	41886	882.1	3.1	0.09	32.0	36		46.9	10.2	2006
Vietnam	54.0	35.0	30.8	52.4	9957	310.1	22.6	0.07	95.5	308	6776	34.8	2.6	2014
Yemen	28.8	16.0	20.7		85	528.0	2.4	0.05	28.3	54	2601	36.7	18.8	2014
Zambia	32.4	37.0	56.8	55.8	7807	743.4	5.1	0.24	17.1	23	4024	57.1	57.5	2015
Zimbabwe		22.0	31.6	44.0	1568	386.9	10.3	0.25	16.5	43	2429	43.2	21.4	2011
Correlation coefficient with GFSI		0.831	0.686	0.727	0.144	0.141	-0.080	0.093	-0.003	0.147	0.808	-0.296	-0.742	

Notes:

1. GFSI includes 113 countries. It ranks countries on a 100-point scale. Higher GFSI means better food security. In 2017, the highest score was 85.6 (Ireland) and the lowest was Burundi (25.1).

2. CPI includes 180 countries and territories. It ranks countries on a 100-point scale. Higher CPI means lower level corruption. In 2017, the highest score was 89 (New Zealand) and the lowest

3. DI includes 165 independent states and two territories. It ranks countries on a 10-point scale. For this table, the original scores out of the 10-point scale has been converted to a 100-point scale by multiplying 10 of the original score. Higher DI means higher level democracy. In 2017, the highest score was 98.7 (Norway) and the lowest was 10.8 (North Korea).

4. TARWR: Total Actual Renewable Water Resources

5. GDP: gross domestic product; PPP: purchasing power parity.

6. IEF includes 180 countries and territories. It ranks countries on a 100-point scale. Higher IEF means higher level economic freedom. In 2017, the highest score was 89.8 (Hong Kong) and the lowest was 4.9 (North Korea).

7. GINI index: World Bank estimate.

8. Poverty headcount ratio: at $1.90 a day, 2011 PPP, % of population.

9. UAE: United Arab Emirates.

Sources: Global Food Security Index: EIU (2017), Global Food Security Index 2017, https://lfoodsecurityindex.eiu.com/Resources, accessed 12 October 2017. Corruption Perception Index: TI (2018), Corruption Perceptions Index 2017, www.transparency.org/news/feature/corruption_perceptions_index_2017, accessed 15 October 2018. Democracy Index: EIU (2018), Democracy Index 2017, https://pages.eiu.com/rs/753-RIQ-438/images/Democracy_Index_2017.pdf, accessed 15 October 2018. Total actual renewable water resources per inhabitant: www.fao.org/nr/water/aquastat/maps/AQUASTAT_water_resources_and_MDG_water_indicator_March_2013.pdf, accessed 15 October 2018. Land area (total, arable land share, and per capita): http://wdi.worldbank.org/table/3.1#, accessed 8 November 2018. Population and density: http://wdi.worldbank.org/table/WV.1#, accessed 8 November 2018. Per capita GDP: https://data.worldbank.org/indicator/NY.GDP.PCAP.PP.CD, accessed 29 January 2019. The Index of Economic Freedom: The Heritage Foundation (2017), 2017 Index of Economic Freedom, www.heritage.org/index/download#, accessed 13 February 2019. GINI index and poverty headcount ratio, World Bank Data, https://data.worldbank.org/topic/poverty?view=chart, accessed 15 March 2019.

A government that is unable to supply adequate food to its citizens is inept.

Part 1

Introduction

Contents

1 Food security: concept and measurement

2 Global food security: an overview

This part introduces you to the basics of food security and provides you with a broad overview of current global food security. Chapter 1 explains the concept of food security and the approaches that can be used to evaluate the level of food security. Chapter 2 highlights the current status of food security at the continental and global levels and identifies major challenges that human beings have to overcome in order to improve future food security for all.

Food security and food systems are integrally related. Food systems affect the level of food output today and food production sustainability for the future. Food systems are also closely interlinked with other important dimensions of food security such as food safety. Thus, the level of food security depends on how good a food system is. As such, it is useful to understand the qualities of a good food system. To facilitate this understanding, a discussion of food systems is appended to Chapter 2.

Chapter 1

Food security

Concept and measurement

Summary

Important concepts about food security and frameworks to evaluate food security are explained in this chapter. In Section 1.1, food is defined and its major features discussed. The history and evolution of the concept of food security is elaborated in Section 1.2. In Section 1.3, it is pointed out that food security can be contemplated/studied at different levels. Finally, in Section 1.4 the main frameworks for analysing/evaluating food security are introduced and their applicability is discussed.

After studying this chapter, you should be able to:
- Define food and explain its major features.
- Define food security and describe the evolution of this concept.
- Explain frameworks for evaluating food security and understand their applicability.

1.1 What is food?

The World Health Organization (WHO) and the Food and Agriculture Organization (FAO) define food in a physiological sense as 'nutritive material taken into an organism and which fulfils needs for maintenance, growth, work, and tissue repair' (WHO and FAO 1974, p. 10). Staple food is defined as 'a food which is regularly consumed in a country or community and from which a substantial proportion of the total calorie supply is obtained, especially by the poorer population sector and in times of food shortage' (WHO and FAO 1974, p. 11). As such, food may embrace any nutritional materials taken by human beings which provide calories (energy), protein, fat and other essential micronutrients, including both animal and vegetable products such as cereals, meats, eggs, dairy products, vegetables, and sugar.

Food has distinctive features. It has an immediate appeal to deep-rooted human feelings because food is a matter of life and death. Major features of food are (Spitz 1985):

- **Time dimension**: Without food, one cannot live for too long. Food has to be obtained within much stricter time constraints than any other necessities of life.
- **Nutritional dimension**: The human body does not effectively store some essential nutritional elements (for example, water-soluble types of vitamins such as vitamin C and the B complex vitamins which need to be replenished regularly). Such nutritional elements need to be taken as part of the diet.
- **Socio-cultural dimension**: Not all edible and nutritionally satisfactory foods are socially, culturally, or psychologically acceptable.
- **Economic dimension**: For most food items, one has to pay to obtain them in the market. Even in semi-subsistence regions food has an implicit price.

1.2 Food security: history and evolution of the concept

Food security concerns the supply of food and access to it. This has been a primary focus of people throughout history. Scarcity of food, starvation, hunger, and famine were various descriptions of food problems prior to, at least, 1974 when a more formal definition of food security was introduced at the World Food Conference. Some researchers suggest that this concept can be traced to well before that time (Gibson 2012). The term food security was 'borrowed, regurgitated and built on numerous age-old ideological and philosophical foundations' (Gibson 2012, p. 511). Before World War I there were numerous mentions of the term food security (Shaw 2007).

However, food security was perceived as an inter-governmental issue only after World War I. According to Shaw (2007), the League of Nations (the forerunner of the United Nations) recognised the need for some form of a multilateral world food security arrangement in rationalising food production and exchange for the benefits of both consumers and producers. However, most governments were preoccupied with post-war recovery. Consequently, international collaboration on food problems did not succeed during the short inter-war era. Nevertheless, the great depression in consumer purchasing power and declining incomes of primary producers in the early 1930s aroused awareness of a need for international participation in staple food problems. At the same time, the negative impacts of chronic malnutrition on children and vulnerable people were revealed. Chronic malnutrition, a problem even in high-income countries, drew world attention to issues of food security (Gibson 2012).

The League of Nations disseminated world hunger statistics for the first time in the 1930s. Subsequently, its Health Division produced a report on nutrition and public health in poor countries. This report also contributed to an initial stage of international collaboration in nutrition policies. Since then, hunger and nutrition issues have been perceived as global issues (Shaw 2007).

In 1945, the FAO was formed under the United Nations (UN). It was the end product of a series of food security-related conferences held during World War II. The most prominent conference was the United States (US) Nutrition Conference for Defense, which determined that conquering hunger was the most important mission for democratic nations. This corresponded with the Four Freedoms initiated by the US President, Franklin D. Roosevelt, which urged for an establishment of a United Nations program for 'freedom from want of food' (Phillips 1981, p. 4).

In 1946, the FAO produced its first *World Food Survey* report. The report revealed that at least one-third of the world population was starving. The Director-General of the FAO, John Boyd Orr, proposed the establishment of the World Food Board (WFB), whose objective was to eradicate hunger through the integration of nutrition, health, agriculture, and trade. As a moral obligation, he believed that a civilised world should be able to feed hungry people even without profit. Simultaneously, trade would play a bridging role to bring food from surplus areas to insufficient ones (Shaw 2007).

In the same period, the International Trade Organization (ITO) was proposed to encourage a reduction in trade barriers, and the International Monetary Fund (IMF) was designed to facilitate the solution of financial problems at the international level. However, the WFB and ITO proposals were not supported by leading economies, such as the US and the United Kingdom (UK). Until 1953, numerous proposals were put forward to solve food insecurity and food surplus problems by national governments and the United Nations, but none was taken seriously by the FAO (Shaw 2007).

From 1950 to 1960, world food production increased by 50%, while the world cereal market continued to suffer with surpluses. However, the food insecurity issue remained unresolved. Hence, a concept called the World Food Reserve (WFR) was popularised and was seen as the most appropriate solution to fix transitory food insecurity. With the WFR, mobile food resources could be delivered to aid emergency needs during disasters. However, because it might drastically reduce world food stocks and lead to market price increases, some national governments did not accept the WFR proposal (Shaw 2007).

In 1955, the FAO concluded that poverty lies at the root of hunger, and the remedy of poverty is economic development (Paulino and Mellor 1984). When an economy is underdeveloped, consumer purchasing power is weak. In such a situation, food for the poor would have to be subsidised. This is not a sustainable solution, considering the cost of subsidies. Hence, world governments rejected both WFB and WFR proposals. This led the US to promote the establishment of the World Food Bank. The World Food Bank proposed loans to poor food-importing countries to buy food. The roles of the World Food Bank also included improving food supply with better nutritional standards, preventing famine, and functioning as a food reserve. By the end of the 1960s, the cereal market continued to be in surplus. The US and Canada implemented plans to reduce cereal production.

The food surplus situation ended in the early 1970s. A drastic change in weather conditions had hampered agriculture production in many exporting countries. World food supply contracted instantly, and many food exporters became importers. Commercial imports became more expensive for developing countries, while food aid dropped from about 17 million tonnes of cereals per year in the 1960s to 7 million tonnes in the early 1970s.

The international food crisis led to the first World Food Conference in 1974 to review food shortages and decide on possible solutions.

The term 'food security' was put forward to a wider audience at the World Food Conference (Smith, Pointing, and Maxwell 1992; Simon 2012; FAO 2015). The conference defined food security as 'availability at all times of adequate world food supplies of basic foodstuff to sustain a steady expansion of food consumption and to offset fluctuations in production and prices'. The quantity and stability of food supplies lay at the centre of this notion, based on the belief that increasing production and improving consumption distribution could resolve food insecurity.

In the early 1980s, the concept of food security evolved from the sole focus on self-sufficiency. In 1983, the FAO expanded the concept to emphasise the importance of the balance between the demand and supply sides of food and the opportunities from world trade in food, and a new definition of food security arose 'ensuring that all people at all times have both physical and economic access to the basic food that they need' (FAO 2003).

The concept of food security continued evolving with inspiration from the World Bank report *Poverty and Hunger* (World Bank 1986). The report distinguished between different situations of food insecurity and proposed appropriate responses. It categorised food insecurity into chronic food insecurity caused by poverty and transitory food insecurity ensuing from natural disasters or economic failure. According to the report, the food shortage portion in chronic food insecurity only represents 5% of the national food supply. Hence, chronic food insecurity would not be eliminated with a 5% increase in the food supply unless inequality in the distribution of food was addressed. Shortage of food is merely one reason for chronic food insecurity. Instead, purchasing power and access rights to adequate food supply are important for malnourished people to maintain active and healthy lives.

The World Bank report, complemented by Sen's theory of famine in relation to 'rights and entitlement' (Sen 1981), showed how famines thrive even without food shortages (CISS 2013; Maletta 2014). Both highlighted the need to incorporate the ideas of access to sufficient food and nutritional balance into the food security concept. The mid-1990s also saw a linking of food security with food safety and preferences (Grover 2010).

In 1996, the World Food Summit redefined food security, using official documents by the FAO and the World Bank in 1970–1995 (FAO 2003) to reflect the complexities and diversity of food security problems and changes in official policy thinking of the time (Clay 2002). The reconstructed definition of food security reads:

> Food security exists when all people, at all times, have physical and economic access to sufficient, safe and nutritious food that meets their dietary needs and food preferences for an active and healthy life'.
>
> (World Food Summit 1996)

The 1996 definition adequately reflects the distinctive features of food. It also adequately embraces and highlights several important aspects or dimensions of food security:

- **Food availability**: This is the most fundamental aspect of food security. Without adequate food availability, there is no need to address other aspects of food security. (*all people … have sufficient … food*)
- **Supply sustainability**: Having food to eat at present is important, but having food to eat in the future is equally important. If 'food availability' cares more about food supply today, then 'supply sustainability' cares more about food availability for the future. (*all people, at all times, have … sufficient … food*)

- **Food quality and safety**: Food needs to be nutritious and safe to consume. Otherwise, the functions of foods are not fulfilled and they may cause health problems. (*safe and nutritious food that meets their dietary needs*)
- **Cultural acceptability**: While available, foods also need to be culturally acceptable. (*food that meets their ... food preferences*)
- **Access to food**: Foods need to be available within a reasonable distance. They also need to be affordable by all people, especially those on low incomes. (*all people ... have physical and economic access to ... food*)

Note that food security should not be confused with food availability or food self-sufficiency (Box 1.1).

BOX 1.1

Food security, food availability, and food self-sufficiency

Food availability and food security: 'Food availability' should not be equated to 'food security'. Food availability is only one dimension, though the most important, of food security. Equating food security to the availability of adequate food supplies has serious drawbacks. For example, it neglects food safety, quality, and nutrition dimensions, and it may lead to a focus on current food supply ignoring sustainability into the future.

Food self-sufficiency and food security: Food security should not be confused with food self-sufficiency either. A high level of food security is not necessarily associated with a high level of food self-sufficiency. Trading on world markets complements domestic production to improve food security.

The level of a country's food self-sufficiency is reflected by its self-sufficiency ratio (SSR). The SSR is equal to domestic production divided by the sum of domestic production plus net imports. If a country's net import is negative, i.e., it net exports a product, this product's SSR will be greater than 100%. The import dependence ratio (IDR) is equal to imports divided by the sum of domestic production plus net imports. If a country does not produce a product or produces very little but imports a large quantity for both domestic consumption and for re-exports (after processing), this product's IDR can be greater than 100%. The sum of SSR and IDR does not have to add up to 100.

Countries with an SSR greater than 100% do not necessarily have a high level of food security (like India). Conversely, countries with a very low SSR do not necessarily have a very low level of food security (like Singapore). Hence, a higher level of food self-sufficiency may be conducive to but does not guarantee a country a high level of food security. Equally, achieving a high level of food security does not require a high level of food self-sufficiency.

1.3 Addressing food security at different levels

Food security issues can be addressed at various levels. At the most aggregate level is global food security. At the next level is food security in each continent or part of it, for example, food security in Africa or food security in Sub-Saharan Africa. Food security issues are more often addressed at the national level. Also attracting attention is food security in regions within a nation. Increasingly, more attention has been given to food security at the household level or even at the individual level.

The foci of food security issues at different levels vary. Approaches needed to address, and balance, the demand and supply of food at different levels are also different. Unless specifically indicated, discussions in this book are chiefly at the global and national levels.

1.4 Frameworks for food security evaluation

To evaluate food security, we need a framework that gives attention to not only the features of food itself, but also the entire range of factors determining the security of food availability and access. There are a number of evaluation frameworks available: for example, Oshaug, Eide, and Eide (1994), Riely et al. (1999), Suresh and Ergeneman (2005), IFRC (2006), EIU (2014), and FAO (2014). Four of them are explained.

1.4.1 The Oshaug–Eide–Eide framework

In an article published in *Food Policy*, Oshaug, Eide, and Eide (1994) proposed a normative food security framework, in which food security is expressed in terms of the adequacy of food supply and the stability of both food supply and access.

Adequacy of food supply means that (1) the overall supply should potentially cover nutritional needs in terms of quantity and quality of all essential nutrients; (2) the food is safe (free of toxic factors and contaminants) and of good quality (taste, texture, etc.); and (3) the types of foodstuffs commonly available (nationally, in local markets, and eventually at the household level) are culturally acceptable (fit the prevailing food or dietary culture).

Stability of supply and access to food implies environmental sustainability and social stability. Environmental sustainability implies protection of the natural resource base used in food production. Social stability addresses conditions and mechanisms for securing food access including the development of policies concerned with income distribution, public welfare safety nets, and fostering community welfare networks.

The normative food security framework proposed by Oshaug, Eide, and Eide (1994) is shown in Figure 1.1. In this figure, each of the two major subdivisions is further expressed in terms of more specific dimensions of food security. Such dimensions can be evaluated by specifying local standards against which performance can be assessed. Below the dotted line are examples of policies, strategies, and means that can help to achieve the targets. Food trade may be an important means to help a country to achieve food security, but it was not explicitly indicated in the original diagram by Oshaug, Eide, and Eide (1994). Figure 1.1 is a slightly modified version of Oshaug, Eide, and Eide (1994) with the trade component added (Zhou 2017).

1.4.2 The FAO framework

The FAO, as a major international body charged with primary responsibilities to ensure global food security, monitors food supplies and provides food supply estimates at the global, regional, and country levels where reliable data are available. Since 1974, when the term food security became widely used, and in particular since the 1996 World Food Summit, when a target to reduce the number of hungry people was set, the FAO has been devising and improving approaches that can help it monitor the global food security status (Table 1.1). The FAO has continuously revised its methodology over the

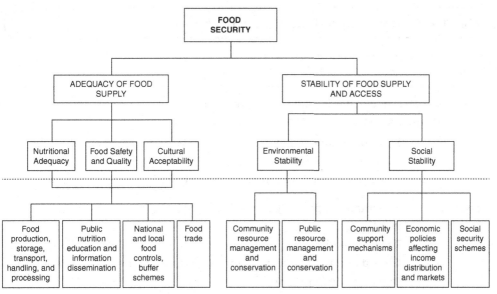

Figure 1.1 A normative food security framework.
Source: Based on Oshaug et al. (1994).

past decades. One recent major revision was introduced in the 2012 *Status of Food Insecurity* (SOFI). In the SOFI 2014 edition, further refinements were introduced. A note on the food security methodology the FAO has developed and changes it has made can be found in FAO (2014). According to the FAO methodological framework, food security is evaluated along four dimensions: availability, access, utilisation, and stability. Under each of these four dimensions, there are specific indicators to be measured (Table 1.1). Using this framework, the FAO has since 2012 provided updates of the status of global food security in its annual SOFI publication.

1.4.3 The Economist Intelligence Unit framework

The Economist Intelligence Unit (EIU) started publishing the Global Food Security Index (GFSI) in 2012 to determine which countries are most and least vulnerable to food insecurity (Table 1.2). The GFSI is a dynamic quantitative and qualitative benchmarking model constructed from 28 unique indicators, which measures drivers of food security across 109 countries. The indicators are placed in three categories or dimensions: affordability, availability, and quality and safety (Table 1.3). The definitions of the indicators and other details about the framework used by the EIU are in the *Global Food Security Index 2014* (EIU 2014).

1.4.4 The USAID framework

In 1999, the US Agency for International Development (USAID) and the Food and Nutrition Technical Assistance (FANTA) published *Food Security Indicators and Framework for Use in the Monitoring and Evaluation of Food Aid Programs* to assist in the identification of food

Table 1.1 Food security indicators used by the FAO

Dimension	Food security indicators
Availability	Average dietary energy supply adequacy
	Average value of food production
	Share of dietary energy supply derived from cereals, roots, and tubers
	Average protein supply
	Average supply of protein of animal origin
Access	Percentage of paved roads over total roads
	Road density
	Rail line density
	Gross domestic product per capita (in purchasing power equivalent)
	Domestic food price index
	Prevalence of undernourishment
	Share of food expenditure of the poor
	Depth of the food deficit
	Prevalence of food inadequacy
Stability	Cereal import dependency ratio
	Percentage of arable land equipped for irrigation
	Value of food imports over total merchandise exports
	Political stability and absence of violence/terrorism
	Domestic food price volatility
	Per capita food production variability
	Per capita food supply variability
Utilisation	Access to improved water sources
	Access to improved sanitation facilities
	Percentage of children under 5 years of age affected by wasting
	Percentage of children under 5 years of age who are stunted
	Percentage of children under 5 years of age who are underweight
	Percentage of adults who are underweight
	Prevalence of anemia among pregnant women
	Prevalence of anemia among children under 5 years of age
	Prevalence of vitamin A deficiency in the population
	Prevalence of iodine deficiency

FAO = Food and Agriculture Organisation.
Source: FAO (2014).

Table 1.2 The Global Food Security Index: selected countries

	2012	2013	2014	2015	2016	2017	2018
Australia	81.1	80.1	81.9	83.8	82.6	83.3	83.7
Bangladesh	34.6	35.3	36.3	37.4	36.8	39.7	43.3
Brazil	67.6	67.0	68.1	67.4	67.6	67.7	68.4
Burundi	22.9	26.3	28.8	25.1	24.0	25.1	23.9
China	62.5	60.2	62.2	64.2	65.5	63.7	65.1
Hungary	70.7	69.0	71.2	71.4	69.3	72.2	72.8
India	45.0	44.4	48.3	50.9	49.4	48.9	50.1
Indonesia	46.8	45.6	46.5	46.7	50.6	51.3	54.8
Israel	77.7	78.4	80.6	78.9	78.9	79.2	78.6
Japan	80.7	77.8	77.8	77.4	75.9	79.5	79.9
Mexico	67.7	66.2	67.1	68.7	68.1	65.8	66.4
Netherlands	86.7	83.2	84.4	85.0	82.6	82.8	84.7
Pakistan	38.5	39.7	43.6	45.7	47.8	47.8	49.1
Singapore	n.a.	79.9	84.3	88.2	83.9	84.0	85.9
South Africa	61.7	61.0	61.1	64.5	62.9	64.0	65.5
South Korea	77.8	71.1	73.2	74.8	73.3	74.7	75.6
United Kingdom	79.0	77.3	81.6	81.6	81.9	84.2	85.0
United States	89.5	86.8	89.3	89.0	86.6	84.6	85.0
Vietnam	50.4	48.6	49.1	53.4	57.1	54.0	56.0
Venezuela	61.6	60.8	62.5	61.7	56.9	50.2	47.4
Zambia	28.5	28.1	32.6	32.9	33.3	32.4	33.7
Highest of the year	**89.5**	**86.8**	**89.3**	**89.0**	**86.6**	**85.6**	**85.9**
Lowest of the year	**18.4**	**20.8**	**24.8**	**25.1**	**24.0**	**25.1**	**23.9**

n.a.: not available.
Source: EIU (2018 and earlier years).
Weighted scores (0–100 where 100 = most favourable).

security hotspots for US food aid programs (Riely et al. 1999). This framework contains three dimensions: availability, access, and utilisation. Figure 1.2 highlights the nature of the relationship of the three dimensions to one another, as well as a brief description of their determinants.

Based on the above four frameworks, it is clear that the two most important dimensions of food security are availability and access. Extending from these two dimensions, each of the four frameworks emphasise other dimensions as well, such as utilisation. It is noted, however, that even for the same dimension, indicators used to measure or evaluate that dimension vary between the four frameworks.

Table 1.3 Food security indicators used by the EIU

Dimension	Food security indicators
1. Affordability	1.1 Food consumption as a share of household expenditure
	1.2 Proportion of population under the global poverty line
	1.3 Gross domestic product per capita (PPP)
	1.4 Agricultural import tariffs
	1.5 Presence of food safety net programs
	1.6 Access to financing for farmers
2. Availability	2.1 Sufficiency of supply
	2.1.1 Average food supply
	2.1.2 Dependency on chronic food aid
	2.2 Public expenditure on agricultural R&D
	2.3 Agricultural infrastructure
	2.3.1 Existence of adequate crop storage facilities
	2.3.2 Road infrastructure
	2.3.3 Port infrastructure
	2.4 Volatility of agricultural production
	2.5 Political stability risk
	2.6 Corruption
	2.7 Urban absorption capacity
	2.8 Food loss
3. Quality & safety	3.1 Diet diversification
	3.2 Nutritional standards
	3.2.1 National dietary guidelines
	3.2.2 National nutrition plan or strategy
	3.2.3 Nutrition monitoring and surveillance
	3.3 Micronutrient availability
	3.3.1 Dietary availability of vitamin A
	3.3.2 Dietary availability of animal iron
	3.3.3 Dietary availability of vegetal iron
	3.4 Protein quality
	3.5 Food safety
	3.5.1 Agency to ensure the safety and health of food
	3.5.2 Percentage of population with access to potable water
	3.5.3 Presence of formal grocery sector

EIU = Economist Intelligence Unit; PPP = purchasing power parity; R&D = research and development.
Source: EIU (2014).

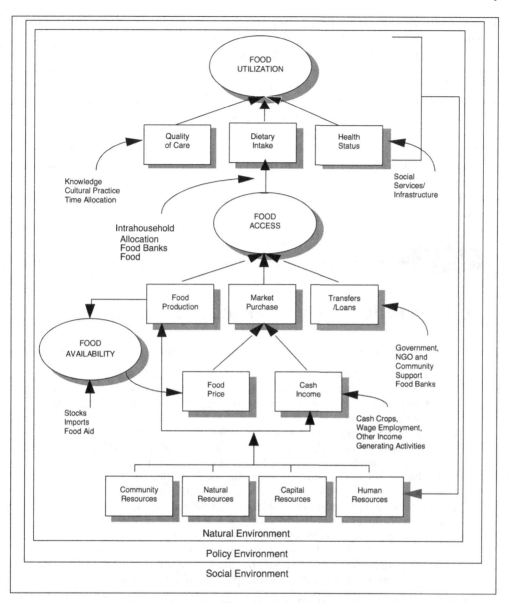

Figure 1.2 Food security conceptual framework used by USAID.
Source: Riely et al. (1999).

The Oshaug–Eide–Eide framework was published in 1994 and represents an early attempt to construct a food security framework. Later frameworks are more 'complicated' or 'fancier'. They include a large number of indicators in evaluating food security. When too many indicators are included, some aspects that are more important in evaluating a country's food security may get overlooked.

The more complicated evaluation frameworks are not necessarily more comprehensive. For example, food security needs to take into account food availability for the present day and the near future and also for the longer term. Hence, a country's food buffer stocks or reserves are important (for the near future) and a country's environment and resource sustainability are also important (for food production in the longer term). Surprisingly, the FAO and EIU frameworks do not give any clear weight to reserve stocks and production sustainability.

One other issue with more complicated frameworks is that they are 'usable' only by well-resourced institutions. It is not practical for individual researchers with limited resources to make use of them. Comparatively, the Oshaug–Eide–Eide framework, while including all key aspects that are important for evaluating a country's food security, is more pragmatic and easy to apply. Especially, it gives researchers the flexibility to tailor their evaluation to include the most important elements in their analysis, while allowing them to omit minor aspects that available resources do not permit.

Several other institutions have also tried to evaluate food security or hunger using different approaches. See Box 1.2 for examples.

BOX 1.2

Other indexes of food security or hunger

There are several other indexes that are related to food security or hunger. For example:

- Rice Bowl Index (RBI), by Syngenta, from 2012, rather than measuring a country's current level of food security, it assesses how robust a country's capacity is to address the challenges of food security, covering 14 Asia-Pacific countries, www.ricebowlindex.com/
- Hunger and Nutrition Commitment Index (HANCI), by the Institute of Development Studies (IDS, UK), from 2012, ranking governments on their political commitment to tackling hunger and undernutrition, focusing on 45 developing countries whose hunger and undernutrition status is considered severe or alarming. www.hancindex.org/the-index/resources/
- Food Security Risk Index, by Maplecroft, a risk analysis and rating firm, from 2010, evaluating the risks to the supply of basic food staples for 163 countries. https://maplecroft.com/about/news/food-security.html.
- Global Hunger Index (GHI), by the International Food Policy Research Institute (IFPRI), from 1992, measuring and tracking hunger globally, regionally, and by country, covering 118 countries, www.ifpri.org/topic/global-hunger-index.

The Global Hunger Index (GHI) reflects a country's food security status chiefly through the hunger situation. It combines several component indicators into one index. Prior to 2015, the GHI had three index components: undernourishment, the weight of children under five, and child mortality (the proportion of children dying before the age of five). In the 2015 calculation, children's weight was replaced with two indicators of child malnutrition – wasting and stunting.

Wasting refers to low weight for height; wasting prevalence is the proportion of children under five whose weight for height is below minus two standard deviations from median weight for height of reference population. Stunting refers to low height for age; stunting prevalence is the proportion of children under five whose height for age is below minus two standard deviations from median height for age of reference population.

The GHI ranks countries on a 100-point scale. Hunger is low if the HGI ≤ 9.9; moderate if 10.0–19.9; serious if 20.0–34.9; alarming if 35.0–49.9 and extremely alarming if ≥ 50.

Table 1.4 The Global Hunger Index: selected countries

	1990	1995	2000	2005	2010	2015	2016	2017	2018
Asia									
Bangladesh	52.2	50.3	38.5	31.0	30.3	27.3	27.1	26.5	26.1
China	25.1	23.2	15.9	13.2	10.0	8.6	7.7	7.5	7.6
India	48.1	42.3	38.2	38.5	32.2	29.0	28.5	31.4	31.1
Indonesia	34.8	32.5	25.3	26.5	24.5	22.1	21.9	22.0	21.9
North Korea	30.1	35.9	40.4	32.4	30.9	28.8	28.6	28.2	34.0
Pakistan	43.6	40.9	37.9	38.3	36.0	33.9	33.4	32.6	32.6
Africa									
Central African Republic	51.9	51.0	51.4	51.0	41.3	46.9	46.1	50.9	53.7
Chad	65.0	60.6	52.0	53.1	48.9	46.4	44.3	43.5	45.4
Madagascar	44.8	45.1	44.1	44.4	36.1	36.3	35.4	38.3	38.0
Niger	64.7	62.7	53.0	42.8	36.5	34.5	33.7	34.5	30.4
Senegal	36.8	36.9	37.9	28.5	24.1	23.2	16.5	18.4	17.2
Zimbabwe	33.3	38.1	40.8	39.2	36.0	30.8	28.8	33.8	32.9
Latin America and The Caribbean									
Brazil	18.2	15.0	12.0	6.7	6.6	<5	<5	5.4	8.5
Chile	6.8	<5	<5	<5	<5	<5	<5	<5	<5
Ecuador	23.8	19.7	20.2	19.0	14.1	14.0	13.9	14.4	11.8
Haiti	52.1	52.1	42.8	45.4	48.5	37.3	36.9	34.2	35.4
Venezuela	16.3	15.3	15.2	13.1	8.4	7.0	7.0	13.0	11.4
Oceania									
Fiji	12.5	11.2	10.1	9.3	8.6	8.7	8.5	8.1	9.0

Sources: based on IFPRI GHI publications from 2015 to 2018.

Review questions

1. How is food defined? What are its major features?
2. How is food security defined?
3. What are the major dimensions of food security?
4. How many possible levels are there at which food security can be discussed?
5. What are the major frameworks for food security evaluation?

> ### Discussion questions
>
> 1. According to the definition of food, would you call anything that human beings consume food? Why?
> 2. There are many definitions of food security. Do you think having many definitions is bad or good? Why?
> 3. Would you come up with your own definition of food security or just simply adapt a ready definition? If the latter, which version would you adapt? Why?
> 4. Out of the available frameworks that can be used to evaluate food security, which one do you prefer? Explain.
> 5. In your view, should a food security evaluation framework be simple and easy to use, or more comprehensive but not necessarily easy to apply?
> 6. If you are going to evaluate the level of food security in your country, which available framework would you use? What is the justification/s for your choice?

References

CISS (Centre for International Security Studies). (2013), *Food Security in Asia: A Report for Policymakers*, The University of Sydney, Australia.

Clay, E. (2002), 'Food security: Concepts and measurement', FAO Expert Consultation on Trade and Food Security: Conceptualising the Linkages, FAO, Rome.

EIU (Economist Intelligence Unit). (2014), *Global Food Security Index 2014: An Annual Measure of the State of Global Food Security*, http://foodsecurityindex.eiu.com/, accessed 30 September 2014.

FAO. (2003), *Trade Reforms and Food Security*, FAO, Rome.

FAO. (2014), *Food Security Methodology*, www.fao.org/economic/ess/ess-fs/fs-methods/fs-methods1/en/, accessed 10 November 2014.

FAO. (2015), *A Short History of FAO*, FAO, Rome. www.fao.org/about/en/, accessed 10 April 2015.

Gibson, M. (2012), *The Feeding of Nations: Redefining Food Security for the 21st Century*, CRC Press, US, Boca Raton, FL.

Grover, V.I. (2010), 'Food security', in Cohen, N. and Robbins, P. (eds), *Green Cities: An A-to-Z Guide*, SAGE Publications, Los Angeles, CA, pp. 187–192.

IFRC (International Federation of Red Cross and Red Crescent Societies). (2006), *How to Conduct a Food Security Assessment: A Step-by-Step Guide for National Societies in Africa*, 2nd edn, IFRC, Geneva, Switzerland. www.ifrc.org/Global/Publications/disasters/food_security/fs-assessment.pdf, accessed 29 September 2014.

Maletta, H. (2014), *From Hunger to Food Security: A Conceptual History*, Universidad del Pacífico, Lima, Peru.

Oshaug, A., Eide, W.B., and Eide, A. (1994), 'Human rights: A normative basis for food and nutrition-relevant policies', *Food Policy* Vol. 19, pp. 491–516.

Paulino, L.A. and Mellor, J.W. (1984), 'The food situation in developing countries: Two decades in review', *Food Policy* Vol. 9, pp. 291–303.

Phillips, R.W. (1981), *FAO: Its Origins, Formation and Evolution*, FAO, Rome.

Riely, F., Mock, N., Kenefick, E., Cogill, B., and Bailey, L. (1999), 'Food security indicators and framework for use in the monitoring and evaluation of food aid programs', United States Agency for International Development, Washington, DC, http://pdf.usaid.gov/pdf_docs/PNACG170.pdf, accessed 10 November 2014.

Sen, A. (1981), *Poverty and Famines: An Essay on Entitlement and Deprivation*, Clarendon Press, Oxford, UK.

Shaw, D.J. (2007), *World Food Security: A History since 1945*, Palgrave Macmillan, UK, Houndsmill, Basingstoke.

Simon, G.A. (2012), 'Food security, four dimensions, history', Basic readings as an introduction to food security for students from the IPAD Master, SupAgro, Montpellier attending a joint training program in Rome, 19–24 March 2012, www.fao.org/fileadmin/templates/ERP/uni/F4D.pdf, accessed 8 August 2015.

Smith, M., Pointing, J., and Maxwell, S. (1992), 'Household food security: Concepts and definition—an annotated bibliography', in Maxwell, S. and Frankenberger, T.R. (eds), *Household Food Security: Concepts, Indicators, Measurements: A Technical Review*, United Nations Children's Fund and International Fund for Agricultural Development, Rome, pp. 135–191.

Spitz, P. (1985), 'The right to food in historical perspective', *Food Policy* Vol. 10, pp. 306–316.

Suresh, B. and Ergeneman, A. (2005), 'A framework for evaluating food security and nutrition monitoring system', *African Journal of Food Agriculture and Nutritional Development* Vol. 5, pp. 3–26, www.ajfand.net/Volume5/No2/Suresh1600.pdf, accessed 10 November 2014.

WHO and FAO. (1974), *Food and Nutrition Terminology*, Terminology Bulletin No. 28, FAO, Rome.

World Bank. (1986), *Poverty and Hunger: Issues and Options for Food Security in Developing Countries*, World Bank, Washington, DC.

World Food Conference. (1974), 'The universal declaration on the eradication of hunger and malnutrition', 5–16 November 1974, FAO, Rome.

World Food Summit. (1996), 'Rome declaration on world food security', 13–17 November 1996, FAO, Rome.

Zhou, Z.Y. (2017), *Achieving Food Security in China: The Challenges Ahead*, Routledge, London.

Further reading

Gibson, M. (2012), *The Feeding of Nations: Redefining Food Security for the 21st Century*, CRC Press, US, Boca Raton, FL. Gibson offers his examination of how the aspiration of global food security has evolved and unfolded. He amalgamates all the disparate elements of food security into one book and sets the record straight about the origins and evolution of the phenomenon while dispelling myths along the way. Part I of the book, Food Security: What Is It, How and Who Does It Affect? is most complementary to the study of Chapter 1.

Simon, G.A. (2012), 'Food security, four dimensions, history', Basic readings as an introduction to food security for students from the IPAD Master, SupAgro, Montpellier attending a joint training program in Rome, 19–24 March 2012. www.fao.org/fileadmin/templates/ERP/uni/F4D.pdf. A useful basic reading on the concept of food security.

Chapter 2

Global food security

An overview

Summary

An overview of the status of global food security is presented in this chapter. Such an overview helps readers grasp food security fundamentals as presented in the rest of the text. Section 2.1 shows the progress towards improved food security since World War II. Section 2.2 depicts the current status of global food security in the early 21st century. Section 2.3 highlights challenges that the human race has to deal with to achieve future food security for all.

Before you read on, note the strong relationship between food security and food systems. Food security is a comprehensive measurement of the performance of a food system. Hence, the level of food security depends on how good a food system is. Generally, if the food system is good, there is improved food security. As such, it is useful to understand what a good food system is. If you are not yet familiar with the concept of food systems, you are advised to read Appendix 2A in this chapter now.

After studying this chapter, you should be able to:
- Describe changes in food availability since World War II at the global, continental, and sub-continental levels.
- Identify continents or sub-continents where severe food insecurity has been prevailing.
- List major challenges that the human race has to handle in its quest to improve future food security.

2.1 Global food security: achievements since World War II

On 2 September 1945, World War II ended. After that, economic reconstruction and recovery took place worldwide. Food availability, which was inadequate and unstable during the War, started to improve gradually. During the 1950s, agricultural policies in many countries focused on increasing domestic production. Some countries also regulated agricultural prices. Soon food surpluses persisted in some rich countries (Gibson 2012, p. 224). During the 1960s, world food production continued growing and food availability improving.

In the late 1960s, grain stocks in exporting countries were very high. Measures were taken by the governments of those countries to reduce food stocks and production capacity. In 1972, global cereal output dropped by 40 million tonnes (mt), partly due to the intended reduction and partly due to poor harvests in parts of the world. This was the first time production had fallen since World War II. Simultaneously, starting in 1972, oil prices soared. Prices of inputs whose production was energy-intensive, such as fertilisers, also increased sharply. Subsequent lower input use, lower yields, and dwindling grain stocks resulted in higher prices. A food crisis, truly at the global scale for the first time, emerged (Simon 2012).

Despite the food crisis, world food production continued increasing (with fluctuations) in the 1970s at a pace largely comparable to that of the 1960s. It was between the 1980s and the early 2010s that food growth was slow, sometimes stagnating or even declining. The global food price crisis in 2006–2007 triggered faster production growth.

Increased food output has resulted in continuous improvements in general food availability around the globe. The FAO uses several indicators to measure the availability of raw food and nutrients from food. Generally, food contains macronutrients and micronutrients, both being essential to human body growth and repair. Three macronutrients are dietary energy, protein, and fats. A minimum amount of each is required for a body to repair, maintain, and grow. This minimum varies between regions and countries depending on various factors such as age, gender, labour strength, climate, and geo-location. For energy, the average dietary energy requirements (ADER) for maintaining body weight are roughly 2350 kilocalories (kcal) per person per day at the global level. The actual availability of energy is measured by the dietary energy supply (DES). When DES is expressed as a percentage of ADER, we derive another important food security indicator: the average dietary energy supply adequacy (ADESA). Energy supply is adequate, on average, if the ADESA is greater or equal to 100. For average daily protein and fat intake, a quantity of around 80 g/capita/day and 50 g/capita/day, respectively, is regarded as adequate.

Data for these indicators from 1961 are available from FAO's Food Balance Sheet (FAO 2018a). In 1961, at the global level, DES was 2196 kcal/capita/day, below the specified ADER. By the early 1970s, DES met the ADER and DES has since continuously increased. The average supply of both protein and fat has also improved and is now above the minimum requirement (Figure 2.1).

The improvement in food supply, however, differed markedly between continents. Since the 1960s, the supply of all the macronutrients in the Americas, Europe, and Oceania has been more than adequate. In Asia and Africa, food shortages existed. Dietary energy supply had only become adequate in the early 1980s in Asia and the early 1990s in Africa. Per capita protein supply, while increasing, was only marginally adequate by the 2010s in both. Per capita fat supply increased much faster in Asia, catching up and then surpassing Africa by the later 1980s (Figure 2.1).

The improvement also differed within a continent. In all the sub-continents of Europe, the supply of all the macronutrients, though varying to some extent, has been above the requirements (Figure 2.2). In the Americas, Northern America's food supply has been adequate.

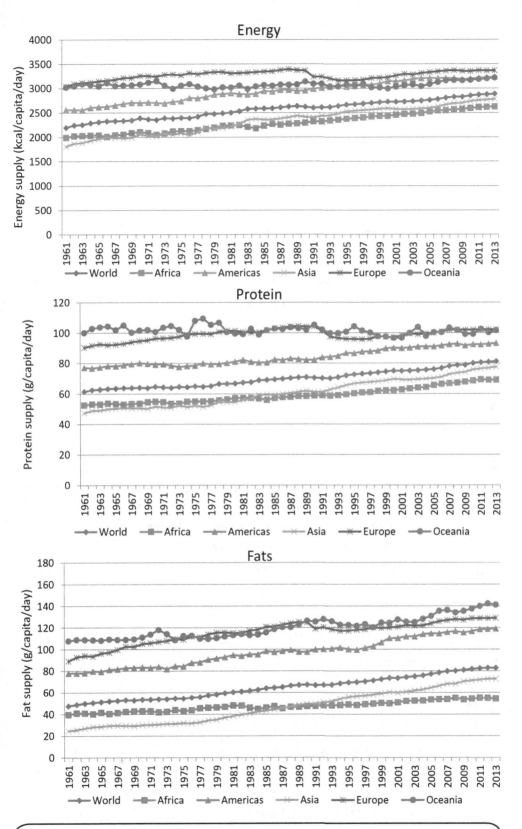

Figure 2.1 Global food supply adequacy.
Source: based on FAO (2018a).

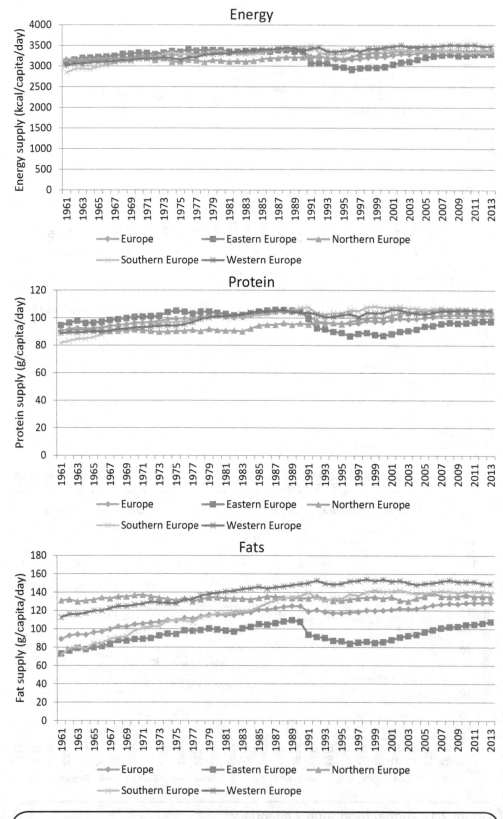

Figure 2.2 Food supply adequacy in Europe and sub-continents.
Source: based on FAO (2018a).

However, food supply was inadequate in all other regions or sub-continents in the early 1960s. The achievement in increasing food supply in Central and South America has been largely comparable and notable. The progress in the Caribbean region has been less impressive and less steady (Figure 2.3).

In Oceania, Australia and New Zealand's food supply has been well above the requirements. The most impressive improvements in food supply occurred in Polynesia (see Figure 2.4). The progress in Melanesia and Micronesia has been less impressive. Their supply of energy and fat has been above requirements but the protein supply has been less adequate.

Most of Asia, with an exception being Western Asia, was starving until the early 1980s. Their supply of all three macronutrients was below requirements (Figure 2.5). The very low supply in Eastern Asia in the early 1960s was due to the very low level of food availability in China where there was a long-lasting, large-scale, and severe famine (starting in late 1958 and ending in mid-1962) (Becker 1996; Dikötter 2010; Song 2013). The improvement in Asia's food availability since the early 1980s, especially in East Asia, has been very impressive. By the early 2000s, the supply of all the macronutrients was above the requirements in Eastern Asia. While not overly impressive, South-Eastern Asia has out-performed Southern Asia since the early 21st century. The performance in improving food supply in Southern Asia is the least satisfactory (Figure 2.5). Central Asia came into being in the early 1990s after the collapse of the USSR (United Socialist Soviet Republic). Its food supply has been largely satisfactory.

In Africa, Southern Africa performed the best in food supply with all macronutrient requirements being nearly met or exceeded. Northern Africa had the most impressive progress in increasing food supply (Figure 2.6). Starting from a very low level of food supply, as for most other subcontinents in Africa, the increase in food supply in Western Africa has also been notable, although protein and fat supply is still below requirements. The achievement in Eastern Africa has been most disappointing. By the 2010s, none of the macronutrient supply requirements had been met. Middle Africa's achievement has not been very satisfactory either; it has performed only marginally better than Eastern Africa.

So far, we have only used food supply, or food availability, to gauge food security achievements. One may rightly argue that, as shown in Chapter 1, food security has several important dimensions and food availability is only one of them. However, food availability is the most important. Food must be available before other dimensions are considered. In this text, a great deal of attention is paid to food availability while accepting that other dimensions of food security are also important.

2.2 Current status of global food security

According to Chapter 1, several frameworks can be used to evaluate the status of food security. From FAO's suite of food security indicators, a couple of them are especially powerful, including ADESA and the 'prevalence of undernourishment' (PoU).

ADESA provides an important index of the adequacy of the food supply in terms of calories in a country or region. The PoU expresses the probability that a randomly selected individual from the population consumes an amount of calories that is insufficient to cover her/his energy requirement for an active and healthy life. It is possible that in a country, the ADESA is well above 100% but the PoU is also very high. This implies that some people in this country do not have an adequate amount of calorie intake, not because there is insufficient food but because it is improperly distributed.

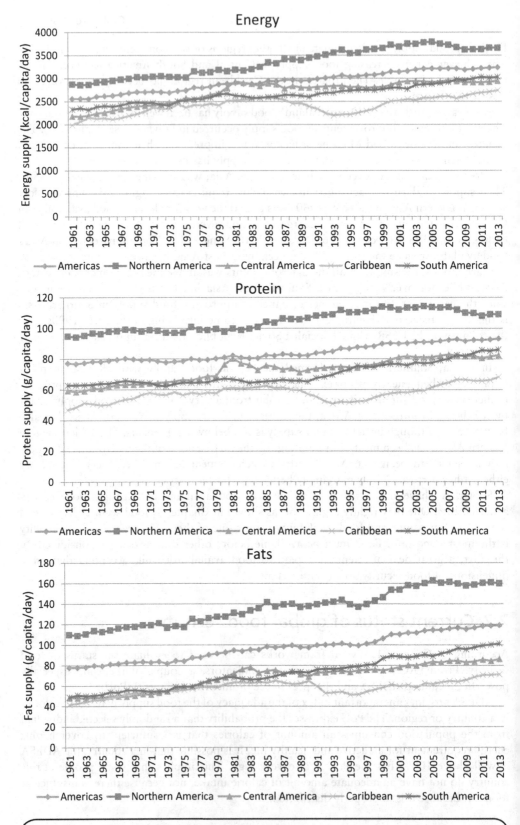

Figure 2.3   Food supply adequacy in Americas and sub-continents.
Source: based on FAO (2018a).

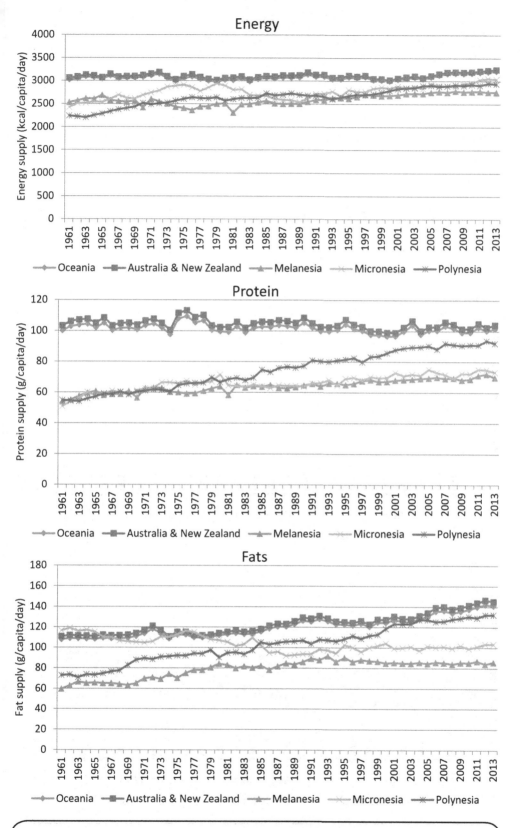

Figure 2.4 Food supply adequacy in Oceania and sub-continents.
Source: based on FAO (2018a).

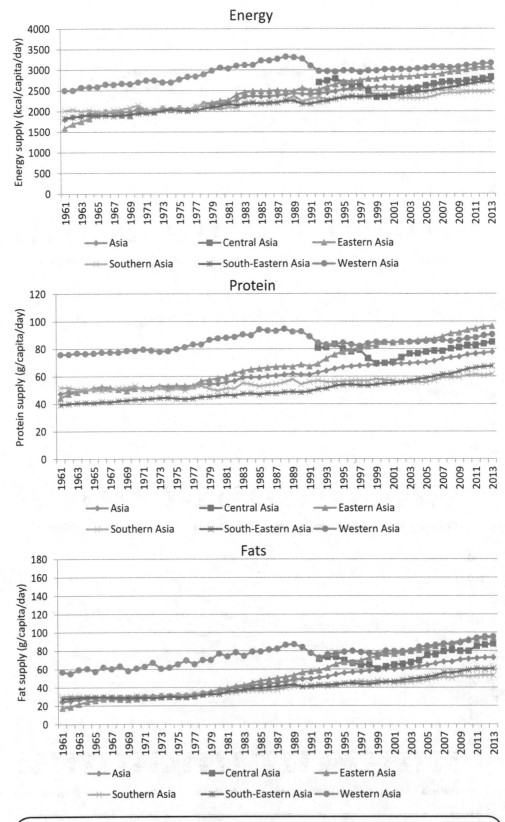

Figure 2.5 Food supply adequacy in Asia and sub-continents.
Source: based on FAO (2018a).

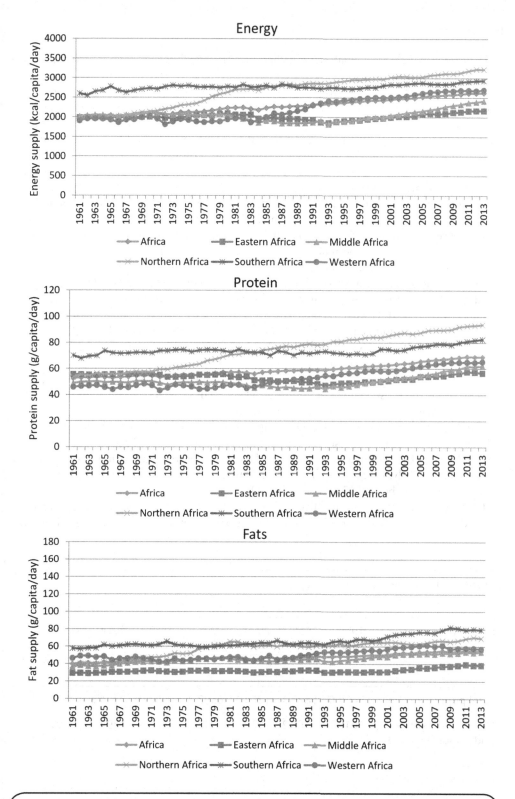

Figure 2.6 Food supply adequacy in Africa and sub-continents.
Source: based on FAO (2018a).

Hence, when ADESA is analysed together with the 'PoU', we are able to derive a broad picture of the overall food security of a country. Generally, if ADESA is greater than 100% and the PoU is below 5%, overall food security is satisfactory. If ADESA is greater than 100% but the PoU is above 5%, then the country's overall food security is not satisfactory. In this case, there is an inequitable income distribution and subsequently, some people do not have the access to food. By applying the PoU to the total population, we get the estimated total number of people at risk of undernourishment in a country.

These three indicators, ADESA, the PoU, and the 'number of people undernourished', provide a good perception of how secure food is in a country or region. These three indicators are related to energy requirements only. They do not cover protein and fats and micronutrients. However, it is common that when calorie intake is short, the intake of other nutrients is also short. Hence, these three indicators adequately reflect food security status. If one is especially interested in details about the intake of other nutrients, one can find them in the full food security indicators database maintained by the FAO (note that such detailed information is chiefly available at the country level, not at the continental or global level) (FAO 2018b).

Table 2.1 shows that at the global level, calorie supply has been adequate in recent decades and improving. The three-year average ADESA (2014–2016) was 123, an improvement of 10 percentage points compared to that of 1990–1992. Unfortunately, the PoU is still as high as over 10% in the 2010s. This means, while the total food supply is more than adequate, over 800 m still live without adequate access to food (Table 2.1).

At the sub-continent level, none in Europe is food insecure. FAO stops reporting food security status for those regions or countries where ADESA is above 100% and the PoU is consistently below 5%. Hence, such data for Europe are not available.

North America has no issues of food insecurity either. Within the Americas, however, other sub-continents are still food insecure (Table 2.2). The Caribbean is the least food secure. Its PoU in 2014–2016 was still as high as 20%. The PoU in Central and South America has been reduced impressively, being close to 5%. The ADESAs achieved in these two sub-continents are also impressive, being 127 by the mid-2010s.

In Oceania, the two economically developed countries, New Zealand and Australia, have no food security concerns. For many other smaller nations in this region, food insecurity still

Table 2.1 Global food security status

Indicators	1990–1992	1995–1997	2000–2002	2005–2007	2010–2012	2014–2016	Growth rate, or, ± percentage points
Total population (m)	5408.0	5820.3	6204.1	6593.3	6997.9	7324.3	1.27
Number of people undernourished (m)	1010.7	966.2	929.6	942.3	820.6	792.5	-1.01
Prevalence of undernourishment (%)	18.6	16.6	14.9	14.3	11.8	10.8	-7.80
ADESA (%)	113	115	116	118	121	123	10.00

Source: based on FAO (2018b).

presents a major challenge. Collectively, these countries' population has been growing at a rate much higher than the global average, at 2.1% annually. The number of their undernourished people did not decline but had grown at an annual rate of 1.4%. The PoU fluctuated over the years from 1990 to 2016, being still as high as 15%, with very limited reduction (Table 2.3).

Asia's current food security is better now than in any other recent times. While its total population has grown at a rate comparable to the global average, its number of undernourished people has dropped at a faster rate. As a result, its PoU has almost halved between 1990 and 2016. In the meantime, its ADESA continuously rose (Table 2.4). However, Asia is still the home to 65% of the world's undernourished.

Within Asia, the food security status in South Asia is the least satisfactory. India contributed significantly to the still large number of undernourished people in this region. East Asia's food security is much better, with major contributions from China. Without China, East Asia's number of people undernourished was actually increasing at an annual rate of 2.4%. Current food security in South-Eastern Asia has also improved compared to the 1990s. Compared to other sub-continents in Asia, food is relatively more secure in the Caucasus and Central Asia. West Asia, however, is cause for concern. Its population is increasing at a rate faster than the global average (2.37% cf. 1.27%) but the number of undernourished is increasing at an even faster rate, being 3.51%. While relatively low previously, its PoU has increased by two percentage points in the mid-2010s compared to that in the early 1990s. In the meantime, its ADESA dropped by six percentage points.

The current food security status in Africa is the most worrisome. Compared to the situation in the early 1990s, its population has increased rapidly (2.49% per annum) and the number of people undernourished has also increased (0.99% per annum) (Table 2.5). It has managed to reduce its PoU by about 8 percentage points to bring it down from 27.6% in the early 1990s to 19.8% in the mid-2010s – still not a good place to be.

North Africa is an exception where food supply poses no major concern at the aggregate level. Also, food security has reached a much higher level in Southern Africa in the mid-2010s. Although its total number of people undernourished has slightly increased, its PoU has declined, approaching 5%. The improvement in Western Africa is also fast and impressive. Its PoU has dropped by a great margin from 24.2% in the early 1990s to 9% in the mid-2010s (being 15.2 percentage points). In the meantime, its ADESA has increased by 18% from 107% to 125%. In East Africa and Middle Africa, the food security situation is the most disturbing. In the former, although its PoU has dropped by an impressive margin – 16%, it was still as high as 32% by the mid-2010s. In the latter, the PoU has actually increased by 8%, being at 41%. Middle Africa's population growth has been the fastest while its ADESA has declined.

Data presented in this section suggest that food security at the global level has generally improved. The improvement, however, is not even. It is very impressive in some parts of the world but far less so in others. At the present time, Middle Africa, Eastern Africa, South Asia, East Asia (without China, Japan, and South Korea), the Caribbean, and Oceania (without Australia and New Zealand) are the least food-secure. Food security in some other regions such as West Africa, South-East Asia and West Asia fares only slightly better. Among these regions, the rising prevalence of undernourishment in West Asia, East Asia (not including China, Japan and South Korea) and especially in Middle Africa is most worrisome.

The above elaboration on food security status is based on geographical locations. Looking at the level of development and the level of income, developed and high-income countries do not have food insecurity problems. Food insecurity is most problematic in the least developed low-income countries. Table 2.6 shows that these countries have the highest PoU and the lowest ADESA.

Table 2.2 Current food security status in Latin America and the Caribbean

Region	Indicators	1990–1992	1995–1997	2000–2002	2005–2007	2010–2012	2014–2016	Growth rate, or, ± percentage points
Latin America and the Caribbean	Total population (m)	453.3	494.3	533.6	569.2	602.8	629.8	1.38
	Number of people undernourished (m)	66.1	65.1	60.4	47.1	38.3	34.3	-2.70
	Prevalence of undernourishment (%)	14.7	13.3	11.4	8.4	6.4	5.5	-9.20
	ADESA (%)	117	119	121	123	126	129	12.00
Caribbean	Total population (m)	34.5	36.7	38.6	40.3	41.7	42.9	0.91
	Number of people undernourished (m)	8.1	9.9	8.2	8.3	7.3	7.5	-0.32
	Prevalence of undernourishment (%)	27	30.9	24.4	23.5	19.8	19.8	-7.20
	ADESA (%)	100	97	107	109	113	115	15.00
Central America	Total population (m)	117.6	130.3	141.7	151.9	162.8	171.9	1.59
	Number of people undernourished (m)	12.6	12.7	11.8	11.6	11.3	11.4	-0.42
	Prevalence of undernourishment (%)	10.7	9.7	8.3	7.6	6.9	6.6	-4.10
	ADESA (%)	126	124	128	128	126	127	1.00
South America	Total population (m)	301.1	327.3	353.3	377.0	398.3	415.0	1.35
	Number of people undernourished (m)	45.4	42.5	40.3	27.2	20.0	19.9	-3.38
	Prevalence of undernourishment (%)	15.1	13.0	11.4	7.2	5.0	4.8	-10.30
	ADESA (%)	115	118	119	123	127	131	16.00

Latin America and the Caribbean = Latin America + the Caribbean; Latin America = Central America + South America.

Source: based on FAO (2018b)

Table 2.3 Current food security status in Oceania

Indicators	1990–1992	1995–1997	2000–2002	2005–2007	2010–2012	2014–2016	Growth rate, or, ± percentage points
Total population (m)	6.6	7.4	8.3	9.1	10.1	10.8	2.07
Number of people undernourished (m)	1.0	1.0	1.3	1.3	1.3	1.4	1.41
Prevalence of undernourishment (%)	15.7	14.6	16.5	15.4	13.5	14.2	-1.50
ADESA (%)	113	114	112	115	115	114	1.00

Source: based on FAO (2018b).

Table 2.4 Current food security status in Asia

Region	Indicators	1990–1992	1995–1997	2000–2002	2005–2007	2010–2012	2014–2016	Growth rate, or, ± percentage points
Asia	Total population (m)	3141.9	3400.2	3629.6	3852.5	4074.0	4248.6	1.27
	Number of people undernourished (m)	741.9	681.7	636.6	665.6	547.0	511.7	-1.54
	Prevalence of undernourishment (%)	23.6	20.1	17.6	17.3	13.5	12.1	-11.50
	ADESA (%)	107	111	111	112	117	120	13.00

(continued)

Table 2.4 (cont.)

Region	Indicators	1990–1992	1995–1997	2000–2002	2005–2007	2010–2012	2014–2016	Growth rate, or, ± percentage points
Caucasus and Central Asia	Total population (m)	67.0	69.5	71.4	74.5	79.1	83.1	0.90
	Number of people undernourished (m)	9.6	8.9	10.9	8.4	7.1	5.8	-2.08
	Prevalence of undernourishment (%)	14.1	12.8	15.3	11.3	8.9	7.0	-7.10
	ADESA (%)	114	112	107	116	119	123	9.00
East Asia	Total population (m)	1275.2	1344.8	1389.0	1430.3	1475.4	1510.6	0.71
	Number of people undernourished (m)	295.4	245.6	221.7	217.6	174.7	145.1	-2.92
	Prevalence of undernourishment (%)	23.2	18.3	16.0	15.2	11.8	9.6	-13.60
	ADESA (%)	107	114	117	118	125	129	22.00
East Asia (exc China)	Total population (m)	66.1	69.3	71.7	73.8	76.1	77.8	0.68
	Number of people undernourished (m)	6.4	9.5	10.4	10.3	11.5	11.3	2.40
	Prevalence of undernourishment (%)	9.6	13.7	14.6	13.9	15.1	14.6	5.00
	ADESA (%)	115	114	115	115	119	123	8.00
Southern Asia	Total population (m)	1217.4	1345.7	1472.8	1592.2	1703.9	1793.5	1.63
	Number of people	291.2	293.7	272.3	319.1	274.2	281.4	-0.14

Region	Indicators	1990–1992	1995–1997	2000–2002	2005–2007	2010–2012	2014–2016	Growth rate, or, ± percentage points
	Prevalence of undernourishment (%)	23.9	21.8	18.5	20.1	16.1	15.7	-8.20
	ADESA (%)	106	107	106	106	109	110	4.00
South Asia (exc India)	Total population (m)	331.1	372.6	413.3	449.1	482.7	511.2	1.83
	Number of people undernourished (m)	81.1	94.7	86.7	85.3	84.3	86.8	0.28
	Prevalence of undernourishment (%)	24.5	25.4	21.0	19.0	17.5	17.0	-7.50
	ADESA (%)	109	108	108	110	111	113	4.00
South-Eastern Asia	Total population (m)	452.2	493.1	532.0	569.0	604.3	633.0	1.41
	Number of people undernourished (m)	137.5	120.8	117.6	103.2	72.5	60.5	-3.36
	Prevalence of undernourishment (%)	30.6	24.7	22.3	18.3	12.1	9.6	-21.00
	ADESA (%)	100	105	106	110	117	120	20.00
West Asia	Total population (m)	130.1	147.2	164.5	186.5	211.3	228.5	2.37
	Number of people undernourished (m)	8.3	12.8	14.1	17.2	18.4	19.0	3.51
	Prevalence of undernourishment (%)	6.4	8.7	8.6	9.3	8.9	8.4	2.00
	ADESA (%)	141	135	134	133	134	135	-6.00

Source: based on FAO (2018b).

Table 2.5 Current food security status in Africa

Region	Indicators	1990–1992	1995–1997	2000–2002	2005–2007	2010–2012	2014–2016	Growth rate, or, ± percentage points
Africa	Total population (m)	646.9	734.4	828.0	934.3	1057.2	1166.4	2.49
	Number of people undernourished (m)	181.7	196.0	210.2	213.0	218.3	230.3	0.99
	Prevalence of undernourishment (%)	27.6	26.6	25.4	22.7	20.7	19.8	-7.80
	ADESA (%)	107	109	110	113	116	117	10.00
Eastern Africa	Total population (m)	203.6	231.7	267.4	306.5	352.6	394.8	2.80
	Number of people undernourished (m)	103.9	117.1	121.6	122.5	118.7	124.2	0.75
	Prevalence of undernourishment (%)	47.2	47.9	43.1	37.8	33.7	31.5	-15.70
	ADESA (%)	89	89	93	97	100	101	12.00
Middle Africa	Total population (m)	72.4	84.9	96.4	111.6	128.5	143.3	2.89
	Number of people undernourished (m)	24.2	31.7	42.4	47.7	53.0	58.9	3.78

Region	Indicators	1990–1992	1995–1997	2000–2002	2005–2007	2010–2012	2014–2016	Growth rate, or, ± percentage points
	Prevalence of undernourishment (%)	33.5	37.6	44.2	43.0	41.5	41.3	7.80
	ADESA (%)	101	94	92	94	96	95	-6.00
Southern Africa	Total population (m)	43.1	48.3	52.2	55.9	59.4	61.3	1.48
	Number of people undernourished (m)	3.1	3.9	3.7	3.5	3.6	3.2	0.13
	Prevalence of undernourishment (%)	7.2	8.2	7.1	6.2	6.1	5.2	-2.00
	ADESA (%)	119	117	119	120	123	127	8.00
Western Africa	Total population (m)	184.6	210.9	240.0	273.7	313.7	349.8	2.70
	Number of people undernourished (m)	44.6	36.6	35.9	32.3	30.2	31.5	-1.44
	Prevalence of undernourishment (%)	24.2	17.3	15.0	11.8	9.6	9.0	-15.20
	ADESA (%)	107	114	116	122	125	125	18.00

(continued)

Table 2.5 (cont.)

Region	Indicators	1990–1992	1995–1997	2000–2002	2005–2007	2010–2012	2014–2016	Growth rate, or, ± percentage points
North Africa	Total population (m)	122.3	133.4	143.6	154.2	166.6	177.4	1.56
	Number of people undernourished (m)	6.0	6.6	6.6	7.0	5.1	4.3	-1.38
	Prevalence of undernourishment (%)	na	na	na	na	na	na	
	ADESA (%)	138	139	139	140	145	148	10.00
Sub-Saharan Africa	Total population (m)	503.8	575.7	655.9	747.7	854.1	949.3	2.67
	Number of people undernourished (m)	175.7	189.3	203.6	206.0	205.5	217.8	0.90
	Prevalence of undernourishment (%)	33.2	31.7	30.0	26.5	24.1	23.0	-10.20
	ADESA (%)	100	102	104	108	110	111	11.00

Note: North Africa (exc Sudan).
Source: based on FAO (2018b).

Table 2.6 Food security status and the levels of development and income

Region	Indicators	1990–1992	1995–1997	2000–2002	2005–2007	2010–2012	2014–2016	Growth rate, or, ± percentage points
Food security and the level of development								
Developed countries	Total population (m)	1159.3	1184.0	1204.5	1228.1	1253.8	1268.7	0.38
	Number of people undernourished (m)	20.0	22.4	21.2	15.4	15.7	14.7	-1.27
	Prevalence of undernourishment (%)	na	na	na	na	na	na	
	ADESA (%)	131	130	133	135	134	136	5.00
Developing countries	Total population (m)	4248.8	4636.3	4999.5	5365.2	5744.1	6055.6	1.49
	Number of people undernourished (m)	990.7	943.8	908.5	926.9	804.9	777.8	-1.00
	Prevalence of undernourishment (%)	23.3	20.4	18.2	17.3	14.1	12.9	-10.40
	ADESA (%)	108	112	112	114	118	120	12.00
Least-developed countries	Total population (m)	523.7	600.3	679.6	765.7	858.2	940.0	2.47
	Number of people undernourished (m)	209.3	245.7	244.3	237.6	237.7	248.7	0.72

(continued)

Table 2.6 (cont.)

Region	Indicators	1990–1992	1995–1997	2000–2002	2005–2007	2010–2012	2014–2016	Growth rate, or, ± percentage points
	Prevalence of undernourishment (%)	40.0	41.6	36.5	31.4	27.7	26.5	-13.50
	ADESA (%)	95	93	97	101	104	105	10.00
Food security and the level of income								
Lower-middle-income economies	Total population (m)	1767.0	1945.8	2122.0	2298.6	2480.2	2627.3	1.67
	Number of people undernourished (m)	407.7	376.9	374.5	420.0	353.0	353.4	-0.59
	Prevalence of undernourishment (%)	22.8	19.2	17.5	18.2	14.2	13.5	-9.30
	ADESA (%)	108	110	109	110	114	115	7.00
Low-income economies	Total population (m)	513.8	584.5	658.6	737.4	822.4	899.1	2.36
	Number of people undernourished (m)	199.2	239.5	238.4	231.5	236.6	247.6	0.91
	Prevalence of undernourishment (%)	39.1	41.4	36.6	31.8	28.7	27.5	-11.60
	ADESA (%)	95	93	96	100	103	104	9.00
Food security and the level of food self-sufficiency								
Low-income food deficit countries	Total population (m)	1657.1	1851.5	2049.1	2254.0	2464.6	2644.3	1.97
	Number of people	460.2	480.6	468.9	512.8	473.8	493.6	0.29

Region	Indicators	1990–1992	1995–1997	2000–2002	2005–2007	2010–2012	2014–2016	Growth rate, or, ± percentage points
	Prevalence of undernourishment (%)	27.6	25.9	22.8	22.7	19.2	18.7	-8.90
	ADESA (%)	103	104	104	106	109	109	6.00
Food security and access to seaport								
Land-locked developing countries	Total population (m)	270.7	304.1	341.6	382.9	430.4	473.2	2.35
	Number of people undernourished (m)	94.4	109.2	112.3	105.2	103.8	107.4	0.54
	Prevalence of undernourishment (%)	35.6	36.6	33.6	28.1	24.1	22.7	-12.90
	ADESA (%)	98	97	99	104	108	110	12.00
Food security and island size								
Small island developing states	Total population (m)	48.9	52.7	56.4	60.0	63.4	66.2	1.27
	Number of people undernourished (m)	10.2	11.9	10.7	10.8	9.7	10.1	-0.04
	Prevalence of undernourishment (%)	24.5	26.7	22.5	21.3	18.2	18.0	-6.50
	ADESA (%)	103	101	108	111	113	115	12.00

Source: based on FAO (2018b).

Table 2.6 also suggests that whether a country has a food deficit (i.e., less than 100% food self-sufficiency), a country is land-locked, or a country is a small island is not critical to a country's food security status. These factors may have an apparent association with a country's food security level if the country also has a low level of development with low income. Otherwise, countries with any of these attributes, but with a high level of development and with a high income, can still enjoy a very high level of food security; for example, Japan (very low level of food self-sufficiency), Switzerland (land-locked), and Singapore (small island).

2.3 Global food security: trends and challenges

In the foreseeable future, if there are no major shocks, e.g., politically, socially, economically, or environmentally, the following trends will prevail:

- Developed and high income countries are most likely to continue enjoying higher levels of food security.
- Developing and poor countries are most likely to continue living with lower levels of food security although some of them may be able to improve their food security to some extent.

Large differences in food security levels between developed and developing countries will remain.Narrowing the differences is possible if those food-insecure countries are willing to improve their weak institutions and their governments are made accountable to their people. Otherwise, it is also possible that their food insecurity may increase. The importance of the quality of a nation's institutions to food security will be repeatedly emphasised in the rest of the text.

There are also major challenges, existing, potential, or emerging, that the human race has to face in its quest to improve food security, including:

- Large-scale man-made shocks to the world due to wars (potential) and terror acts (emerging).
- Large-scale nature-induced and/or man-induced shocks, i.e., impacts resulting from climate changes (emerging and ongoing), damage to food production resulting from extreme weather events (ongoing regionally, but potential on a larger scale).
- Widespread epidemics that have significant impacts on food production and transportation/ distribution (potential).
- Inadequate public and private investment in R&D (research and development) to continue improving agricultural productivity and to explore new sources of food (existing and ongoing).
- Disturbances to global trade institutions or resorts to increasing trade restrictions by national policies (existing and emerging).

Future food security of all nations, no matter poor or rich, will be affected by these challenges. How to handle such challenges will be a recurring theme in the rest of the text when we discuss food security fundamentals. In the next three parts, we will first examine what affects food demand and supply and market equilibrium. This provides a valuable framework with which we can analyse how factors that affect food demand or supply can be influenced to ensure food supply is adequate to meet the demand. In Part 5, examples of how various countries have influenced demand and supply for improved food security are given. Finally in Part 6, we pull together all the threads addressed in the earlier parts to pinpoint and emphasise what ultimately matters if a country really wants to improve its level of food security.

Review questions

1. What are useful indicators to measure the level and adequacy of food availability?
2. At the global level, to what extent, has food availability improved since the early 1960s?
3. Since the early 1960s, which continents' food availability has improved or deteriorated?
4. Identify the sub-continents whose food availability has improved or deteriorated since the early 1960s. Which one has the most improved food availability? Which one the least?
5. The two databases maintained by the FAO, 'Food Balance Sheets' and 'Food Security Indicators', can be very useful in informing us of food security status at the global, continental, sub-continental or country levels. What would be the major indicators which you would use to highlight your country's current food security status? Explain your choice of the indicators.
6. Related to Review Question 5, produce a one-page outline that highlights your country's current food security status.

Discussion questions

1. Food security has several dimensions. In your view, which dimension is most important and should receive more attention? Why?
2. In Figure 2.1, for all three macronutrients, their availability in Asia was below that in Africa in the early 1960s. Explain why.
3. Explain: why in Figure 2.1, the availability of all three macronutrients in Asia started to exceed that in Africa from the early 1980s.
4. Figure 2.6 shows the level of food security in Eastern Africa has been very unsatisfactory. Investigate what the major causes could be.
5. In addition to the major challenges that the human race has to handle to improve future food security, as listed in Section 2.3, are there any other major challenges, either existing, potential or emerging?

References

Becker, J. (1996), *Hungry Ghosts: China's Secret Famine*, John Murray, London.
Dikötter, F. (2010), *Mao's Great Famine: The History of China's Most Devastating Catastrophe, 1958–1962*, Walker, New York.
FAO. (2018a), 'Food balance sheets', www.fao.org/faostat/en/#data/FBS, accessed 15 August 2018.
FAO. (2018b), 'Food security indicators', www.fao.org/faostat/en/#data/FS, accessed 6 August 2018.

Gibson, M. (2012), *The Feeding of Nations: Redefining Food Security for the 21st Century*, Boca Raton, FL, CRC Press, US.

Simon, G.A. (2012), 'Food security, four dimensions, history', Basic readings as an introduction to food security for students from the IPAD Master, SupAgro, Montpellier attending a joint training program in Rome, 19–24 March 2012, www.fao.org/fileadmin/templates/ERP/uni/F4D.pdf, accessed 8 August 2015.

Song, Y.Y. (ed) (2013), *Database of the Chinese Great Leap Forward and Great Famine*, Fairbank Center for Chinese Studies, Harvard University, Boston, USA.

Further reading

Gibson, M. (2012), *The Feeding of Nations: Redefining Food Security for the 21st Century*, Boca Raton, FL, CRC Press, US. Part III of the book provides a more detailed overview of changes in global food security over the 20th century and also the first several years of the 21st century.

Shaw, D.J. (2007), *World Food Security: A History since 1945*, Houndsmill, Basingstoke, Palgrave Macmillan, UK. This book provides a much more comprehensive account of the numerous attempts made since World War II to provide food security for all.

Appendix 2A

Global food system

2A.1 What is a food system?

A food system is defined as a system that embraces all the elements (environment, people, inputs, processes, infrastructure, institutions, markets, and trade) and activities that relate to the production, storage, processing, distribution, retailing, preparation and consumption of food, and the outputs of these activities, including socio-economic and environmental outcomes (Hueston and McLeod 2012; Chase and Grubinger 2014).

Food systems emerged with the dawn of civilisation when agriculture, including the domestication of animals, set the stage for permanent settlements. Inhabitants could grow more crops and raise more animals than necessary to feed those who tended them. This changed human culture; unlike earlier hunter-gatherers, agriculturalists did not need to be in constant motion to find new sources of food. Cultivating grain allowed for drying and storage of some of the harvest for later consumption. Different grain cultures emerged in each of the cradles of civilisation: maize in Mexico, rice in China, and wheat and barley in the Middle East.

Since agriculture began, food systems have constantly evolved, each change bringing new advantages and challenges. Today, food systems have become extremely complex. In reality, any of the above-mentioned 'elements' and 'activities' can change over time and vary between regions (Hueston and McLeod 2012; Chase and Grubinger 2014).

Food systems affect food security. To improve food security for today and for the future, food systems need to be sustainable. A sustainable food system is one that is able to generate food not only for the current generation but also for future generations (FAO, UNCTAD, UNIDO, and World Bank 2015).

Agriculture adds to greenhouse gas (GHG) emissions and thus contributes to climate change. It has the potential to reduce GHG emissions. Hence, a sustainable food system should be climate-smart and simultaneously increase agricultural productivity. In addition to agricultural production, other 'elements' and 'activities' such as transportation of inputs and outputs, food consumption, and associated activities like transformation of certain crops/vegetables/fruits are all important dimensions of sustainable food systems.

A food system's sustainability is influenced by natural and human factors. Through smart, sensible, and responsible human choices, we can help to make our food systems sustainable, achieving food security for today and for the future.

2A.2 Levels of the food systems

Food systems function at a hierarchy of levels (Hueston and McLeod 2012; Chase and Grubinger 2014):

- Individual.
- Household.
- Local.
- Regional.
- National.
- Global.

Each of these levels reflects and responds to social, cultural, political, economic, and environmental conditions, whether in a household kitchen or through a nation's food policies.

The levels in this hierarchy also interact. For example, consider asparagus. When consumers are convinced that asparagus is packed with health benefits, more individuals are likely to buy and eat it. Their household budget affects the amount of money they spend on asparagus. Their decisions to buy locally produced or imported asparagus have the potential to affect the revenues of local, regional, and national asparagus producers and companies selling asparagus, or the revenues of those in other countries that produce and sell asparagus. The same is true for most foods we eat.

Individual food systems: This level of the food system is focused on personal decisions about food, which include how to acquire, prepare, serve, give away, eat, store, and clean it. These decisions and resulting behaviours are influenced by many factors including life experience, cultural and social factors, and the need to balance different values such as affordability and quality. The decisions a person makes about food can differ depending on circumstances and can change over time. For example, people often follow a different diet when they eat out compared to cooking at home, and few people eat the same way they did as a teenager once they reach middle age. When aggregated at the household level, individual decisions about food help us understand how families interact with food systems.

Household food systems: Most households are groups of people, often related, that live together and function as a unit. In terms of food, they may eat together, share a household food budget, and affect one another's eating behaviours, especially through parental influence on children. The proportion of income spent on food is lower for households with higher income and higher for households with lower income. As income rises, households increase their expenditure on food. Generally, the increase in food expenditure is less than their income increase. Hence, the proportion of income spent on food decreases when household income increases. Understanding food systems at the household level helps us paint a picture of food systems on a larger scale, at the local, regional, and national levels.

Local food systems: There is no universally accepted definition of a local food system. Local foods are often based on a geographical concept related to the distance between food producers and consumers. Local food systems are frequently associated with direct marketing of 'local foods' from farms to consumers or to retailers and institutions in the same geographic location as the farms. Direct-to-consumer markets include farm stands and farmers' markets. Direct-to-retailer sales include convenience shops, supermarkets, and restaurants. Institutions include schools, hospitals, prisons, and retirement villages.

Regional food systems: As for local food systems, regional food systems are place-based. Here, the 'place' is conceived more broadly. There is distinct boundary between local and regional food systems. 'Regional' is often thought to include a cluster of 'locals'. In general, regional food systems aggregate smaller local communities in order to accommodate larger scales of production and economic activity. In a regional food system, direct marketing is not paramount; rather, regional identity has value in the food marketplace to consumers and producers (e.g., producers in the Barossa Valley of South Australia are proud of the wine grapes and the subsequent wines they produce, which are highly sought after by consumers). Together, regional food systems within a nation make up the national food system.

National food systems: The food system at the national level is easier to define than a local or regional food system because the geographic boundaries are clear. In addition, many features of the food system as a whole are set up on a national basis, such as most food policies and regulations (e.g., food safety, product labelling). Characteristics of national food systems can be described and compared using various criteria, such as dietary intake (rice is the staple in Japan and South Korea) and the levels of food processing (a high portion of food is processed in high-income countries such as the USA and the UK). Private-sector initiatives are also part of national food systems, as are educational efforts and consumer actions. All national food systems combined make up the global food system.

The global food system: At this topmost level, the food system is inevitably diverse and complex, involving everything from subsistence farming to multinational food companies. Inputs used for food production and food outputs are moved around the globe. Examples of food and food ingredients moved include animals and animal products, plants and plant products, minerals, and vitamins. Food processing supplies are also moved around the globe, including for example processing equipment, packaging and chemicals such as disinfectants and preservatives. Agricultural inputs are moved, too, from feed to fertiliser, to vaccines and pharmaceuticals, to planting and harvesting equipment. In the recent decades, international trade in agri-food and other food ingredients has increased. As a result, one processed food sold in a country may include ingredients from multiple countries.

2A.3 Food systems and food security

The delineations above point out that food systems have strong impacts on the levels of food output today and food production sustainability for the future. In particular, food systems are integrally related to food safety. Contamination can occur at any point in the food system, and prevention and control strategies can be implemented at any point. The scale and complexities of today's food systems contribute to the likelihood and magnitude of food-borne illness. The more complex, the more opportunities for things to go wrong; the larger the scale, the more people are potentially affected. These features of food systems are closely interlinked with important dimensions of food security, as demonstrated in Chapter 1. In other words, the level of food security, either at the regional, national, or global level, depends greatly on the performance of the food systems. In this sense, the level of food security is an important measurement of how well the food systems perform.

Everyone eats; therefore, everyone relies on, and thus is a participant in, food systems; locally or globally. Consequently, individuals' decisions about food, i.e., how they choose to acquire, prepare, serve, give away, eat, store, and clean food, have significant influence on many aspects of food systems such as resource utilisation, environmental quality, production sustainability, and national food policies. Each and every one of us can choose to consume food responsibly to help the food systems to function well at all levels, hence contributing to improved global food security.

The evolution of food systems over time and their sophistication in the present day also mean that, unlike those in the times when subsistence was dominant, it is no longer feasible for the majority of the people on the planet to produce their own food. Food has to be produced and distributed through more complex division of labour and cooperation, hence, requiring effective managing and coordination at various levels of our modern society. Within a country, it is largely the national government's responsibility to first ensure adequate food availability to the citizens and ultimately achieve and maintain a high level of food security for all.

Discussion questions

1. Do you think the level of food security is a good measurement of the performance of a food system? Why?
2. As an individual, your 'food system' is focused on personal decisions about food. How are your personal decisions about food related to many aspects of higher level of food systems such as resource utilisation, environmental quality, production sustainability, and national food policies? Can you make any improvements to your 'individual food system'?

References

Chase, L. and Grubinger, V. (2014), *Food, Farms, and Community: Exploring Food Systems*, University of New Hampshire Press, Lebanon, NH. Chapter 1: Introduction to Food Systems, pp. 1–15.

FAO, UNCTAD (United Nations Conference on Trade and Development), UNIDO (United Nations Industrial Development Organization) and World Bank. (2015), 'All food systems are sustainable', in Advisory Notes by the HLTF (High-Level Task Force) Working Groups to Respond to the 5 'Zero Hunger Challenge' Elements, FAO, Rome, pp. 31–37.

Hueston, W. and McLeod, A. (2012), 'Overview of the global food system: changes over time/space and lessons for future food safety', in Institute of Medicine (US) (ed), *Improving Food Safety through a One Health Approach: Workshop Summary*, National Academies Press, Washington, DC, pp. 189–197.

Part 2

Food security

Demand side

Contents

3 Population and food demand

4 Income and food demand

5 Other determinants of food demand

Food has to be purchased and consumed on a regular basis. How much food consumers demand is affected by many factors. Similarly, how much food producers supply is also affected by many factors. Understanding how such factors affect food demand and supply is of crucial importance in understanding how policies are used to manage and balance food demand and supply and ultimately to better manage and improve a country's food security. In this part, we first discuss how some key factors affect food demand. In the next part we will study factors that affect food supply.

Among the factors that have the most important impact on food demand are population and income. In Chapters 3 and 4, we focus, respectively, on how population and income affect food demand. In Chapter 5, we discuss the impact of some other important factors on food demand.

Before you read on, it is recommended that you first study Appendix 3A. Appendix 3A helps you to revise (if you have done some previous study) or understand (if you have not done any at all) the basics of demand and supply.

Chapter 3

Population and food demand

Summary

This chapter addresses how population impacts on food security. It first shows how population change affects food demand. It then discusses how human beings have tried to feed the fast expanding population since World War II and how future population expansion will affect food demand and food security.

After studying this chapter, you should be able to:
- Explain how food demand is affected by population change.
- Discuss how future population change will impact on food demand and food security.
- Formulate your own opinion as to how our human society should handle future population increase for better food security.

3.1 Population growth and food demand

Suppose, initially, the population is one million in the Rasian Republic, or Rasia (a hypothetical country). The demand curve for rice by the Rasians is D_1 in Figure 3.1 (all three demand curves in Figure 3.1 are based on the demand schedules contained in Table 3A.3 in Appendix 3A: Columns 1 and 4 for D_1, Columns 1 and 6 for D_2 and Columns 1 and 8 for D_3). The supply curve by Rasian rice producers is S_1 in Figure 3.1 (based on the supply schedule, Columns 1 and 4 in Table 3A.5).

According to Figure 3.1, the rice market in Rasia reaches its equilibrium at Point E_1, where D_1 and S_1 intersect. The equilibrium price is $0.8 per kg. At this price, the quantity demanded by consumers is 120 kt.

Intuitively, the more people, the more food is needed. Now, *ceteris paribus* (meaning hold everything else constant), the total population is increased to 1.5 million. As a result, the total demand for food increases. This will lead to a shift in the demand curve to the right, from D_1 to D_2 (Figure 3.1).

Because there is no supply change, now D_2 and S_1 intersect at E_2. At this new equilibrium, the price goes up, from P_1 to P_2, and the total quantity demanded increases from Q_1 to Q_2. (Note if you have trouble understanding the above, turn to Appendix 3A at the end of this chapter and study the appendix first.)

If the population further increases to 2 million, then the demand curve shifts further to D_3. Now, without any supply change, D_3 and S_1 intersect at E_3. At this new equilibrium, the price goes up further, from P_2 to P_3, and the total quantity demanded increases from Q_2 to Q_3.

Hence, when the population increases, with everything else held constant, total demand for food will increase. Of course, if the population decreases, total demand will decrease.

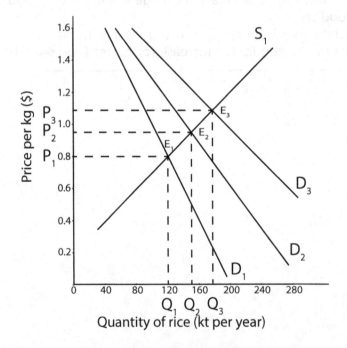

Figure 3.1 Impact of population change on food demand.

However, in most countries, especially in most developing countries where food is largely insecure, total population has increased. (Recently, population has decreased only in some developed countries such as Japan where food security generally is not an issue.)

Not only does population size affect food demand, other attributes of population such as gender and age structure also affect food demand. Males generally require more food than females. Young people require more food than elderly ones.

However, in terms of total quantity demanded, the size of population has the most significant impact. Hence, the focus in this chapter is on the impact on food demand by total population. How other attributes of population may affect the quantity and composition of food are dealt with elsewhere.

3.2 Population growth in the past

Human population has increased enormously over the course of its existence and has reached 7.6 billion in 2018. The population increase in the 20th century was explosive (Figure 3.2). During this century alone, over 4 billion people were added. Data show that it took a long time for world total population to reach 1 billion. It took only 125 years for the population to reach the second billion. In recent decades, each increase of a billion in the population has taken just 12 years (Table 3.1). According to forecasts, population growth will slow down to some extent. But in less than 40 years, by 2055, the total population will reach 10 billion, over 2 billion more than today's population (Table 3.1).

Despite the fast population increase, human beings have managed to feed themselves most of the time. Nonetheless, managing to feed the large and still-increasing number of people remains challenging. The pressure on the ecosystem to extract more food has been so significant as to cause environmental damages.

At the regional level, Asia has been the most crowded continent with its population being almost 60% of world's total (Figure 3.3). After World War II, all continents, except

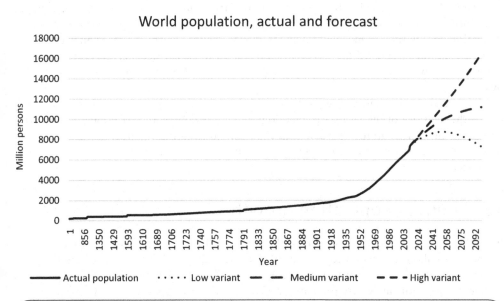

Figure 3.2 World population, actual and forecast.
Source: based on Roser and Ortiz-Ospina (2017) and UNPD (2017).

Table 3.1 Number of years taken for human population to increase by 1 billion

	Year reached	Number of years taken
1 billion	1803	From beginning of human existence
2 billion	1928	125
3 billion	1960	32
4 billion	1975	15
5 billion	1987	12
6 billion	1999	12
7 billion	2011	12
8 billion	2023F	12
9 billion	2037F	14
10 billion	2055F	18

F: forecast. UNPD (2017) provides three sets of forecasts at different population growth rates, high, medium, and low. The forecasts used in this table are the medium variant.
Source: based on Roser and Ortiz-Ospina (2017) and UNPD (2017).

Europe, experienced fast population expansion. Between 1950 and 2015, the average annual population growth rate was the highest in Africa (2.58%), followed by Latin America and the Caribbean (2.05%). For Asia, Oceania, and North America, this rate was 1.78%, 1.77%, and 1.12%, respectively. The growth rate was the lowest in Europe, being only 0.46% (Figure 3.3).

If we look at regional growth rates at a shorter time interval (every ten years), they all experienced a fast increase after World War II till the 1960s or 1970s (Figure 3.4). Since then, population growth rates in most continents started to decline. The only exception was Africa, where it continued rising till the 1990s when it started to slowly decline. Currently, Africa's population growth rate still remains at a very high level (>2%). Europe's rate has been the lowest.

These trends in population suggest that (1) Asia has had the greatest challenge as it had to feed the majority of the world's population; and (2) regions with fast population growth have faced and will continue to face tough challenges to feed the ever-increasing number of mouths. In the next section, we examine the prospects of population growth and how they may affect food security.

3.3 Trends in population growth

By 2058, i.e., in 40 years, it is projected that the world's total population will increase by another 2.5 billion, compared to that in 2018 (UNPD 2017). The increase of another 2.5 billion is gigantic. Further, most of the increased population will be in those countries, sub-continents, or continents where food availability has been very poor.

Figure 3.5 shows that at the continental level, Africa's population will continue increasing at an annual rate greater than 2% till the early 2040s. After that, it may take another 40 years

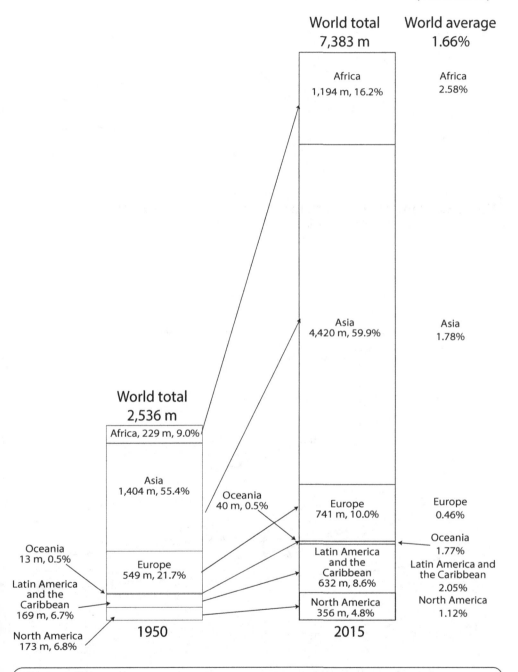

Figure 3.3 World population growth (1950–2015).

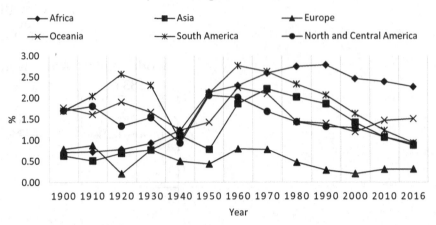

Figure 3.4 Population growth rates at the continent level (1900–2016).
Source: based on Roser and Ortiz-Ospina (2017).

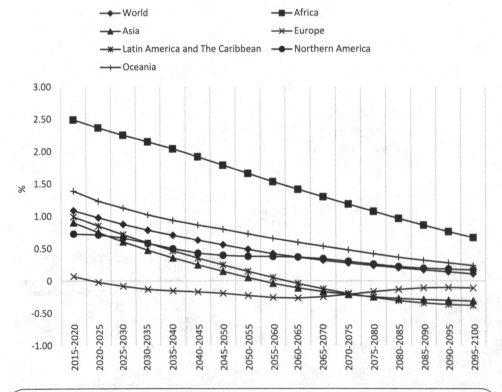

Figure 3.5 Population growth rates, forecast (medium fertility, 2015–2100).
Source: UNPD (2017).

(i.e., until the early 2080s) for its population growth rate to reduce to 1%. By then, all other continents will have a population growth rate that is way below 0.5% or is negative. Due to this very fast growth, from 2015 onwards, a very large portion of the world's increased population will be in Africa. By 2100, Africa's population will amount to 4.5 billion and account for about 40% of the world's total, only slightly behind Asia (Figure 3.6).

In Chapter 2, it was pointed out that, currently, food is least secure in most sub-continents in Africa. These sub-continents also had very fast population growth (Table 2.5). Hence, feeding the extra people in Africa in the years to come is a huge challenge.

In some other countries or sub-continents, such as India and South Asia, food is less insecure compared to those in Africa. However, the annual net increase in population is still very large. The current total population in South Asia is about 1.9 billion. The annual growth rate for the next 15 years is forecast to gradually decline from the current 1.2% to 0.9% by 2030 (UNPD 2017). This implies that around 19 million people will be added to its total population each year from now till 2030. Feeding such a large and increasing number of mouths in South Asia also presents huge challenges for human society.

Will we human beings be able to produce enough food to feed all the mouths? Most probably, yes. Given that human beings have done a marvellous job in the past of producing enough food for the large population, it is most likely we will be able to do so as well in the future (this, however, does not mean that everyone will have an adequate amount of food due to distribution issues, which will be discussed later in the text). There are various means at human beings' disposal to increase food output, such as more efficient use of resources, better protection of the natural environment, adequate investment in research and development, all of which will be dealt with in later chapters.

Despite the possibility that human beings may be capable of producing enough extra food to meet the needs of future population increase, some fundamental questions should draw our attention: Is the planet Earth capable of accommodating more human population? What will be the impact on the health of the Earth's ecosystem? Should the ever-expanding demand for food by human beings be curtailed by reducing human population?

The direct and significant impact of population change on food demand as depicted in Figure 3.1 clearly suggests that controlling human population increase is very effective in reducing the pressure to have more food produced, hence helping improving food security. Regions and countries with high population growth but low food security should seriously consider planning and curtailing their population expansion as an important approach to helping improve their food security.

Review questions

1. How do some attributes of population affect the demand for food (such as geographical locations – living in mountainous areas or plains, rural or urban – age composition, or the population size)? Which one do you think has the greatest impact on food demand?
2. What has happened to the population size of our world over time (from 1–2018)? What are the periods during which the population increased fastest?
3. What is likely to happen to the size of the global population in the future?
4. Which continents will have higher population growth in the future? Are they currently food secure?
5. Which continents will have a higher total population in the future? Are they currently food secure?

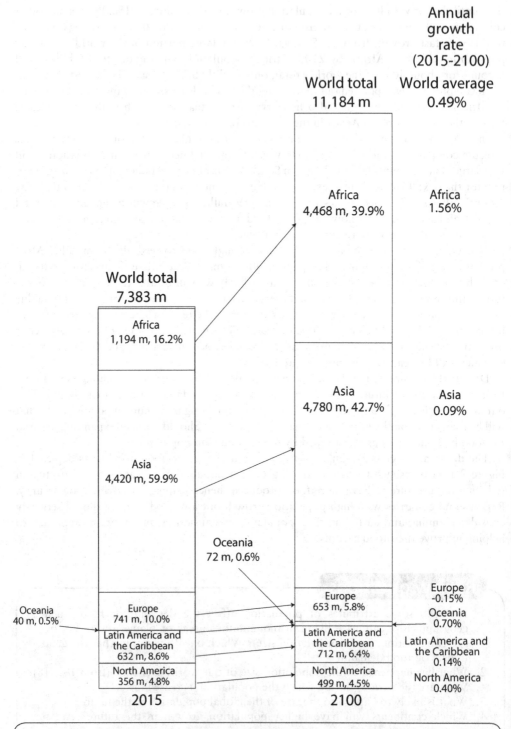

Figure 3.6 World population growth, forecast (medium fertility, 2015–2100).

Discussion questions

1. Based on what you understand now, what relationships do you observe between population growth and the level of food security?
2. Depending on your answer to Discussion Question 1 above, what is your opinion on future population growth?
3. If our population grows as has been forecasted, what do you think about human beings' ability to feed the rising population in the future?

References

Roser, M. and Ortiz-Ospina, E. (2017), 'World population growth', https://ourworldindata.org/world-population-growth/#long-run-historical-perspective-country-trends-in-the-last-500-years, accessed 9 August 2017.

UNPD. (2017), *World Population Prospects: The 2017 Revision*, DVD edition, United Nations: Department of Economic and Social Affairs, Population Division.

Appendix 3A

Basics of demand and supply

Households demand all sorts of goods and services. Firms transform various inputs into different kinds of goods and services. Goods and services are exchanged in the markets between households and firms at a price. Goods and services together are referred to as products. Generally, goods are tangible and services are intangible.

The amount of a product that consumers demand is affected by a number of factors. Similarly, the amount of a product that producers are willing to supply is also affected by a number of factors. Understanding how product demand and supply is affected is necessary to understanding the discussion in the rest of the text. This understanding is also crucial for us to understand policies that are used to manage the demand and supply of a product. In this appendix, we first discuss the most influential factors that affect the demand for a product, followed by discussion on factors affecting product supply. Finally, we bring demand and supply together to see how they jointly determine (1) the price of a product in the market, (2) the quantity of the product demanded by consumers, and (3) the quantity of the product supplied by producers.

3A.1 Demand

Demand for a product can be affected by:

- The price of the product itself.
- The number of consumers, or the population.
- Consumer income.
- Consumer tastes and preferences.
- Price expectations.
- Prices of related products.

Rice is a product. Taking rice as an example in a hypothetical country, called the Rasian Republic or Rasia. Initially, the price of rice is $0.8 per kg. The amount of rice John demands at this price is 120 kg per annum. If the price increases to $1.0 per kg, he would buy 100 kg. If the price drops to $0.6 per kg, he would buy 140 kg. Or, if the rice is free, he would demand 200 kg, and if the rice costs $2.0 kg, he would not buy any. The quantity of rice John would buy at different prices can be listed in a table as shown in Columns 1 and 2 in Table 3A.1. This relationship between the price and the quantity demanded is called a demand schedule. So, the first two columns in Table 3A.1 are John's demand schedule.

As suggested by John's demand schedule, generally, the quantity of a food demanded by a consumer increases when the price of that food drops and decreases when the price of that food increases, *ceteris paribus* (meaning hold everything else constant). This relationship is referred to as the law of demand. That is, with everything else held constant, the quantity demanded of a product is inversely related to its price.

John's demand schedule can be depicted in a plane diagram as shown in Figure 3A.1. Conventionally, the horizontal axis of the plane indicates the quantity of a product; the vertical axis indicates the price. Each pair of numbers, i.e., the price and the corresponding quantity demanded, such as $2.0 and 0 kg, $1.2 and 80 kg, and $0.8 and 120 kg, determines a unique point on the plane. Connecting all the points gives us a line as shown in Figure 3A.1

The negatively sloped line is referred to as the demand curve – showing the inverse relationship between the price of the product and the quantity demanded. It allows us to find the quantity demanded by a buyer at any possible selling price by moving along the curve. For example, when the price increases from $0.8 to $1.0, the quantity of rice demanded

Table 3A.1 Individual and market demand schedule

Price	Individual demand		Total population	Market demand
	John	Sally		
($/kg)	(kg)	(kg)	(person)	(kg)
(1)	(2)	(3)	(4)	(5)
2.0	0	0	2	0
1.8	20	20	2	40
1.6	40	40	2	80
1.4	60	60	2	120
1.2	80	80	2	160
1.0	100	100	2	200
0.8	120	120	2	240
0.6	140	140	2	280
0.4	160	160	2	320
0.2	180	180	2	360
0.0	200	200	2	400

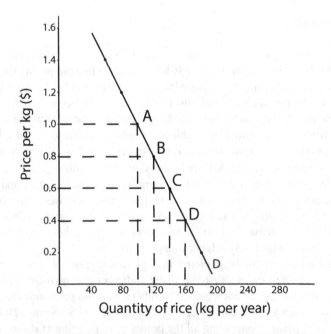

Figure 3A.1 An individual buyer's demand curve for rice.

drops to 100 kg (moving on the demand curve from Point B to Point A). If subsequently, the price dropped from $1.0 to $0.6 or $0.4, then there would be a movement along the demand curve from Point A to Point C or to Point D, and the quantity demanded increases. Hence, when the price of rice changes, there is a movement along the demand curve, and there is an associated change in the quantity of rice demanded.

Figure 3A.1 shows the demand for rice by one individual, John (hence, individual demand). Suppose there are *only* two individuals in the market; Sally is the other one. For simplicity, the quantity of rice demanded by Sally at different prices is exactly the same as John's (as shown in Table 3A.1). Then, total demand in this market, or, market demand, is the sum of the quantity demanded by all individuals at different prices. That is, when the price is $0.8, market demand is 240 kg (120 kg + 120 kg); when the price is $0.6, market demand is 280 kg. Figure 3A.2 shows the market demand curve. When the price changes, similarly, there will be movements along the demand curve. For example, when the price decreases from $1.0 to $0.6, there will be a movement from Point A to Point B. Total quantity of rice demanded in the market increases from 200 kg to 280 kg.

Now suppose that total population in Rasia is one million. Assume that the demand schedule for rice of every individual in this country is exactly the same as that of John and Sally as in Table 3A.1. Then, Column 4 in Table 3A.2 is Rasia's demand schedule for rice. Note different units used in diagrams: some of them being kilogram (kg), others kilo tonnes (kt).

Rasia's demand curve for rice can be shown as D_1 in Figure 3A.3. Once we know the market price, a quick look at the demand curve will tell us how much rice all the consumers in Rasia will buy. For example, if the price is $0.8, the total quantity of rice demanded is 120 kilo tonnes.

In addition to 'the price of the food', there are 'other factors' that can also result in changes in the quantity consumers will buy. Important such 'other factors' have been listed above. Taking 'consumer tastes and preferences' as an example. Assume people in Rasia have become extremely fond of having rice. *Ceteris paribus*, they will buy 40 kt more rice at

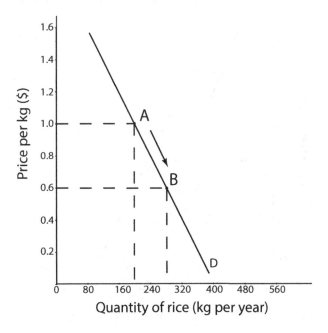

Figure 3A.2 Market demand curve for rice.

Table 3A.2 Market demand schedule for rice in Rasia with preference change

Price	Individual demand	Total population	Market demand, different preferences		
			Normal	Fond	Not fond
($/kg)	(kg)	(person)	(kt)	(kt)	(kt)
(1)	(2)	(3)	(4)	(5)	(6)
2.0	0	1000000	0	40	
1.8	20	1000000	20	60	
1.6	40	1000000	40	80	0
1.4	60	1000000	60	100	20
1.2	80	1000000	80	120	40
1.0	100	1000000	100	140	60
0.8	120	1000000	120	160	80
0.6	140	1000000	140	180	100
0.4	160	1000000	160	200	120
0.2	180	1000000	180	220	140
0.0	200	1000000	200	240	160

each price (Column 5 in Table 3A.2). This will lead the demand curve to shift to the right, to D_2 (Figure 3A.3). That is, at the same price, the quantity of rice Rasian consumers will buy increases by 40 kt. For example, at the price of $0.8 per kg, consumers now demand 160 kilo tonnes rather than 120 kilo tonnes. Conversely, if the consumers have somehow become

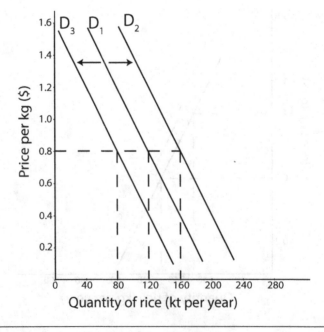

Figure 3A.3 Market demand for rice in Rasia.

Table 3A.3 Market demand schedule for rice in Rasia with population change

Price	Individual demand	Total population	Market demand	Total population	Market demand	Total population	Market demand
($/kg)	(kg)	(person)	(kt)	(person)	(kt)	(person)	(kt)
(1)	(2)	(3)	(4)	(5)	(6)	(7)	(8)
2.00	0	1000000	0	1500000	0	2000000	0
1.80	20	1000000	20	1500000	30	2000000	40
1.60	40	1000000	40	1500000	60	2000000	80
1.40	60	1000000	60	1500000	90	2000000	120
1.20	80	1000000	80	1500000	120	2000000	160
1.00	100	1000000	100	1500000	150	2000000	200
0.80	120	1000000	120	1500000	180	2000000	240
0.60	140	1000000	140	1500000	210	2000000	280
0.40	160	1000000	160	1500000	240	2000000	320
0.20	180	1000000	180	1500000	270	2000000	360
0.00	200	1000000	200	1500000	300	2000000	400

less fond of rice, the quantity of rice demanded drops by 40 kt at each corresponding price (Column 6 in Table 3A.2) and the demand curve will shift to the left, to D_3 (Figure 3A.3). At the price of $0.8 per kg, consumers now demand 80 kilo tonnes rather than 120 kilo tonnes, a decrease of 40 kt.

Similarly, when the population increases, the total amount of food will increase by the amount of food demanded by each extra person at the prevailing market price. In Table 3A.3, when the population increases from 1 million to 1.5 million, total market demand for rice also increases at each price (Column 6). For example, when the price is $0.8 per kg, the total demand rises from 120 kt to 180 kt. The extra 60 kt demand for rice (an increase of 50%) is due to the increase in population of 0.5 million (also an increase of 50%). When the population increases to 2 million, i.e., an increase of 100%, the demand for rice also increases by 100% (Column 8). Figure 3.1 of this chapter shows how the demand curve has shifted.

Generally, when each of the 'other factors' changes (other than 'the price of the product itself'), holding everything else constant, the demand for a product will change, leading to a shift in the demand curve. As such, we call these 'other factors' 'demand curve shifters', or just 'demand shifters'. When the demand curve shifts to the right, we say the demand has increased. Otherwise, we say the demand has decreased.

Let us keep in mind the difference in the expressions we used. When 'the price of the product itself' changes, we say there is *a change in the quantity demanded* of the food, and there is *a movement along the demand curve*. When there is a change in any of the demand shifters, we say there is *a change in demand*, and there is *a shift to a new demand curve*. Understanding such differences is essential to avoid confusion in the study of demand.

3A.2 Supply

Like the demand for a product, the supply of a product can also be affected by a number of factors. The most influential factors that affect product supply include:

- The price of the product itself.
- The cost of production inputs.
- Technological progress.
- The number of producers.
- Price expectations.
- Prices of related products.

Again, taking rice as an example. Initially, the price of rice is $0.8 per kg. The amount of rice Sarah, a rice producer in Rasia, is willing to supply at this price is 6 tonnes per annum. When the price increases to $1.0 per kg, she would supply 8 tonnes. If the price drops to $0.6 per kg, she would supply 4 tonnes. If the price is at $0.2 per kg or lower, she is not willing to supply any. The quantity of rice Sarah would be happy to supply at different prices can be listed in a table, as shown in Columns 1 and 2 in Table 3A.4. This relationship between the price and the quantity supplied is called a supply schedule. So, the first two columns in Table 3A.4 are Sarah's supply schedule.

Generally, the quantity of rice supplied increases when the price of rice increases and decreases when the price of rice decreases, *ceteris paribus*. This is referred to as the law of supply. That is, everything else held constant, the quantity supplied of a product is positively related to its price.

The law of supply can be depicted in a diagram (Figure 3A.4). The positively sloped curve is referred to as the supply curve – showing the positive relationship between the price of the

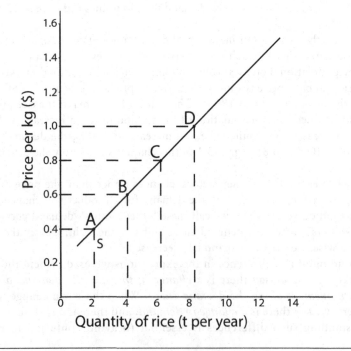

Figure 3A.4 An individual producer's supply curve for rice.

Table 3A.4 Individual and market supply schedule

Price	Individual supply		No. of producers	Market supply
	Sarah	Adam		
($/kg)	(t)	(t)	(No.)	(t)
(1)	(2)	(3)	(4)	(5)
2.0	18	18	2	36
1.8	16	16	2	32
1.6	14	14	2	28
1.4	12	12	2	24
1.2	10	10	2	20
1.0	8	8	2	16
0.8	6	6	2	12
0.6	4	4	2	8
0.4	2	2	2	4
0.2	0	0	2	0
0.0	0	0	2	0

product and the quantity supplied. The supply curve allows us to find the quantity supplied by a producer at any possible selling price by moving along the curve. For example, when the price increases from $0.8 to $1.0, the quantity of rice supplied increases to 8 tonnes (moving on the supply curve from Point C to Point D). If subsequently, the price dropped from $1.0 to $0.6 or $0.4, then there would be a movement along the supply curve from Point D to Point B or to Point A, and the quantity supplied drops. Hence, when the price of rice changes, there is a movement along the supply curve, and there is an associated change in the quantity supplied.

Figure 3A.4 shows the supply of rice by one producer, Sarah. Suppose there are only two rice producers; Adam is the other one. Assume the quantity of rice supplied by Adam at different prices is exactly the same as Sarah's (as shown in Columns 1 and 3 in Table 3A.4). Then, total supply to the market, or, market supply, is the sum of the quantity supplied by all producers at different prices. That is, when the price is $0.8, market supply is 12 tonnes (6 tonnes + 6 tonnes); when the price is $1.0, market supply is 16 tonnes (see Column 5 in Table 3A.4). Figure 3A.5 shows the market supply by all the producers, Sarah and Adam. When the price increases from $0.6 to $1.0, there will be a movement along the supply curve from Point A to Point B. Total quantity of rice supplied in the market increases from 8 tonnes to 16 tonnes.

Imagine, in fact, there are also many other rice producers in Rasia in addition to Sarah and Adam. Together there are 20,000 rice producers and they supply a much larger quantity of rice to the market at various prices. Columns 1 and 4 in Table 3A.5 are their supply schedule.

When the total number of producers is 20,000, the market supply curve is shown as S_1 in Figure 3A.6 (based on Columns 1 and 4 in Table 3A.5). Once we know the market price, a quick look at the supply curve will tell us how much rice all the producers in Rasia are willing to supply. For example, if the price is $0.8, the total quantity of rice supplied is 120 kilo tonnes.

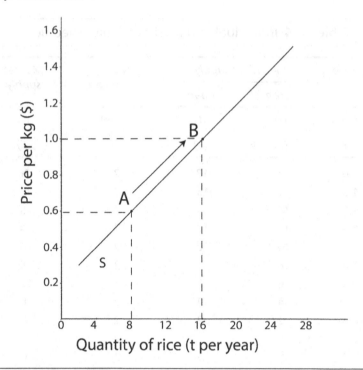

Figure 3A.5 Market supply curve for rice.

Table 3A.5 Market supply schedule for rice in Rasia with changes in the number of producers

Price	Individual supply	No. of producers	Market supply	No. of producers	Market supply	No. of producers	Market supply
($/kg)	(t)	(1000)	(kt)	(1000)	(kt)	(1000)	(kt)
(1)	(2)	(3)	(4)	(5)	(6)	(7)	(8)
2.0	18	20	360	25	450	15	270
1.8	16	20	320	25	400	15	240
1.6	14	20	280	25	350	15	210
1.4	12	20	240	25	300	15	180
1.2	10	20	200	25	250	15	150
1.0	8	20	160	25	200	15	120
0.8	6	20	120	25	150	15	90
0.6	4	20	80	25	100	15	60
0.4	2	20	40	25	50	15	30
0.2	0	20	0	25	0	15	0
0.0	0	20	0	25	0	15	0

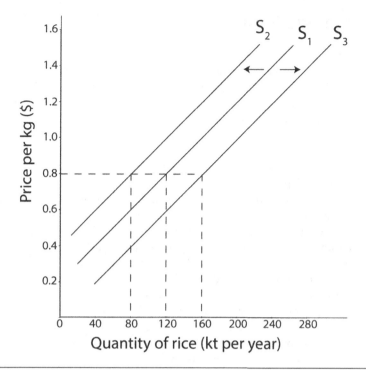

Figure 3A.6 Market supply of rice in Rasia.

Ceteris paribus, when the number of producers increases, total amount of rice supplied will increase. In Table 3A.5, when the number of producers increases from 20,000 to 25,000, total market supply of rice also increases at each price (Column 6). For example, when the price is $0.8 per kg, the total supply rises from 120 kt to 150 kt. If the number of producers decreases from 20,000 to 15,000, total market supply of rice decreases at each price (Column 8). For example, when the price is $0.8 per kg, the total supply drops from 120 kt to 90 kt (Column 8). Figure 3A.6 shows how the supply curve has shifted.

In addition to 'the price of the product itself', there are 'other factors' that can also result in changes in the quantity producers will supply. Important such 'other factors' have been listed above.

When each of the 'other factors' changes, the supply of the product will change, leading to a shift in the supply curve. As such, we call these 'other factors' 'supply curve shifters' or just 'supply shifters'. When the supply curve shifts to the right, we say the supply has increased. Otherwise, we say the supply has decreased.

Again, as in the demand study, it is important to remember the difference in the expressions we use. When 'the price of the product itself' changes, we say there is *a change in the quantity supplied* of the product, and there is *a movement along the supply curve*. When there is a change in any of the supply shifters, we say there is *a change in supply*, and there is *a shift in the supply curve*.

3A.3 Market equilibrium

In the market, how is the total quantity demanded and supplied determined and at what price? Bringing together market demand and market supply will enable us to determine the quantity and price. In Figure 3A.7, D_1 and S_1 are the same as in Figure 3A.3 and 3A.6. At the price of $0.8 kg, producers are willing to supply 120 kilo tonnes of rice to the market and consumers are willing to buy 120 kilo tonnes. The rice market has reached an equilibrium (Point E in Figure 3A.7). The price of $0.8 kg is the equilibrium price and the quantity of 120 kilo tonnes is the equilibrium quantity.

The market will not be at an equilibrium at any price other than $0.8 kg. If the price is $1.0 kg, producers are happy to supply more to the market (from 120 kilo tonnes to 160 kilo tonnes) but consumers are only willing to buy 100 kilo tonnes rather than the previous 120 kilo tonnes. There will be an excess of 60 kilo tonnes. Conversely, if the price is $0.6 kg, producers are only willing to supply 80 kilo tonnes to the market but consumers are happy to buy 140 kilo tonnes. There will be a shortage of 60 kilo tonnes.

When the market is not at the equilibrium, producers or consumers will make adjustments. If the price is too high and there is a surplus, some producers will be willing to reduce their price so that they can sell more. This exerts a downward pressure on the price towards the equilibrium. Otherwise, if the price is too low and there is a shortage, some consumers are willing to offer a higher price to entice producers to sell to them. This exerts an upward pressure on the price towards the equilibrium. If there is no intervention in the market, the adjustments by producers and consumers will generally lead the price to return to the equilibrium point. This, of course, does not imply that in reality markets will always operate exactly at the point of equilibrium. Nonetheless, choices by sellers and buyers will generally result in the market operating somewhere close to the equilibrium point.

By bringing demand and supply together in Figure 3A.7, we have built a demand–supply model. This model is very useful to help us analyse how markets may behave when there are changes to those influential factors. This demand–supply model can also be used to help us evaluate the effectiveness of some policies that affect food demand and supply and hence food security (see Appendix 9A).

3A.4 Responses to price changes

As noted earlier, people respond to price changes. When the price of a product increases, a consumer generally will respond by buying less, and *vice versa*. For a producer, when the price of a product increases, s/he will respond by selling more, and *vice versa*.

To measure how consumers and producers respond to price changes, the concept of price elasticity is used. The price elasticity is defined as the percentage change in the quantity demanded (or supplied) of a product divided by the percentage change in price. Hence, the elasticity tells us the increase or decrease in quantity demanded (or supplied) (in %) of a product in response to a 1% change in price.

For example, assume, the price elasticity of demand for product A is -1.5 and B -0.4. These two elasticities tell us that if each of their prices increases by 1%, the quantity demanded of Product A will drop by 1.5% and B by 0.4%. As such, consumers are more responsive to the price change of Product A.

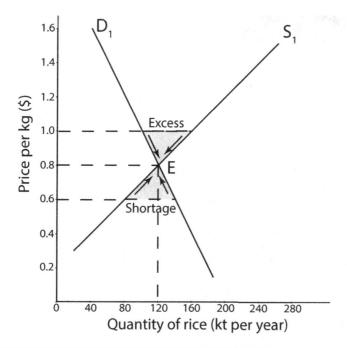

Figure 3A.7 Rice market equilibrium in Rasia.

The price elasticities of demand are always negative because price and quantity always change in opposite directions. Conventionally, the negative sign is dropped and the price elasticity of demand is just reported as 1.5 or 0.4.

A price elasticity of supply is used to measure how producers respond to price changes. Assume, the price elasticity of supply for product A is 1.9 and B 0.3. They tell us that if each of their prices increases by 1%, the quantity supplied of Product A will increase by 1.9% and B by 0.3%. Producers are said to be more responsive to the price change of Product A.

It is noted, however, producers often cannot respond to price changes during a very short time period as limited by their production capacities or growing season. Typically, supply becomes more elastic the longer producers have to adjust their production.

The price elasticities of supply are always positive because price and quantity always move in the same direction. That is, when the price of a product rises, the quantity supplied also increases.

If the price elasticity of demand is greater than 1, it is said that the demand for the product is more responsive, or elastic. If less than 1, the demand is less responsive, or inelastic. If equal to 1, the demand is unitary elastic.

Similarly, if the price elasticity of supply is greater than 1, the supply is more responsive, or elastic. If less than 1, the supply is less responsive, or inelastic.

People's demand for a product also responds to their income changes. That is, when their income increases, they may buy more or less of a product. Income-related responses are discussed in Chapter 4.

Review questions

1. A movement along a demand curve and a shift in demand curve are caused by different factors. What will cause a movement along a demand curve? What will cause a shift in demand curve?
2. Each of the following two changes: a change in the quantity demanded of a product and a change in demand for a product, is caused by one of the following: a change in the price of the product itself or a change in any one of the 'demand shifters'. Match each change to its cause.
3. Draw demand curves using the demand schedules as shown in Table 3A.3 when the population is 1, 1.5 and 2 million, respectively.
4. A movement along a supply curve and a shift in supply curve are caused by different factors. What will cause a movement along a supply curve? What will cause a shift in supply curve?
5. Each of the following two changes: a change in the quantity supplied of a product and a change in the supply of a product, is caused by one of the following: a change in the price of the product itself or a change in any one of the 'supply shifters'. Match each change to its cause.
6. Draw supply curves using the supply schedules as shown in Table 3A.5 when the number of producers is 15,000, 20,000, and 25,000, respectively.
7. Explain, if a market is left without intervention, why we can expect that the market will operate somewhere close to its equilibrium.

Chapter 4

Income and food demand

Summary

This chapter addresses the impact of income on food security. Research has repeatedly confirmed that, for a given population, income is the single most important factor that affects the demand for food. Not only does it affect the amount of food demanded, it also affects the composition of food demanded. In this chapter, we first, in Section 4.1, introduce the concept of income elasticity of demand and discuss how it can be used to measure how consumer demand responds to income changes. We then, in Section 4.2, show how the level of income affects the quantity and composition of food demanded. In Section 4.3, we demonstrate how food demand is related to income changes at the national level. Finally, in Section 4.4, we shed some light on the importance of developing adequate policies to improve consumer income and developing proactive food policies to respond to consumer income changes, especially in developing countries.

After studying this chapter, you should be able to:
- Discuss how the quantity of food demanded is affected by income change.
- Explain how the composition of food demanded is affected by income change.
- Describe the likely quantity and composition of food demanded by people living in absolute poverty.

4.1 Consumer demand and income change

Consumers' demand for a product responds to their income changes. That is, when their income increases, they may buy more or less of a product. Table 4.1 illustrates the changes in food consumption and income in China. You will see that as Chinese consumers' income increases, their demand for grains and pork increases. For grains, however, after consumption reaches 254 kg per capita per annum, it starts to decline although the income still increases. For pork, consumption continues increasing, though at a slower rate, when the income becomes higher. The consumption trends for poultry meats, poultry eggs, and aquatic products are the same as that of pork when income increases.

To measure how consumers respond to income changes, the concept of income elasticity of demand is used. Income elasticity is defined as the percentage change in the quantity demanded of a product divided by the percentage change in income. Hence, the income elasticity tells us the increase or decrease in quantity demanded (%) in response to a 1% change in income.

Assume, for a given income level, the income elasticity of Product A (say, pork) is 1.8 and B (say, rice) 0.6. They tell us that if consumer income increases by 1%, the quantity demanded of pork will increase by 1.8% and rice by 0.6%. As such, pork is said to be more income responsive and rice less income responsive. Similar to price elasticities, if an income elasticity is great than 1, the demand for that product is income elastic; if less than 1, income inelastic.

Income elasticities are usually positive but, they can be negative for some products. If the income elasticity is positive, when consumer income increases, the quantity demanded of a product increases. Otherwise, a negative income elasticity means the quantity demanded of a product decreases when consumer income increases.

The relationship between the size of income elasticities and consumer income can be shown intuitively in a diagram. In Figure 4.1, the vertical axis represents income elasticity. The horizontal axis represents income. Initially, income elasticity is 0 when income is 0. When income rises, the quantity demanded of rice or cassava increases. At this stage, the demand is very income elastic – rising income elasticity (people have to get more rice or cassava to curtail hunger). With increased consumption of rice or cassava, hunger becomes less acute

Table 4.1 Changes in food consumption and income in China (kg, ¥, 1978=100)

	1978	1980	1985	1990	2013	2015
Per capita GDP	385	427	661	768	7373	8126
Grain	196	214	254	238	149	135
Vegetable oil	1.6	2.3	5.1	5.7	12.0	10.0
Pork	7.7	11.2	14.0	16.6	19.8	20.1
Poultry	0.4	0.8	1.6	1.7	7.2	8.4
Eggs	2.0	2.3	5.0	6.3	8.2	9.5
Aquatic products	3.5	3.4	4.9	6.5	10.4	11.2

Source: SSB, various years.

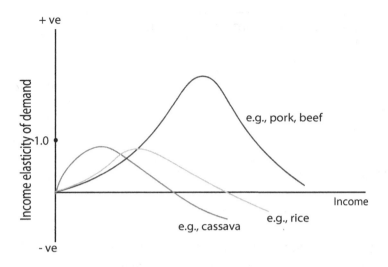

Figure 4.1 Relationships between income elasticities and income change.

and consumers have more money to afford more expensive foods of higher nutrition such as pork or beef. Hence, the demand for rice or cassava becomes less and less income elastic. The demand for pork or beef, however, becomes more and more income elastic.

When consumer income is high enough, consumption of starchy food like rice or cassava may plateau (the income elasticity is 0), or may start to decline (the income elasticity becomes negative), as shown by the data for China in Table 4.1. Starchy food like rice or cassava are replaced at a greater rate by other foods of higher nutrition such as pork or beef.

Generally, when income improves, people consume more and more pork or beef. However, when income is high enough, the increase in the consumption of pork or beef also slows down – a person can only eat so much of a certain food. The income elasticity of demand for pork or beef, however, generally will not become negative. That is, when consumer income is high enough, the increase in the consumption of pork or beef becomes very small with any further income increase but total consumption does not drop.

It is noted that the income elasticity curves as shown in Figure 4.1 are indicative only and do not cover all possible situations. Suppose that cassava is traditionally the staple for a community. As a result, it is very unlikely that the consumption of cassava will be completely replaced even though income has reached a very high level. This means the income elasticity of demand for cassava becomes negative over a certain income range but then as income continues rising, it approaches zero again. That is, the consumption of cassava remains at a certain level. The same is true for rice or wheat. When they are traditionally taken as staple, no families would ever completely eliminate rice or wheat flour from their diet. Data in Table 4.2 lend support to this claim.

In Table 4.2, since 2000, per capita rice and wheat consumption in China's urban areas has largely remained around 40–44 kg and wheat flour around 11–12 kg. In rural areas, this consumption has continued declining. When rural income further increases, it may be expected that the per capita consumption of rice and wheat will also remain at a certain level, though this level is likely to be higher than that in urban areas: rural residents need a higher intake of dietary energy for physical work.

Table 4.2 Income and consumption of rice and wheat in China (2000–11, ¥, kg)

	Rural Residents			Urban Residents		
	Per capita income	Paddy rice	Wheat	Per capita income	Rice (milled)	Wheat flour
2000	2253	n.a.	n.a.	6280	46	17
2001	2366	123	77	6860	44	15
2002	2476	123	76	7703	44	12
2003	2622	119	73	8472	44	13
2004	2936	117	72	9422	42	12
2005	3255	113	68	10493	42	12
2006	3587	112	66	11760	41	12
2007	4140	109	64	13786	42	12
2008	4761	111	63	15781	45	13
2009	5153	106	60	17175	43	12
2010	5919	102	58	19110	40	11
2011	6977	97	55	21810	39	12

Source: SSB, various years.

4.2 Income change and food demand

4.2.1 Income and the quantity of food demanded

Food is available in the market but at a cost. If one has the necessary disposable income, one can afford to buy food from the market. When consumers' income increases, their ability to access food improves.

As shown in the previous section, how an income increase may affect food demand depends on what kind of food it is. For some foods, the demand increases when consumer income increases (e.g., pork or beef). For others, the demand may increase, remain constant, or decrease when the income increases to a certain range (e.g., cassava or rice).

In poorer countries, income is a strong demand shifter. When consumer income rises from a very low level, we can expect the demand curve for some foods to shift to the right due to the impact of income increase, as shown in Figure 4.2.

4.2.2 Income and the composition of food demanded

Consumer income also affects the composition of food demanded. When consumer income is low, generally more staple food is consumed. When consumer income increases, they will demand more food that is protein-rich but less food that is starchy. As shown in Table 4.1, the composition of food consumption for Chinese consumers in 2015 is vastly different from that in 1978.

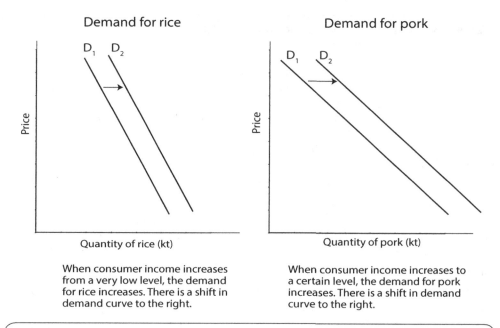

Demand for rice

When consumer income increases from a very low level, the demand for rice increases. There is a shift in demand curve to the right.

Demand for pork

When consumer income increases to a certain level, the demand for pork increases. There is a shift in demand curve to the right.

Figure 4.2 Effect of an income increase on demand for rice and pork.

As Japan's consumer income increased, consumption composition also experienced major changes. In 2015, Japan's per capita GDP was about two times higher than that in 1965 (at the 1965 constant price). Compared with 1965, energy intake from rice dropped by more than half (there was also a minor drop in sugar and 'other' foods). Energy intake from other foods, especially meats, oils and fruits, increased (Table 4.3).

Similar changes have also occurred elsewhere, for example, India and South Korea (Gandhi and Zhou 2014; Song and Kwon 2017).

4.2.3 Income disparities and food demand

Low-income consumers demand more lower-value food but much less higher-value food. The opposite is true for those consumers with high incomes. Hence, food demand patterns differ notably between consumers of different incomes.

In urban China, the consumption of rice and wheat started to decline from the early 1980s and by the early 2000s it had been largely stabilised. Nonetheless, between consumers of different income groups, it is still very clear that lower income residents consume more wheat (Figure 4.3; urban residents only, similar data for rural residents are not available). For higher-value food such as aquatic products, consumption by low-income groups is much lower in both rural and urban areas (Figure 4.4). In fact, except for grain, data show that the consumption level of all other foods is much lower for the low-income quintile, e.g., fruits (Figure 4.5).

In India, similar patterns exist. Table 4.4 indicates that residents with the lowest income (the first decile) in rural areas spend a very large share of their income on food, being 65%. Expenditure by these rural poor (the first decile) on cereals is also relatively high. The same is true for urban poor. For the tenth decile (the richer people in the society), the same shares are much lower, being 46% in rural areas and 32% in urban areas. Their shares of expenditure on cereals are also much lower.

Table 4.3 Changes in major food items consumed in Japan (kcal per capita per day)

	1965		2015		± in kcal in 2015 over 1965 (%)
	(yen, kcal)	(% of total)	(yen, kcal)	(% of total)	
Per capita GDP (yen, constant price, 1965=100)	331280		959799		189.7
Rice	1090	44.3	534	22.1	-51.0
Meats	157	6.4	406	16.8	158.6
Oils	159	6.5	359	14.8	125.8
Wheat	292	11.9	331	13.7	13.4
Sugar	196	8.0	194	8.0	-1.0
Aquatic	99	4.0	101	4.2	2.0
Vegetables	74	3.0	74	3.1	0.0
Soybean	55	2.2	73	3.0	32.7
Fruits	39	1.6	62	2.6	59.0
Other	298	12.1	284	11.7	-4.7
Total*	2459	100.0	2418	100.0	

*In Japan, per capita daily energy intake underwent an increase after WWII till 1996, peaking at 2,670 kcal/capita/day (Hirasawa 2017). Since then, there has been a downward trend, due to reasons such as population aging, increased automation of activities, health concerns, etc. The estimated energy need for Japanese people is 2413 kcal/capita/day.

Source: MAFF (2018).

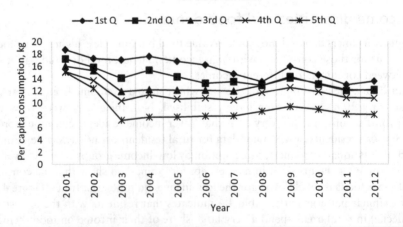

Per capita consumption of wheat flour in urban China

Figure 4.3 Per capita wheat consumption and income level.
Source: based on SSB, various issues.

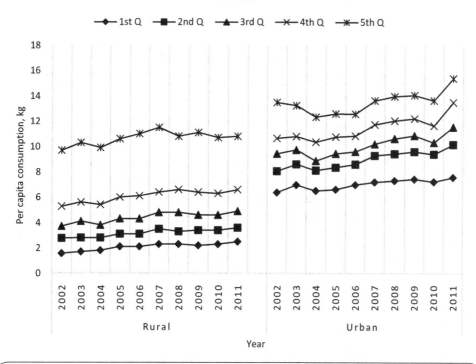

Figure 4.4 Per capita consumption of aquatic products and income level.
Source: based on SSB, various issues.

Similar to China, wealthier people spend much more money, compared to their poor counterparts, on foods of high value and better nutrition. Figure 4.6 reveals that the expenditure on 'dairy foods', 'eggs, fish and meats', and 'fruits' by rich people is about 10, 7, and 20 times more than that by the poorest residents, respectively.

4.3 Income and food demand: international experiences

The discussion in the previous section points out that food demand is significantly affected by consumer income. This relationship has been confirmed by global experiences. Figure 4.7 shows the relationship between income changes and food consumption of chosen countries (with the majority being developing countries). It is clear from their experiences that when consumer income improves, food consumption improves. When income worsens, food consumption deteriorates (FAO 2018; World Bank 2018).

In both Brazil and China, the continuous improvement of consumer income has been accompanied with improved food consumption. Generally, when energy intake is above ADER (average dietary energy requirements), further improvement in food intake is reflected by the increased consumption of food of animal origin. Looking at the graphs of Brazil and China, the proportion of their energy intake from animal products has increased impressively. The other country whose experience is similar to that of Brazil and China is South Korea,

Table 4.4 Share of expenditure on food and cereals in India, 2009–2010 (per person, 30 days)

MPCE Decile Class	Expenditure Rural					Expenditure Urban				
	Total	Food	Share	Cereal	Share	Total	Food	Share	Cereal	Share
	Rs	Rs	%	Rs	%	Rs	Rs	%	Rs	%
1	453	294	64.9	107	23.6	599	370	61.8	111	18.5
2	584	376	64.3	123	21.0	831	491	59.1	129	15.5
3	675	428	63.4	129	19.1	1012	583	57.6	138	13.7
4	761	480	63.1	138	18.1	1196	659	55.1	146	12.2
5	848	527	62.1	140	16.5	1398	741	53.0	154	11.0
6	944	574	60.7	144	15.3	1633	835	51.1	167	10.2
7	1063	636	59.8	152	14.3	1931	939	48.6	172	8.9
8	1221	704	57.7	157	12.8	2330	1059	45.5	188	8.1
9	1470	827	56.3	168	11.4	3051	1285	42.1	196	6.4
10	2517	1157	46.0	187	7.4	5863	1845	31.5	212	3.6

MPCE: monthly per capita consumer expenditure.
Source: NSSO (2011).

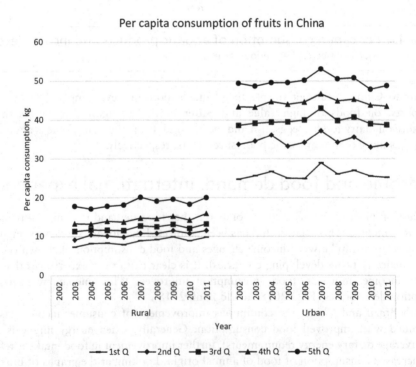

Per capita consumption of fruits in China

Figure 4.5 Per capita fruit consumption and income level.
Source: based on SSB, various issues.

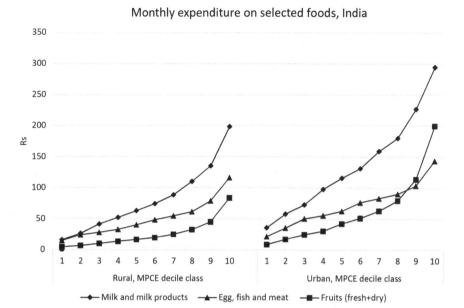

Figure 4.6 Monthly per capita consumer expenditure, by income group, India, 2009–2010.
Source: NSSO (2011).

though it is no longer a developing country. India and Indonesia seem to also follow the path of Brazil and China (the intake of animal products in India and Indonesia is lower, perhaps, partly, due to their dietary customs).

Most other countries in Figure 4.7 exhibited notable income fluctuations. Fluctuations in food intake then followed in these countries. Among them, the income drop in Afghanistan, Central African Republic, Madagascar, and Zimbabwe has caused major deterioration in their food intake.

North Korea and Congo, two of the poorest countries in the world, have so far failed to get their average energy intake to reach the ADER (their per capita GDP data are not available). In Figure 4.7, other countries that have not managed to reach the ADER or have slid below the ADER include Afghanistan, Central African Republic, Ethiopia, Haiti, Madagascar, Zambia, and Zimbabwe.

Note that in Figure 4.7, only the intake of one of the three macronutrients (i.e., energy) is shown. When dietary energy intake (kcal/capita/day) is high, then the intake of protein and fats would be generally high as well. If the energy intake is below the ADER, then the daily intake of protein and fats would most likely be inadequate. Similarly, if the proportion of energy from animal products is high, then protein and fat intake is also likely to be higher.

4.4 Income and food security

The deliberations in this chapter reinforce the fact that improving consumers' disposable income is crucially linked to the improvement of a country's food security. Improvement in income is accompanied by increased food intake and subsequently an improvement in food security. Otherwise, food intake can hardly improve and food security suffers.

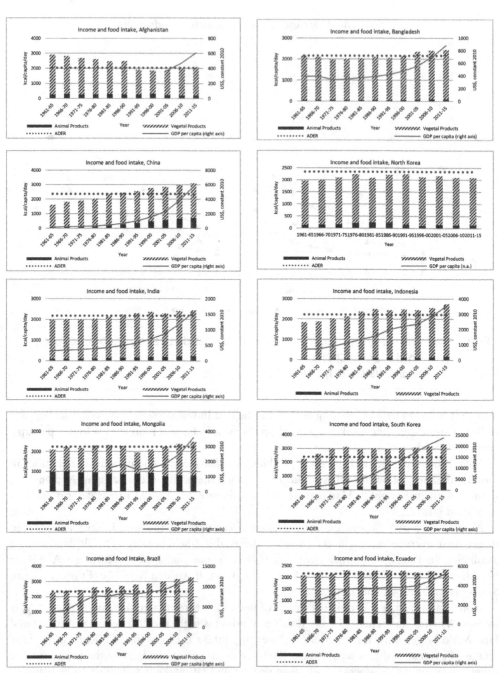

Figure 4.7 Income and food consumption in various countries.
Source: FAO (2018) and World Bank (2018).

For many developing countries that have low levels of food security, their policy efforts must be focused on improving consumer income if they really care about helping their citizens to improve food security. Efforts should also be devoted to equitable income distribution.

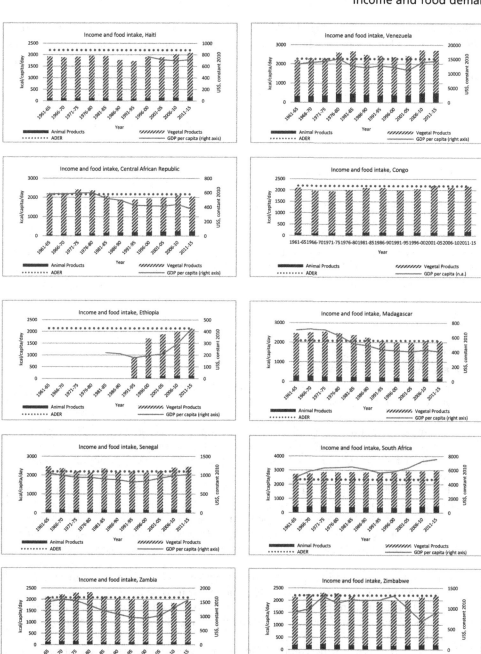

Figure 4.7 (*Continued*)

For those developing countries that have made notable progress in improving income and food security (such as Brazil and China), if they wish to sustain and further improve their food security, they must also have policies that can help their citizens to maintain or further increase their income. If their income rises to a level comparable to that in many developed countries,

83

then their chance of sustaining a high level of food security will be much enhanced. Data from the FAO and EIU (The Economist Intelligence Unit) clearly confirm that stable high incomes are associated with higher levels of food security, such as in Singapore, the Netherlands, and Australia.

Improving the income of the poor is particularly important. The discussion in Section 4.2 clearly shows that it is poor people who have a lower intake of food, often below the ADER, and also often have food of lower quality. Indeed, the UN has in 1943 established that '... the first cause of hunger and malnutrition is poverty' (Gibson 2012, p. 202). The FAO again in 1955 emphasised that poverty lies at the root of hunger (Paulino and Mellor 1984). This points to the strong need for any country to raise the income of the poor if they wish to raise food security in their country.

Another important revelation from the examination of the relationships between income and food demand is related to food diversity and quality. It has been shown in Section 4.2 that if consumer income improves from a very low level, per capita demand for most food will increase. Once a certain income level has been reached, the demand for some food may reduce, chiefly staple food or food of low value. However, the demand for food of high value and high quality will continue rising. As such, when consumer income improves, food policies need to be adjusted and to be responsive to meet the changing demand.

Review questions

1. Draw a graph similar to Figure 4.2 to show how the demand curves for rice and pork would shift if consumers' income fell.
2. Choose a developing country that you are familiar with. Assume that this country's economy is expanding steadily and the income of its residents also improves steadily. Would you be able to identify one food item for which demand is likely to undergo a fast increase initially followed by a slow increase? Briefly discuss how and why.
3. Choose a developing country that you are familiar with. Assume that this country's economy is expanding steadily and the income of its residents also improves steadily. Would you be able to identify one food item for which demand is likely to undergo a fast increase initially followed by a slow increase and then the demand declines when the income becomes even higher? Briefly discuss how and why.
4. As far as food demand is concerned, how do you think the behaviour of very rich people and very poor people may differ when their income increases?
5. Describe the change in the composition of food consumed in your family in the past 20 years. What are the likely causes? Would income change be considered a major cause?
6. Describe the change in the composition of food consumed in your country in the past 20 years. What are the likely causes? Would income change be considered a major cause?

Discussion questions

1. Rice is the staple for many Asian countries. Is it possible for the income elasticity of demand for rice to become negative? Explain. If you can, find a few countries as examples where you believe the income elasticity of demand for rice has become negative.
2. Would you think income inequalities and absolute poverty have a similar impact on the poor's food security? Why?
3. The quantity and composition of food demanded are generally affected by income changes. Discuss the likely differences in changes in the quantity and composition of food demanded between developing and developed countries.
4. When a developing country experiences fast economic growth, why would its government's food policies need to be responsive and dynamic? If not, how would that affect the country's food security?

References

FAO. (2018), 'Food balance sheet', www.fao.org/faostat/en/#data/FBS, accessed 12 September 2017.

Gandhi, V.P. and Zhou, Z.Y. (2014), 'Food demand and the food security challenge with rapid economic growth in the emerging economies of India and China', *Food Research International*, Vol. 63, pp. 108–124.

Gibson, M. (2012), *The Feeding of Nations: Redefining Food Security for the 21st Century*, Boca Raton, FL, CRC Press, US.

Hirasawa, A. (2017), 'Food security measures in Japan since World War II', in Zhou, Z.Y. and Wan, G.H. (eds), *Food Insecurity in Asia: Why Institutions Matter*, ADB Institute, Tokyo, Ch. 5, pp. 89–138.

MAFF (Ministry of Agriculture, Forestry and Fisheries, Japan). (2018), 'Food self-sufficiency ratio', www.maff.go.jp/j/wpaper/w_maff/h28/h28_h/trend/part1/chap1/c1_1_01.html, accessed 25 October 2018.

NSSO (National Sample Survey Office). (2011), *Level and Pattern of Consumer Expenditure 2009–2010*, http://mospi.nic.in/Mospi_New/site/inner.aspx?status=3&menu_id=31, accessed 17 February 2019.

Paulino, L.A. and Mellor, J.W. (1984), "The food situation in developing countries: Two decades in review', *Food Policy*, Vol. 9, pp. 291–303.

Song, J.H. and Kwon, T.J. (2017), 'Food security in the Republic of Korea and the Democratic People's Republic of Korea: Why the difference?', in Zhou, Z.Y. and Wan, G.H. (eds), *Food Insecurity in Asia: Why Institutions Matter*, ADB Institute, Tokyo, Ch. 6, pp. 139–191.

SSB (State Statistical Bureau). (2012), *China Statistical Yearbook*, various years, China Statistical Press, Beijing.

World Bank (2018), 'World development indicators', http://datatopics.worldbank.org/world-development-indicators/, accessed 19 September 2017.

Chapter 5

Other determinants of food demand

Summary

Discussed in Chapters 3 and 4 were the two most important factors that affect food demand: population and income. As noted in the introduction to this part, there are also other factors that affect food demand. In this chapter, how some of these other factors affect food demand is explained. Generally, changes in the prices of related foods and in consumer tastes and preferences cause changes in demand. How they influence food demand is the subject of Section 5.1. There are also some special or emerging forces that affect food demand, directly or indirectly, such as urbanisation, globalisation, and age and gender. In Section 5.2, we address how they affect food demand.

After studying this chapter, you should be able to:
- Describe how changes in prices of related foods and changes in consumer tastes and preferences will affect the demand for food.
- List and discuss how any other important factors may affect food demand.

5.1 Other conventional determinants of food demand

5.1.1 Prices of related foods

Two products, A and B, are related if we use Product A in place of Product B (e.g., having a lamb chop for dinner instead of a piece of beef steak) or if we use Product A together with Product B (e.g., potato chips and tomato sauce). In the former, the two products are referred to as substitutes. In the latter, they are called complements.

For related products, the price change in one product may affect the demand for the other. Taking rice and wheat flour as an example. Demand for wheat flour increases if the price for rice increases because they are substitutes. This leads the demand curve for wheat flour to shift to the right because consumers will substitute rice for wheat flour. If the related products, A and B, are complements, the price increase in Product A will lead to the decline in demand for Product B because the demand for A has fallen. The demand curve for Product B shifts to the left.

Depending on local dietary culture, some food ingredients are complements to the cooking of many dishes. One example is onion. While onions may be used as the main ingredient for a dish in some cases, in India and many other parts of South Asia they are used as an important complementary ingredient in many dishes.

Changes in prices of related foods generally would not have very large and negative impacts on the management of a country's food economy and food security. However, there are occasions when managing the prices of related foods can be very beneficial or critical. For example, in South Korea, during times of food shortage, imported wheat was processed into wheat flour and then sold at a low price to encourage consumers to substitute it for rice (Song and Kwon 2017). In Box 5.1 is another example where wheat flour was used to ease the demand for rice in China.

BOX 5.1

The magic of substitutes

Traditionally, wheat is the staple for Northern Chinese and rice for Southern Chinese. There was a severe shortage of food by 1976, when the infamous Cultural Revolution ended (see the section on China in Chapter 11 for more details). Food had to be imported. While both wheat and rice were scarce, China chiefly imported wheat (see Table 5.1), for the following reasons:

1. Wheat and rice are substitutes. Although it is not the staple food for Southerners, people would consume it when the alternatives were limited. At that time, food was supplied to residents through rations. In the monthly rations, the portion of rice was reduced and that of wheat increased for people in Southern China.
2. The price for rice was higher than that for wheat (see Table 5.1). Exporting rice to achieve a higher unit value and importing wheat at a lower unit value is financially sensible. Table 5.1 shows that during those years, wheat export from China was negligible while rice export was relatively high. While China did import some rice, the amount of wheat imported was much larger.
3. The world rice market is a very thin market (a market in which trading volume is low). As such, when a buyer buys a large quantity, the price will go up. As seen

from Table 5.1, had China imported a large amount of rice, the price would have gone up enormously, working against its financial interest. The wheat market, however, is 'thick' (a market in which trading volume is high and hence, the level of price volatility is low). In the early 1980s, world wheat exports were in the order of over 90 mt. China's import, though in large quantity (13 mt), was less than 1/6 of the supply. At the same time, world rice export was at 12 mt. Had China not imported wheat but instead imported rice, the rice supply would not have been sufficient to meet China's demand anyway.

Table 5.1 Import and export of wheat and rice, China and the world (1976–1982)

	Import			Export		
	Quantity	Value	Unit value	Quantity	Value	Unit value
	1000 t	US$ (m)	$/t	1000 t	US$ (m)	$/t
	Wheat China					
1976	2753	468	170	0.040	0.010	250
1977	7600	1272	167	0.044	0.010	227
1978	8467	1459	172	0.005	0.001	200
1979	9544	1883	197	0.025	0.006	240
1980	11774	2609	222	0.157	0.041	261
1981	13779	2982	216	0.017	0.007	412
1982	14651	3051	208	0.030	0.011	367
	Wheat world					
1976	65732	11232	171	62674	9594	153
1977	63692	9338	147	66751	8350	125
1978	71244	10866	153	75863	9953	131
1979	75153	13740	183	71839	11738	163
1980	88839	18695	210	90178	16804	186
1981	92126	19537	212	95522	17963	188
1982	99105	19199	194	95744	16514	172
	Rice China					
1976	504	153	304	1444	451	312
1977	367	113	309	1186	287	242
1978	527	173	328	1676	497	296
1979	501	170	340	1466	423	289
1980	511	206	402	1381	513	371
1981	667	277	415	687	263	383
1982	612	208	341	784	237	302
	Rice world					
1976	8446	2896	343	8814	2502	284
1977	9832	3309	337	10720	2902	271

1978	9995	3940	394	9491	3373	355
1979	11957	4621	387	11376	3786	333
1980	12575	5369	427	12794	5011	392
1981	13488	6507	482	12887	5837	453
1982	11300	4592	406	11946	4210	352

Source: based on FAOSTAT, FAO (2019).

By the mid-1980s, China's own production had expanded quickly and, soon after, it was able to export more cereals to the world market. In the 1990s, for some years, it net-exported cereals to the world market. Nonetheless, as a strategy, taking advantage of the substitutability of rice and wheat helped China enormously in the late 1970s and the early 1980s when it was economically very poor.

Other countries have also made use of the substitutability of grains to manage their food economy. For example, when Japan and South Korea were experiencing serious food shortages after World War II, they imported wheat to feed the population although rice is the staple in both countries (see the section on South Korea and Japan in Chapter 12 for more details; also see Hirasawa 2017; Song and Kwon 2017).

References

FAO. (2019), 'FAOSTAT – Trade', www.fao.org/faostat/en/#data/TP, accessed 20 February 2019.

Hirasawa, A. (2017), 'Food security measures in Japan since World War II', in Zhou, Z.Y. and Wan, G.H. (eds), *Food Insecurity in Asia: Why Institutions Matter*, ADB Institute, Tokyo, Ch 5, pp. 89–138.

Song, J.H. and Kwon, T.J. (2017), 'Food security in South Korea and North Korea: Why the difference?', in Zhou, Z.Y. and Wan, G.H. (eds), *Food Insecurity in Asia: Why Institutions Matter*, ADB Institute, Tokyo, Ch 5, pp. 139–191.

Given that onions are such an important ingredient complementary to the cooking of many dishes in India, higher onion prices can cause a huge headache to many. Not only can such high prices become a burden for the public, they can also result in enormous shock to the Indian politicians (see Box 5.2).

BOX 5.2

The power of complements

Some foods are complementary to each other. Some complementary foods can be very important to the lives of people in some cultures. Onion is one such food to Indians.

Onion is an indispensable ingredient of most Indian cooking, providing the pungent foundation for different kinds of curries and other dishes. The demand for onion is in every corner of the country (Bhowmick 2013).

In recent decades, the supply of onion seems to have been a recurring issue, causing problems to producers, consumers, and politicians. When there is an oversupply, farmers suffer (Fresh Plaza 2016). When there is a supply shortage, consumers suffer. In either case, politicians are challenged.

The challenge is more acute for politicians when the public's demand for onion cannot be adequately met, which is often accompanied by skyrocketing prices. They have to handle this challenge with great diligence. Otherwise, their jobs will be on the line.

Since the 1980s, there have been several occasions when Indian governments were brought down by high onion prices. It is believed that onion prices were the decisive factor in the 1998 state elections in Delhi and Rajasthan and were responsible for bringing down the central government in 1980 (Editorial of The Hindu 2010; Bhowmick 2013).

To meet the country's huge and rising demand, efforts are needed to improve the management of the onion supply chains, with particular attention to improving technologies, distribution, and infrastructure related to the onion supply chains. As an integral part, trade in onion should also be a regular element of the country's onion supply chain management.

Until the onion supply chain management is substantially improved, governments in India may find their fates will continue depending on this pungent bulb.

References

Bhowmick, B. (2013), 'How onions could bring down the Indian government', http://world.time.com/2013/10/24/why-an-onion-crisis-brings-tears-to-indian-eyes/, accessed 25 February 2019.

Editorial of The Hindu. (2010), 'The political price of onions', www.thehindu.com/opinion/editorial/The-political-price-of-onions/article15607000.ece, accessed 25 February 2019.

Fresh Plaza. (2016), 'Indian onion crisis: Farmers dumping produce', www.freshplaza.com/article/2157335/indian-onion-crisis-farmers-dumping-produce/, accessed 25 February 2019.

5.1.2 Changes in tastes and preferences

When consumer tastes and preferences change in favour of a product, the demand for that product will increase and the demand curve for that product will shift to the right. When a product falls out of favour, the demand for that product will decline and the demand curve will shift to the left. In Appendix 3A, we had a hypothetic example where people in Rasia become extremely fond of rice. Hence, at a given price they buy more rice than previously. This leads the demand curve for rice to shift to the right (see Figure 3A.3).

While tastes and preferences for food may vary among people of different geographical regions or ethnic backgrounds, consumer tastes and preferences for most foods are relatively stable. Changes in tastes and preferences can occur but that is most likely a slow process. Such changes can be triggered by increased availability of different foods due to improved food transportation facilities and through increased exposure to diverse cuisines due to interregional or international travels.

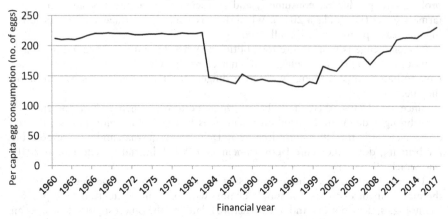

Figure 5.1 Changes in Australia's per capita egg consumption.
Source: 1960–1970: Australian Bureau of Statistics (ABS), Report on Food Production and the Apparent Consumption of Foodstuffs and Nutrients in Australia; 1971–1999: ABS Apparent Consumption of Foodstuffs (and Nutrients), Australia; 2000–2017: Australian Egg Corporation Limited Annual Reports

Research findings concerning the impact of food on health can also affect tastes and preferences. Take eggs as an example. For many decades, from the mid-20th century, it was believed that diet had an impact on cholesterol levels in humans. Since eggs contain cholesterol, eating eggs was believed to raise cholesterol and therefore be bad for health. This certainly discouraged people from eating eggs.

Recently, research has shown that most of the cholesterol in our body is made by our liver. Cholesterol in foods has only a small effect on our LDL (low density lipoprotein) cholesterol (commonly referred to as 'bad cholesterol'). Hence, the cholesterol in eggs has only a small effect on blood LDL cholesterol. On the other hand, eggs are very nutritious. They contain good quality protein, lots of vitamins and minerals, and mostly the healthier polyunsaturated fat. The egg industry capitalised on such research findings and increased their information dissemination activities, advising consumers that eating eggs is fine. Consequently, egg consumption has steadily increased in recent years in many countries. In Australia, per capita egg consumption in 2000 was 166 and by 2017 it was 231 (Australian Bureau of Statistics 2000; Australian Egg Corporation Limited 2018; see Figure 5.1). It may increase further.

5.2 Special factors and food demand

There are some special and emerging forces that also affect food demand, directly or indirectly.

Urbanisation: Urbanisation (the increase in the proportion of the population living in urban areas) has occurred at a much faster rate in recent decades around the globe, especially in many developing countries. In 1950, about 30% of the world's population lived in urban areas. By 2015, this proportion increased to 54%. In actual numbers, it increased from 749 million in 1950 to 3,957 million in 2015. In less developed regions, the urban population increased from 18% in 1950 to 49% in 2015; or from 302 million to 2,971 million in the same time period. The level of urbanisation is expected to further increase (Figure 5.2). By 2050, some 66% (or 6,338 million) of the world's population will live in urban areas.

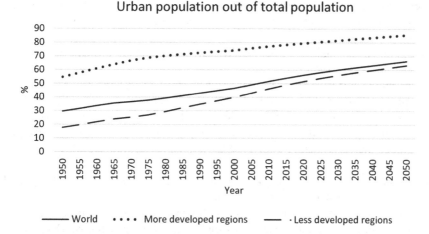

Figure 5.2 Level of urbanisation (1950–2050).
Source: Based on Population Division (2014), World Urbanization Prospects: The 2014 Revision, CD-ROM Edition, United Nations, Department of Economic and Social Affairs.

Urbanisation can affect food demand directly, such as reduced needs for foods of high energy, e.g., cereals. In most cases, however, it affects food demand indirectly through:

● Increased income: after rural people move to urban areas, their income generally increases.
● Changes in tastes and preferences: these new urban dwellers will also be readily exposed to more and diverse food dietary practices.

Ultimately, the quantity and composition of foods demanded by these new urban residents will change (Gandhi and Zhou 2014). They may increasingly demand, and afford, higher priced foods with more protein and less calories. A report by the International Food Policy Research Institute (IFPRI) (2017) on global food policy has taken an in-depth look at how rapid urbanisation is reshaping food systems, and its impact on food security and nutrition for rural and urban populations.

Rapid urbanisation may also worsen urban malnutrition. Urban malnutrition has been a problem in low socio-economic pockets of large cities, especially in poorer countries. Many large cities today are concentrated in Asia and Africa. Future fast urbanisation growth will also take place in these regions. The urban poor may be unable to afford enough food to meet their nutritional requirements (for example, Morris 2001; Mohiddin, Phelps and Walters 2012).

Climate zones: The Earth has three main climate zones – tropical, temperate, and polar. The amount of food needed by human bodies to maintain body growth differs in different zones. Generally, human bodies require less calories in tropical regions and thus less dietary energy is demanded.

Land terrain: Everything else being equal, people living in hilly and mountainous areas require more dietary energy to get around compared to people living in plain areas.

Age: Human bodies have different nutrition needs at different ages. Younger people require more nutrition of all kinds. Older people demand less high-energy and fatty foods but more protein-rich foods. Thus, a society with a higher portion of younger people requires more food.

Gender: Females generally consume less food. This factor, however, is unlikely to have any major impact on the total amount of food demanded in a society because the male–female ratio is generally stable.

Occupation: Those engaged in heavy physical work, such as farmers or road workers, require higher intakes of food.

Status of public infrastructure: In places where road conditions are poor and modern transportation facilities are lacking, people will need to consume more food to move around.

Food storage and transportation technologies: Advancement in such technologies makes it possible to transport food longer distances, improving food availability across regions. This can induce increased demand for food as well as changes in the composition of food demanded.

Social-cultural factors: In some societies, food in excess of need may be provided or consumed, for example, when entertaining guests, or when showing that one is rich. This increases food demand but often results in severe food wastage. In some affluent communities, people grow up with plenty and regard throwing food away as acceptable. Demand for food will be reduced if wastage is reduced.

Purchasing through the Internet: This, together with the fast expansion of parcel delivery services, has made it possible and easy for anyone with access to the Internet to buy foods from elsewhere, including from other countries. This may increase the amount demanded of certain foods and affect the composition of food demand.

Globalisation: Globalisation (the increase in interactions of people through the growth of the international flow of money, ideas, and culture) has also gathered momentum in recent decades. As a result, people are exposed to ways of eating that are completely new, influencing their tastes and preferences. While globalisation may affect the total amount of food demanded to some extent, it is likely to chiefly affect the composition of food demanded. In some cases, it will affect the country of origin of the foods consumed – imported foods replacing domestically produced foods. IFPRI's 2018 Global Food Policy Report focuses on the impacts of globalisation and the recent growing anti-globalisation related to food security (IFPRI 2018).

Understanding how the above special and emerging factors affect food demand has important implications for food policies. In countries where urbanisation increases at a faster rate with more people increasingly interacting with the rest of the world, government policy innovations are needed to prepare their food systems to cater for the changing demand for foods. Food demand can also be managed by improving public infrastructure helping to reduce the human body's needs for food. Governments may also devise incentives to reduce food wastage.

Review questions

1. Wheat flour and rice are substitutes. When people use more wheat flour, they will eat less rice and *vice versa*. Draw a diagram similar to Figure 3A.7; the market is in equilibrium with the equilibrium price being $0.8 per kg, and the corresponding quantity traded is 120 kt. Then, show how the demand curve for rice may shift:
   1. When the price of wheat flour drops; and
   2. When the price of wheat flour rises.
      Point out whether the resulting quantity of rice traded and the price of rice will be higher or lower for each situation.
2. Can you think of any factors other than those discussed so far that may affect the amount of food demanded? Explain how.

Discussion questions

1. In your community, do people provide excessive food to entertain their guests? Do people try to buy more food for themselves in public eating places as a way to show off that they are rich? If not, what may have led to such behaviours? If yes, what can you suggest to your community to change their behaviours?
2. You may conduct a small survey in your neighbourhood to verify the extent of food waste. If the waste is serious, try to understand why and make use of your wisdom to influence your neighbourhood to avoid food waste.

References

Australian Bureau of Statistics (2000) and earlier years. *Reports on Food Production and the Apparent Consumption of Foodstuffs and Nutrients in Australia; and Apparent Consumption of Foodstuffs (and Nutrients), Australia,* Australian Government, Canberra.

Australian Egg Corporation Limited (2018) and earlier years. *Australian Eggs Annual Reports,* www.australianeggs.org.au/who-we-are/annual-reports/, accessed 4 October 2018.

Gandhi, V.P. and Zhou, Z.Y. (2014), 'Food demand and the food security challenge with rapid economic growth in the emerging economies of India and China', *Food Research International,* Vol. 63, pp. 108–124.

IFPRI (International Food Policy Research Institute). (2017), *2017 Global Food Policy Report,* www.ifpri.org/publication/2017-global-food-policy-report, accessed 3 March 2018.

IFPRI. (2018), *2018 Global Food Policy Report,* www.ifpri.org/publication/2018-global-food-policy-report, accessed 8 October 2018.

Mohiddin, L., Phelps, L. and Walters, T. (2012), 'Urban malnutrition: A review of food security and nutrition among the urban poor', www.nutritionworks.org.uk/our-publications/programme-review-and-evaluation/2011/153-urban-malnutrition-a-review-of-food-security-and-nutrition-among-the-urban-poor, accessed 8 October 2018.

Morris, S.S. (2001), 'Targeting urban malnutrition: A multi-city analysis of the spatial distribution of childhood nutritional status', *Food Policy,* Vol. 26, pp. 49–64.

Population Division. (2014), *World Urbanization Prospects: The 2014 Revision,* CD-ROM Edition, United Nations, Department of Economic and Social Affairs, New York.

Song, J.H. and Kwon, T.J. (2017), 'Food security in the Republic of Korea and the Democratic People's Republic of Korea: Why the difference?' in Zhou, Z.Y. and Wan, G.H. (eds), *Food Insecurity in Asia: Why Institutions Matter,* ADB Institute, Tokyo, Ch 6, pp. 139–191.

Further reading

IFPRI (International Food Policy Research Institute), *Global Food Policy Reports.* This Report Series was first published in 2011 and all past reports can be obtained from http://gfpr.ifpri.info/past-reports. The Reports focus on a distinct theme each year. The *2017 Global Food Policy Report* takes an in-depth look at how rapid urbanisation is reshaping food systems, and its impact on food security and nutrition for rural and urban populations. The 2018 Report focuses on the impacts of globalisation and the challenge of growing anti-globalisation pressures on food security.

Part 3

Food security

Supply side

Contents

6 Natural resources and food supply

7 Technological progress and food supply

8 Other determinants of food supply

Like the demand for a product, the supply of a product is also affected by a number of factors. In Appendix 3A, we highlighted those factors that are conventionally regarded as more influential shifters to the supply of a product.

The extent to which each of the supply shifters impacts on the supply of a product differs. Specific to the supply of food, some of them seem to have also become less critical over time, such as the number of producers. The trend around the globe is that fewer producers are now producing more food.

There are three important shifters to food supply: the availability and quality of natural resources, technological progress, and weather conditions. In this part, we address how they affect food supply.

In Chapters 6 and 7, we examine how the endowment of natural resources and technological progress affect food supply, respectively. In Chapter 8, we discuss the impact of other important shifters, such as input costs, weather conditions, and other emerging forces, on food supply.

Before you read on, make sure you are still fresh with the basics of demand and supply. Otherwise, you need to review the contents of Appendix 3A.

Chapter 6

Natural resources and food supply

Summary

This chapter explains how the quantity and quality of natural resources affects food supply. Section 6.1 introduces the essential resources needed for food production: water, land, light, temperature, and air. Section 6.2 discusses recent changes in the availability of water and land, the two most important natural resources for food production. Section 6.3 highlights the importance of the quality of natural resources to food production. Preserving both quantity and quality of natural resources for sustainable use is addressed in Section 6.4. Finally, Section 6.5 points out that although a lack of natural resources is disadvantageous to a country in terms of food supply from domestic sources, it does not prevent a country from achieving a high level of food security.

It is noted that changes in resource use efficiency also affect food supply. That is, with a given quantity and quality of resources, the advent of better methods that can make their use more efficient can also boost food output, shifting the supply curve to the right. This kind of influence, however, will be addressed in the next chapter on technological progress. In this chapter, it is implied that resources are made use of to their maximum efficiency at a given technological level.

After studying this chapter, you should be able to:
- Enumerate and explain the most crucial natural resources to food production.
- Discuss the importance of quantity and quality of natural resources to food supply.
- Outline the availability of two important natural resources, water and land, at the global and continental levels and note how the availability differs between continents.
- Form your own thoughts about the importance of resource availability to a country's food security.

6.1 Natural resources: indispensable for food production

Key resources essential for plant growth include water, air, soil/land, light, and temperature. Water provides moisture for, and ducts nutrients to, plants. Air allows plants to breathe. Air and water also provide most of the carbon, hydrogen, and oxygen that plants need for growth. Soil physically supports plants and stores and supplies nutrients (through water) to plants. Important elements that are essential for plant photosynthesis (in addition to carbon, hydrogen, and oxygen) such as nitrogen, potassium, phosphorus, sulphur, calcium, and magnesium come chiefly from the soil. Important micronutrients including boron, copper, iron, manganese, molybdenum, and zinc also come from the soil. Light is essential for plants to carry out photosynthesis. Temperature affects plants' physiological processes. Among all of the above, water, however, is the most important resource. Without water, no plants can be grown.

Plants can be consumed by human beings directly as food. They are also essential in providing human beings with food of animal origin. Hence, resources needed for plant growth are crucial in the supply of foods of both vegetal and animal origins.

Concern about population outgrowing food supply goes back at least as far as Malthus (Thomas Robert Malthus, 1766–1834, was an English scholar. In *An Essay on the Principle of Population*, he argued that population multiplies geometrically and food arithmetically; therefore, whenever the food supply increases, population will rapidly grow to eliminate the abundance). Rapid population growth since World War II and growing recognition of the impact of human induced damages to the natural environment, including climate change, has reignited these concerns. In the next section, changes in the availability of fresh water, agricultural land, and other key natural resources are discussed.

6.2 Resource availability and food supply

6.2.1 Water availability and use in agriculture

Based upon levels of salinity (the saltiness or amount of salt dissolved in water), water can be classified as fresh water (<0.05%), brackish water (0.05–<3%), saline water (3–<5%), or briny water (≥5%). Much of all the water on Earth (97% of the planet's crust water) is saline – chiefly found in seas and oceans – and cannot be directly used for most human activities. Fresh water, which can be directly used by human beings for most activities, only accounts for about 3% of the planet's total water.

Fresh water exists in three states: liquid, solid (ice), and gas (invisible water vapour in the air; clouds are accumulations of water droplets, condensed from vapour-saturated air). Of the 3% of fresh water, a little over 2/3 (68.7%) is solid – frozen in glaciers and polar ice caps. The remaining unfrozen fresh water is found mainly as ground water, with only a small fraction present above ground or in the air.

Fresh water on Earth is replenished by precipitation. Precipitation is the amount of rain, snow, hail, etc. that falls at a given place within a given period, usually expressed in centimetres of water. For the whole planet, the annual precipitation falling on land is about 110,000 km³ per year (in the early 2010s). About 56% of this amount is evapotranspired by forests and natural landscapes and 5% by rainfed agriculture.

The remaining 39% or 43,000 km³ per year is converted to surface runoff and groundwater. Surface runoff (or overland flow) is the flow of water that occurs when excess stormwater, meltwater, or other sources flow over the Earth's land surface. Groundwater is the water found underground in the cracks and spaces in soil, sand, and rock. It is stored in, and moves slowly through, geologic formations of soil, sand, and rocks called aquifers.

Surface runoff and groundwater replenishment are called 'renewable freshwater resources'. Part of this water is removed from rivers or aquifers by installing infrastructure. This removal of the water is called water withdrawal.

In FAO statistics, three types of water withdrawal are distinguished: municipal (including domestic), industrial, and agricultural (including irrigation, livestock and aquaculture). A fourth type of anthropogenic water use is the water that evaporates from artificial lakes or reservoirs associated with dams. At the global level, the withdrawal ratios (without the fourth type) are 12% municipal, 19% industrial, and 69% agricultural in the early 2000s (Table 6.1).

The share of fresh water withdrawal for agricultural production is significant. This share, however, differs notably between continents and regions, according to Table 6.1. At the continent level, for example, this share is 81% in Africa and Asia but is just 21% in Europe. At the sub-continental level, it is 91% in South Asia but only 5% in Western Europe. Differences in climate and the importance of agriculture in the economy are chiefly responsible for such large variation in this ratio between continents and regions. The same is true at the country level.

Global fresh water withdrawals have increased significantly since the early 20th century (Figure 6.1). After evaporation from reservoirs (an anthropogenic consumptive water use) is added, over 4,000 km^3 were withdrawn annually in the early 2010s (Figure 6.1B)

The trend in Figure 6.1 shows that the increase in water withdrawal has slowed down over the last few decades. However, given that the total population will increase by over 2 billion by 2050, total demand for water will further increase. According to OECD, by 2050, almost 5,500 km^3 will be demanded annually based on its baseline projections (Figure 6.2).

Figure 6.2 suggests that by 2050, total water demand in OECD countries is likely to decline to some extent. In the emerging economies and developing countries, water demand will increase by a large margin. Overall, global water demand is projected to increase by some 55% according to the baseline scenario. This increase is chiefly due to growing demand from manufacturing (400%), thermal electricity generation (140%), and domestic use (130%). Water demand by the agricultural sector (irrigation and livestock combined) will decline to some extent as shown in Figure 6.2. One reason for this decline as suggested by the OECD is the limited scope for expanding irrigation water use due to competition from other sectors (OECD 2012). Another reason could be more efficient water use in agriculture.

Across the globe:

- Water is unevenly distributed across different locations. The 'Food security and related variables' table provides a glimpse of total actual renewable water resources (TARWR) per inhabitant for major countries around the globe. The difference in the water endowment between countries is enormous, from as low as 7 m^3 in Kuwait to as high as 84,483 m^3 in Canada.
- Over a year, water may be not available in a timely manner. Hence, annual per capita TARWR may be high but there may still be shortages during the year.
- Consequently, water shortage occurs in parts of the globe at various times. It may be absolute shortage/scarcity or it may be seasonal shortage/scarcity. Crop failure is caused by such shortages.

Table 6.1 Water withdrawal by sector and region (around 2010)

Continent Regions	Subregions	Total withdrawal by sector						Total water withdrawal	Total freshwater withdrawal	Freshwater withdrawal as % of IRWR
		Municipal		Industrial		Agricultural				
		km³/year	%	km³/year	%	km³/year	%	km³/year	km³/year	
World		464	12	768	19	2769	69	4001	3853	9
Africa		33	15	9	4	184	81	227	220	6
Northern Africa		14	13	3	3	89	84	106	101	215
Sub-Saharan Africa		19	16	6	5	96	79	121	119	3
	Sudano Sahelian	2.1	5	0.6	1	40.2	94	42.8	42.8	26.8
	Gulf of Guinea	6.5	39	2.6	16	7.4	45	16.5	16.5	1.7
	Central Africa	1.3	45	0.5	19	1.0	36	2.8	2.8	0.1
	Eastern Africa	3.0	15	0.3	1	16.8	84	20.1	20.1	7.0
	Southern Africa	5.5	22	2.1	9	16.9	69	24.6	23.0	8.5
	Indian Ocean Islands	0.6	4	0.2	1	13.5	94	14.3	14.3	4.2
Americas		123	14	321	37	415	48	859	855	4
Northern America		79	13	289	47	241	40	610	605	10
	Northern America	68.0	13	281.5	53	179.8	34	529.3	526.0	9.3
	Mexico	11.4	14	7.3	9	61.6	77	80.3	79.5	19.4
Central America and Caribbean		8	23	6	18	20	59	33	33	5
	Central America	3.3	27	1.3	11	7.5	62	12.1	12.1	1.9

Continent Regions / Subregions	Total withdrawal by sector						Total water withdrawal	Total freshwater withdrawal	Freshwater withdrawal as % of IRWR
	Municipal		Industrial		Agricultural				
	km³/year	%	km³/year	%	km³/year	%	km³/year	km³/year	
Caribbean-Greater Antilles	4.0	19	4.6	22	12.0	58	20.5	20.5	22.2
Caribbean-Lesser Antilles and Bahamas	0.4	60	0.1	23	0.1	18	0.6	0.5	9.7
Southern America	**36**	**17**	**26**	**12**	**154**	**71**	**216**	**216**	**2**
Guyana	0.1	5	0.2	8	1.8	87	2.1	2.1	0.6
Andean	10.9	18	3.9	7	45.2	75	60.1	60.1	1.1
Brazil	17.2	23	12.7	17	44.9	60	74.8	74.8	1.3
Southern America	7.9	10	9.0	11	62.4	79	79.3	79.1	5.7
Asia	**234**	**9**	**253**	**10**	**2069**	**81**	**2556**	**2421**	**20**
Middle East	**25**	**9**	**20**	**7**	**231**	**84**	**276**	**268**	**55**
Arabian Peninsula	3.9	11	0.9	3	29.5	86	34.3	30.1	492.2
Caucasus	1.7	10	2.9	17	12.3	73	16.9	16.9	23.1
Islamic Republic of Iran	6.2	7	1.1	1	86.0	92	93.3	93.1	72.5
Near East	13.6	10	14.9	11	103.3	78	131.8	128.0	46.3
Central Asia	**7**	**5**	**10**	**7**	**128**	**89**	**145**	**136**	**56**
Southern and Eastern Asia	**202**	**9**	**224**	**10**	**1710**	**80**	**2135**	**2017**	**18**
South Asia	70.2	7	20.0	2	912.8	91	1003.1	889.6	46.0
East Asia	93.8	14	158.0	22	469.4	65	725.8	721.5	21.2

(continued)

Table 6.1 (cont.)

| Continent Regions | Subregions | Total withdrawal by sector | | | | | | Total water withdrawal | Total freshwater withdrawal | Freshwater withdrawal as % of IRWR |
| | | Municipal | | Industrial | | Agricultural | | | | |
		km³/year	%	km³/year	%	km³/year	%	km³/year	km³/year	
	Mainland Southeast Asia	7.5	4	6.6	4	164.4	92	178.4	178.2	9.4
	Maritime Southeast Asia	25.7	11	39.1	17	163.4	72	228.2	228.0	5.9
Europe		**69**	**21**	**181**	**54**	**84**	**25**	**334**	**332**	**5**
Western and Central Europe		**51**	**21**	**131**	**53**	**66**	**27**	**248**	**246**	**12**
	Northern Europe	2.7	31	4.9	55	1.2	14	8.8	8.8	1.1
	Western Europe	21.0	21	73.5	74	4.9	5	99.4	98.7	15.9
	Central Europe	9.3	23	27.6	68	3.6	9	40.5	40.5	16.3
	Mediterranean Europe	17.9	18	25.0	25	55.9	57	98.8	97.8	23.1
Eastern Europe		**18**	**21**	**50**	**58**	**18**	**21**	**86**	**86**	**2**
	Eastern Europe	4.3	22	10.6	53	5.1	25	20.0	20.0	14.7
	Russian Federation	13.4	20	39.6	60	13.2	20	66.2	66.2	1.5
Oceania		**5**	**20**	**4**	**15**	**16**	**65**	**25**	**25**	**3**
	Australia and New Zealand	5	20	4	15	16	65	25	24	3
	Other Pacific Islands	0.03	30	0.01	11	0.05	59	0.1	0.1	0.1

Source: Based on FAO (2018a), AQUASTAT database 2018, www.fao.org/nr/water/aquastat/data/query/index.html?lang=en.

- Over the past decades, water shortage has increasingly become a major issue in some parts of the globe, especially in countries that are heavily populated. The water-shortage problem has become more and more acute in both China and India, the two most populous countries on Earth.
- Looking into the future, freshwater availability in some countries will become more and more strained. Often in such countries, water management is lacking or less effective (Gandhi and Namboodiri 2007). Less effective water management exacerbates water shortages. How water availability will affect food production in these countries deserves close attention.

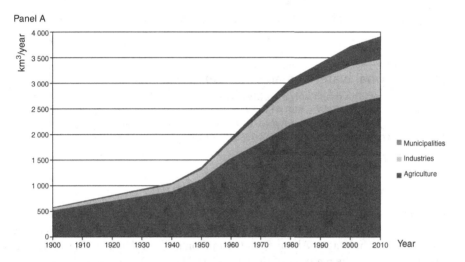

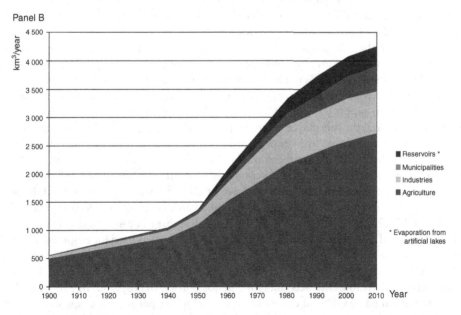

Figure 6.1 Global water withdrawal over time.
Source: FAO (2018b), water uses, http://www.fao.org/nr/water/aquastat/water_use/index.stm.

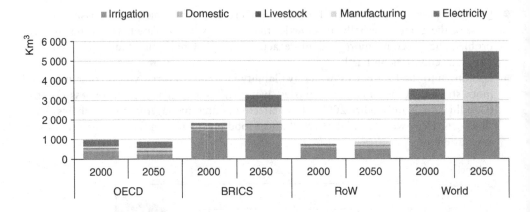

Figure 6.2 Global water demand by 2050, OECD forecast.

Notes: This graph only measures blue water demand and does not consider rain-fed agriculture. RoW = Rest of the World.

Source: OECD 2012, http://www.oecd.org/environment/indicators-modelling-outlooks/oecd-environmental-outlook-1999155x.htm.

6.2.2 Land availability and use in agriculture

Out of a total of 510.1 million km², some 71% (361 million km²) of the Earth's surface is covered by ocean. Land accounts for the rest 29% (149 million km²). Some 71% of the land (104 million km²) is habitable. About 50% (51 million km²) of the habitable land is used for agricultural purposes. The majority of the agricultural land (77%, or 40 million km²) is used for livestock production. The rest 23% (11 million km²) is for crop production (for land use definitions and global surface area allocation, see Box 6.1).

Although more than three-quarters of agricultural land is used for the rearing of livestock (through a combination of grazing land and land used for animal feed production), meat and dairy products provide only 17% of global caloric supply and 33% of global protein supply. The rest is provided by crops. In other words, the 11 million km², or 23% of, agricultural land used for crop production supply 83% of calories and 67% of protein, respectively. Hence, in feeding the world population, the role played by crops (produced on one quarter of the agricultural land) is far greater than that played by livestock products (produced on three quarters of the land).

According to the FAO, global agricultural land stood at 4873 million ha (1 km² = 100 ha) in 2016. This represents an increase of 8.7% compared to the area in 1965 (4481 million ha). Figure 6.5 shows land use since 1965 and also the forecast till 2050 according to the FAO. It suggests that the use of agricultural land seems to have peaked around 2000. In 2000, agricultural land was 4955 million ha, the highest so far. By 2050, it is forecast to be 4911 million ha.

Out of the total agricultural land in 2016, 1592 million ha was used for cropland. According to Figure 6.5, the cropland area will further increase from the current 1592 million ha in 2016 to 1661 million ha by 2050. Cropland is composed of 'arable land' and 'land under permanent crops'. Arable land accounts for a major portion of cropland. In 1961, arable land was 1292 million ha (93.6%, of cropland), and land under permanent crops was 88 million ha (6.4% of cropland). By 2016, arable land was 1424 million ha (89.5%), and land under permanent crops was 168 million ha (10.5%). The share of land used for permanent crops had undergone an increase, from 6.4% in 1961 to 10.5% in 2016. In absolute terms, the area had almost doubled from 88 million ha in 1961 to 168 million ha in 2016.

BOX 6.1

Land use definitions and land area breakdown

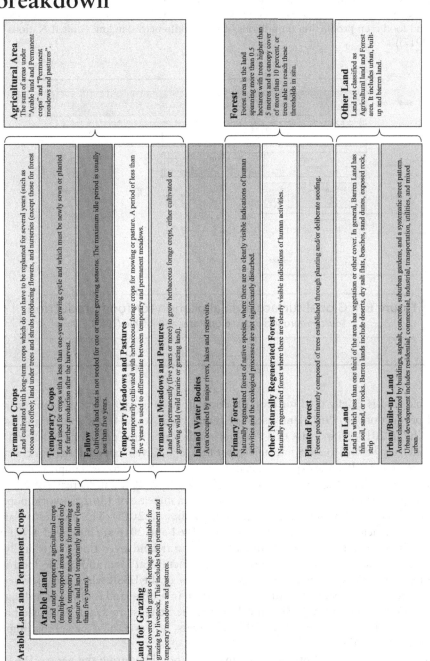

Arable Land and Permanent Crops

Arable Land
Land under temporary agricultural crops (multiple-cropped areas are counted only once), temporary meadows for mowing or pasture, and land temporarily fallow (less than five years).

Land for Grazing
Land covered with grass or herbage and suitable for grazing by livestock. This includes both permanent and temporary meadows and pastures.

Permanent Crops
Land cultivated with long-term crops which do not have to be replanted for several years (such as cocoa and coffee); land under trees and shrubs producing flowers, and nurseries (except those for forest production after the harvest.

Temporary Crops
Land used for crops with a less than one-year growing cycle and which must be newly sown or planted for further production after the harvest.

Fallow
Cultivated land that is not seeded for one or more growing seasons. The maximum idle period is usually less than five years.

Temporary Meadows and Pastures
Land temporarily cultivated with herbaceous forage crops for mowing or pasture. A period of less than five years is used to differentiate between temporary and permanent meadows.

Permanent Meadows and Pastures
Land used permanently (five years or more) to grow herbaceous forage crops, either cultivated or growing wild (wild prairie or grazing land).

Inland Water Bodies
Area occupied by major rivers, lakes and reservoirs.

Primary Forest
Naturally regenerated forest of native species, where there are no clearly visible indications of human activities and the ecological processes are not significantly disturbed.

Other Naturally Regenerated Forest
Naturally regenerated forest where there are clearly visible indications of human activities.

Planted Forest
Forest predominantly composed of trees established through planting and/or deliberate seeding.

Barren Land
Land in which less than one third of the area has vegetation or other cover. In general, Barren Land has thin soil, sand, or rocks. Barren lands include deserts, dry salt flats, beaches, sand dunes, exposed rock, strip

Urban/Built-up Land
Areas characterized by buildings, asphalt, concrete, suburban gardens, and a systematic street pattern. Urban development includes residential, commercial, industrial, transportation, utilities, and mixed urban.

Agricultural Area
The sum of areas under "Arable land and Permanent crops" and "Permanent meadows and pastures".

Forest
Forest area is the land spanning more than 0.5 hectares with trees higher than 5 metres and a canopy cover of more than 10 percent, or trees able to reach these thresholds in situ.

Other Land
Land not classified as Agricultural land and Forest area. It includes urban, built-up and barren land.

Figure 6.3 Land use definitions for agricultural and non-agricultural land cover.

Figure 6.3 contains a number of land use definitions and combined categories, particularly in relation to agriculture. The groupings and definitions are based on the UN Food and Agriculture Organization (FAO) and are therefore consistent with most international data sources.

Shown in Figure 6.4 below is the breakdown of the Earth's surface area by functional and allocated uses, down to agricultural land allocation for livestock and food crop production (in millions of square kilometres, m km² (United Nations 2017)).

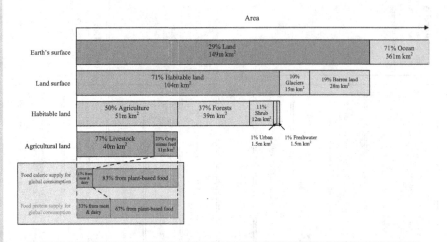

Figure 6.4 Global surface area allocation for food production.
Source: reproduced based on Roser and Ritchie (2018).

Arable land is chiefly used for crop production. Around 50% of arable land is used for cereal production. In 1961, land used for cereal crops was 648 million ha and was 718 million ha in 2016, an increase of 11%. During the same time period, global cereal output increased from 887 mt to 2849 mt, an increase of 225%. Given that land used for cereal crops only increased by 11%, the expansion in output was chiefly due to yield improvement; which increased from 13,532 kg/ha in 1961 to 39,668 kg/ha in 2016, an increase of 193%. The output expansion of 225% surpassed the population increase of 136.2% (world population increased from 3090 million in 1961 to 7383 million in 2015). The indexes of land use, cereal output, yield, and the population between 1961 and 2016 are displayed in Figure 6.6.

At the continental level, variation in agricultural land over time is generally small (Figure 6.7, Panel A). The sharp variation in agricultural land and arable land in Asia and Europe in the early 1990s is due to the collapse of the USSR when some former USSR members returned to being part of Asia. Variation in arable land is also small (Figure 6.7, Panel B). For the Americas, Asia, and Europe, the increase in arable land use has been relatively small. Their increases in yields of cereals, however, have been most impressive (Figure 6.7, Panel C).

In contrast, arable land use in Africa increased notably during the period 1961–2016, by 54%. Since 2000, arable land use is still increasing by a large margin in most parts of Africa except in Southern Africa. Fast population increase was responsible for the notable increase in the use of land for crops. Africa's cereal yield has been the lowest in the world.

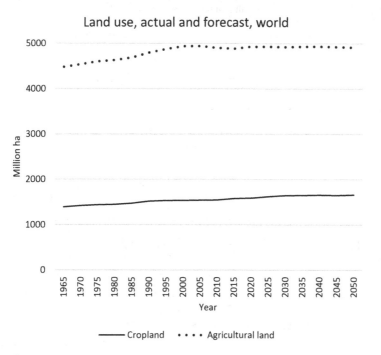

Figure 6.5 Changes in land use, 1965–2050 (actual and forecast).

Note: data between 1961 and 2016 are actual in five-year average; e.g., the average of 1961–1965 is indicated as 1965. Numbers beyond 2015 are predictions.

Source: FAO (2018c), FAOSTAT database, Land Use, 1965–2015; Alexandratos and Bruinsma (2012), 2020–2050.

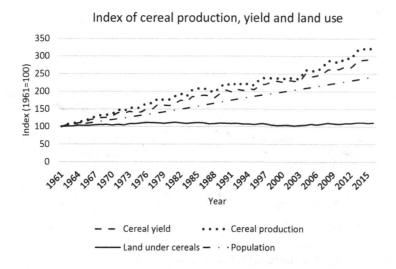

Figure 6.6 Index of arable land use for cereal and output (1961–2016, 1961=100).

Source: FAO (2018c), FAOSTAT database, Crops, 1965–2016; United Nations (2017).

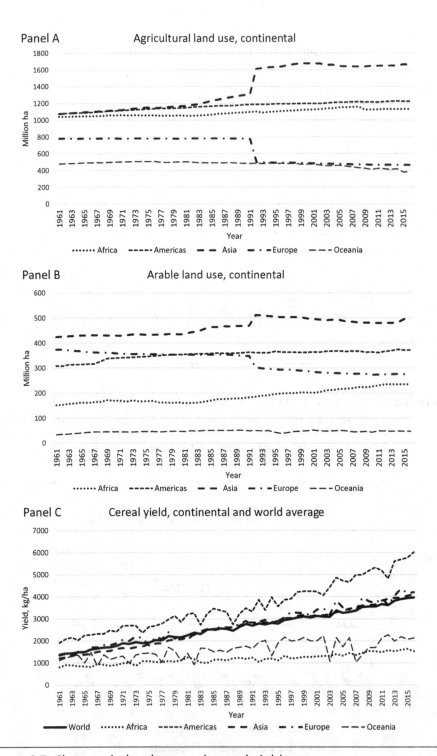

Figure 6.7 Changes in land use and cereal yield.

Note: The sharp variation in agricultural land and arable land use in Asia and Europe in the early 1990s is due to the collapse of the USSR; some former USSR members returned to be part of Asia.

Source: based on FAO (2018c), FAOSTAT database, Crops, and Land Use.

Looking to the future at the global level, expansion in land for agricultural purposes is likely minimal. Agricultural land is projected to slowly increase from 4870 million ha in 2016 to 4933 million ha in 2040. After that it will likely drop to 4911 million ha by 2050. Cropland is likely to slowly expand by another 68 million ha by 2050 (from 1593 million ha in 2016 to 1661 million ha in 2050).

Cropland expansion can be achieved either by converting land for grazing to land for cropping, or by encroaching into forests (which currently covers 37% of the land, or 3900 million ha) (refer to Box 6.1). How the extra cropland expansion can be achieved is unsure. Deforestation is a threat to the environment.

For some countries, the lack of land availability will remain a major constraint in expanding food production to meet the needs of a growing population. In the past, productivity improvement has played a major role in increasing domestic food output. In the future, food production expansion will need to continue relying, or even more, on productivity improvement through smart and increased investment in research and development, which will be addressed in the next chapter. Some countries will have to rely on trade to meet their requirements for food.

6.2.3 Availability of other important natural resources

Other natural resources also play a crucial role in food production. The discussion below focuses on the importance of the availability of three such natural resources: biodiversity, fish stocks, and phosphorous.

6.2.3.1 Biodiversity

Biodiversity is short for biological diversity. It is the variety that exists among organisms within their environments. There are three levels of biodiversity:

- Genetic diversity is the most basic level. It refers to the variety of genes present in the members of a species.
- Species diversity refers to the variety of species in a specific place or among a specific group of organisms.
- Ecosystem diversity refers to the variety of physical settings on the Earth, such as deserts, lakes, forests, and coral reefs, and their populations of plants and animals. If an ecosystem disappears, so do the species that live only in that ecosystem.

The human population has expanded very quickly recently and so has its impact on the environment. Some human activities, many of which are related to increasing food production, have seriously threatened biodiversity. For example, large-scale monoculture or monocropping (where the same species is grown year after year), based on scale efficiencies in machinery, often leaves little space for local flora and fauna. This is detrimental to the preservation of genetic diversification and species diversification. Unsustainable felling of forests or large-scale encroachment on forests for land expansion is extremely harmful to ecosystem diversification.

The preservation of biodiversity has the potential to lead to discoveries of valuable genetic materials and species that can significantly improve future food output. Protecting biodiversity has become one of the greatest challenges facing humankind.

6.2.3.2 Fish stocks

As an important food, fish provides human beings with protein. About three billion people get a fifth of their protein from fish, making it a more important protein source than beef (*The Economist 2014*). Overfishing, however, has presented an ever-increasing threat to the sustainable use of this valuable protein source.

Overfishing is the removal of a species of fish from a body of water at a faster rate than that at which it reproduces. This results in those species either becoming depleted or underpopulated in that given area. Overfishing is happening all over the globe.

Overfishing can happen in water bodies of different sizes, such as ponds, rivers, lakes, or oceans. Overfishing in oceans in particular has been a growing concern and has attracted much attention. According to the FAO, a third of fish stocks in the oceans have been over-exploited (FAO 2018d). Overfishing has been largely attributed to the global mismanagement of fish stocks. Improving the management of ocean fish stocks requires the joint efforts of all parties to avoid potentially undermining international efforts.

6.2.3.3 Availability of phosphorus

One other vital natural resource that will critically affect future food supply is phosphorus.

Although phosphorus shortage is not as well-known as other popular issues, it is no less significant. Phosphorus is an essential nutrient for all forms of life. All living organisms require a daily phosphorus intake to produce energy. Without phosphorus, there is no life (Faradji and de Boer 2016). Phosphorus, however, is limited in supply although there are different views on how limited its supply is (Cordell, Drangert, and White 2009; Cornish 2010; Cho 2013).

Crop yields will be severely compromised in the future if phosphorus one day becomes short. Food supply and subsequently food security will suffer. Some experts argue that significant physical and institutional changes should be made to the way we currently use and source phosphorus. Programs that develop ways to use phosphorus more efficiently and that recapture and recycle phosphorus are urgently needed (Cordell, Drangert, and White 2009; Cornish 2010; Elser and Bennett 2011).

6.3 Resource quality and food supply

While resource availability or quantity is very important to food production, their quality is also very important. When resources are of poor quality, e.g., the water and land are being polluted, the output from such resources may be lower and the quality of foods produced inferior. In extreme circumstances, such resources may be so damaged or polluted as to be no longer usable for food production.

The term 'water stress' has been recently used to describe not only when demand for water is greater than the amount of water available at a certain period in time (water scarcity) but also when the quality of water restricts its usage. Without due protection of water quality, an area may suffer from very high levels of water stress while it has no water scarcity – because the supplies of water, while plentiful, have been contaminated, by salt, for example.

Contaminated water pollutes the soil/land. Foods produced with such contaminated water and soil may be harmful to the health of human beings. Polluted water will also have dire consequences for other plants in the ecosystem and subsequently for any other animals that rely on such plants.

In countries and regions with water scarcity but high population, it is even more pressing to protect water. According to OECD projections, by 2050, 2.3 billion more people than today (in total, over 40% of the global population, i.e., 4 billion) will be living in river basins under severe water stress, especially in North and South Africa, and South and Central Asia (OECD 2012).

Soil quality also affects food supply. Soil pollution has occurred in many countries and especially in less developed countries. Polluted soil may contain high levels of salinity or acidity or other substances that may limit plant growth, resulting in reduced output. When planted on soil heavily polluted with harmful substances (e.g., heavy metals), crops can accumulate those toxins through their roots and transfer them to seeds or other edible parts of the crops, causing human health problems (Zhang et al. 2015). Severely polluted soil/land may be no longer suitable for producing any food and this reduces a country's food output, especially in many less developed countries.

Protecting air quality has also become ever more important. Many of us take having fresh air for granted. However, air pollution is widespread in many countries, both developed and developing, but especially in emerging economies. Heavily polluted air affects food production through its impact on the strength of sunlight and air temperatures. Heavy smog filters the sunlight which in turn reduces the photosynthesis of plants. Temperatures may also become lower, reducing plant growth. In addition, polluted air also affects the quality of surface water and soil – pollutants in the air brought down by rainfall. 'Heavy acid rain' (with a pH lower than 5.0) and 'very heavy acid rain' (with a pH lower than 4.5) can cause serious damage to crops, trees, and fish and result in soil pollution (USEPA 2017).

6.4 Resource sustainability and food supply

In Chapter 1, we made it very clear that the sustainability of food production is an important dimension of food security. That is, we accept that having food to eat at present is important, but so is having food to eat in the future. Prior to 2017, the GFSI compiled by the EIU did not take sustainability into consideration. In its 2017 GFSI compilation, the EIU has included sustainability as an important aspect (see Box 6.2).

BOX 6.2

EIU's move to include sustainability

In Chapter 1, a comment was made that the FAO and EIU 'do not give any clear weight to reserve stocks and production sustainability' in their frameworks used for measuring food security. In 2017, the EIU acknowledged that food security 'cannot be measured without considering the potential risks that exposure, extreme weather, and natural resource depletion pose to agriculture and supply chains and how countries are building resilience against such risks'. It decided to incorporate natural resources and resilience in its GFSI compilation.

In its 2017 updated index, the GFSI featured a new environmental category that recognises the growing emphasis on resource conservation, climate change adaption, and sustainable agriculture practices. With factors, such as temperature change, land deforestation, and depletion of water resources, the Natural Resources and Resilience category measures future impacts on the countries in the GFSI.

The new category is a stand-alone addition to the GFSI that does not affect the country-by-country data the EIU has been measuring since 2012. The new section allows users to see food security scores for the 113 nations in the GFSI, based on the existing models; then they see how country scores shift when the environmental factors are added.

To access the GFSI with the additional category of Natural Resources and Resilience, follow the usual link to EIU's GFSI website: https://foodsecurityindex.eiu.com/

Source: '2017 updated Global Food Security Index released', http://foodsecurity.dupont.com/2017/09/26/2017-updated-global-food-security-index-released/, accessed 12 October 2017.

Sustainable food production requires us to use scarce natural resources sustainably. This can be achieved through adequate resource management and conservation. Sustainable resource use has received increased attention since the 1960s, chiefly led by developed countries. Paying attention to resource sustainability in developing countries started much later, in the late 20th century and more so at the beginning of the 21st century.

Efforts to protect the environment and sustain the resource base in many developed countries have seen their resource policies well-developed, more effectively implemented, and adequately reinforced. This has resulted in much better resource protection in countries such as Australia, Japan, the Netherlands, and Germany. For many economically less developed countries, such as China and India, while sustainable use policies have been developed, they are often not effectively carried out or adequately reinforced through necessary judicial mechanisms.

In the future, it is in those emerging and developing economies that more attention should be given to sustainable resource use. In many of these countries, per capita natural resource availability, especially fresh water and land, is low. Making things worse, the lack of effort to protect the environment in the past has already resulted in wide deterioration in water, soil, and air quality. Inaction by these countries will lead to further deterioration of essential food-producing resources and undermine their food supply.

6.5 Is resource availability deterministic on food security?

Given that natural resources are essential in food production, does resource availability determine a country's food security? That is, if a country is rich in, or short of, natural resources, will the country's food security be affected? The answer is no: resource availability does not determine a country's food security.

A rich endowment of natural resources is conducive to the production of more food but does not necessarily lead to increased food production and subsequently increased food availability (e.g., in Ecuador, Venezuela, and Zimbabwe). On the other hand, lack of natural resources does not necessarily mean that food availability will be poor (e.g., Singapore, Israel, and Japan). This is simply due to the fact that food availability can be achieved through either domestic production or imports or a combination of both (food imports will be discussed in Part 4; further discussions will be made in Part 5 on why resource availability does not determine a country's food security).

Indeed, in spite of natural resource shortages, domestic food production can still be boosted through adequate investment in research and development (R&D); the Netherlands is an example of this. R&D can also help overcome the rigid constraints of lack of natural resources, as can be seen in Israel. In Israel, fresh water supply has been increased through desalination and waste water recycling (Box 6.3). The intensive use of greenhouses has allowed Israel to 'create' arable land from areas that otherwise are hardly arable. In the future, with the aid of technological progress, more fresh water can be produced through desalination and waste water recycling; and more arable land can be created through vertical farming (Despommier 2009).

BOX 6.3

Israeli water experiences

Israel's national goal is to supply water to all consumers sustainably, based on approved requirements for quality, quantity, efficiency, and economic feasibility. To this end, Israel has set specific targets to gradually reduce its reliance on natural potable water by 2050. The key policy initiatives aim to reduce demand by:

- Requiring by law that all water supplies are metered.
- Monitoring water reuse and the use of brackish water in agriculture.
- Promoting drip irrigation and reuse of treated domestic wastewater in agriculture.

The government also aims to increase potable water supply by constructing large-scale desalination facilities.

Efforts are also being made to use economic instruments. Significant increases in water tariffs have taken place or are planned in all sectors. Prices for effluent and brackish water are lower to encourage their use for irrigation. A quota of potable water is allocated to the agricultural sector each year; farmers who opt to exchange part of this quota for alternative sources can secure the volume of wastewater they will procure at a fixed price.

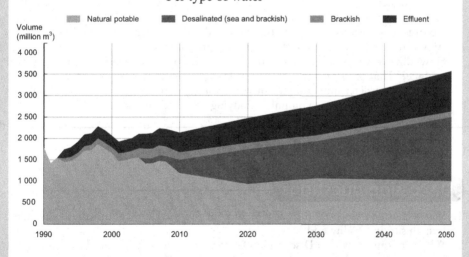

Figure 6.8 Israel's water consumption outlook to 2050.

Note: The statistical data for Israel are supplied by and under the responsibility of the relevant Israeli authorities. The use of such data by the OECD is without prejudice to the status of the Golan Heights, East Jerusalem, and Israeli settlements in the West Bank under the terms of international law.

Source: OECD (2012), *OECD Environmental Outlook to 2050: The Consequences of Inaction*, www. keepeek.com/Digital-Asset-Management/oecd/environment/oecd-environmental-outlook-to-2050/ water_env_outlook-2012-8-en#page36, accessed 2 November 2017.

Review questions

1. What are the major kinds of resources that are essential for food production? Why/ How are they so essential?
2. Resource is a supply shifter. Increased or reduced availability of food production resources will affect the prices of inputs and subsequently lead to a shift in the supply curve. Draw a diagram similar to Figure 3A.7; the market is in equilibrium with the equilibrium price being $0.8 per kg, and the corresponding quantity traded is 120 kt. Then, show how the supply curve for rice may shift:

    1. A quarter of the rice paddy land has been diverted for industrialisation in Rasia; and
    2. Rasia is short of fresh water supply but it has invented a magic way to desalinise seawater very cheaply. Now more fresh water is available at a price that is half of the previous price.

    Specify whether the resulting quantity of rice traded and the price of rice will be higher or lower for each situation.
3. Can you develop a diagram of 'global water allocation for agriculture' similar to 'global surface area allocation for food production' in Box 6.1? (FAO AQUASTAT database, www.fao.org/nr/water/aquastat/data/query/index.html?lang=en, provides necessary statistics.)
4. Can you develop a similar diagram to the one in Review Question 3 for your country of residence? (You can also get data for your country from FAO AQUASTAT database.)
5. How is the total area of your home country used for different purposes? Can you develop a diagram for your country similar to 'global surface area allocation for food production' in Box 6.1? Compare your diagram with those of your classmates. (You can obtain the needed data for your country from FAOSTAT database, www. fao.org/faostat/en/#data. In the 'Inputs' sub-database, click 'Land Use' link.)
6. Why is resource quality important for food production?
7. How does your country's natural resource endowment compare to the world average? That is, is it rich or poor? In your view, is your country's resource endowment a determining factor in your country's food security? Why? (You may revisit this question after you finish studying the whole book.)

Discussion questions

1. Water is utterly essential for any life. In your opinion, is there a water crisis facing human survival? Why and how?
2. Whether your answer to Discussion Question 1 is yes or no, what do you think the human race should do to make use of water resources smartly (and sustainably) to benefit human beings as well as the ecosystem of the planet? (What is the ecosystem? Can we say it encompasses everything in it, including human beings?)
3. Are there any major issues in human beings' use of the limited surface of the Earth? If so, what are they?
4. In addition to FAO's forecasts on agricultural land and cropland use, are there other forecasts? Do they agree with each other? Why?

5. In your view, in the future, will there be sufficient arable land for human beings to produce food crops? Provide your justifications.
6. What major problems can you identify in human use of the aquacultural resources? What are the solutions you would propose to fix these problems?
7. Discuss with your classmates on whether resource availability in your country of residence is deterministic on its food security.

References

Alexandratos, N. and Bruinsma, J. (2012), 'World agriculture towards 2030/2050: The 2012 revision,' *ESA Working paper No. 12-03*, FAO, Rome, www.fao.org/docrep/016/ap106e/ap106e.pdf, accessed 19 October 2018.

Cho, R. (2013), 'Phosphorus: Essential to life – Are we running out?' https://blogs.ei.columbia.edu/2013/04/01/phosphorus-essential-to-life-are-we-running-out/, accessed 5 March 2019.

Cordell, D., Drangert, J.O., and White, S. (2009), 'The story of phosphorus: Global food security and food for thought', *Global Environmental Change*, Vol. 19, pp. 292–305.

Cornish, P. (2010), 'A postscript to "Peak P"– an agronomist's response to diminishing P reserves', www.regional.org.au/au/asa/2010/plenary/sustainability/7452_cornish.htm, accessed 4 May 2019.

Despommier, D. (2009), 'The rise of vertical farms', *Scientific American*, Vol. 301, Issue 5 (November 2009), pp. 80–87.

The Economist. (2014), 'In deep water; governing the high seas' (2014, February 22), No. 410, 51-n/a, https://search-proquest-com.elibrary.jcu.edu.au/docview/1501904646?accountid= 16285, accessed 3 March 2019.

Elser, J. and Bennett, E. (2011), 'A broken biogeochemical cycle', *Nature*, Vol. 478, pp. 29–31.

FAO. (2018a), FAO AQUASTAT database, www.fao.org/nr/water/aquastat/data/query/index.html?lang=en, accessed 9 October 2018.

FAO. (2018b), 'Water uses', www.fao.org/nr/water/aquastat/water_use/index.stm, accessed 1 November 2017.

FAO. (2018c), 'FAOSTAT database', www.fao.org/faostat/en/#data, accessed 6 January2018.

FAO. (2018d), 'State of fisheries and aquaculture in the world 2018', www.fao.org/state-of-fisheries-aquaculture/en/, accessed 3 March 2019.

Faradji, C. and de Boer, M. (2016), 'How the great phosphorus shortage could leave us all hungry', https://theconversation.com/how-the-great-phosphorus-shortage-could-leave-us-all-hungry-54432, accessed 4 March 2019.

Gandhi, V. and Namboodiri, N.V. (2007), 'Water resource development and institutions in India: Overview and profile', in Crase, L.and Gandhi, V. (eds), *Reforming Institutions in Water Resource Management*, Earthscan, London, Ch. 8, pp. 146–166.

OECD (2012), 'OECD environmental outlook to 2050: The consequences of inaction', www.oecd.org/environment/indicators-modelling-outlooks/oecd-environmental-outlook-1999155x.htm, accessed 2 November 2017.

Roser, M. and Ritchie, H. (2018), 'Yields and land use in agriculture', published online at OurWorldInData.org, https://ourworldindata.org/yields-and-land-use-in-agriculture, accessed 30 October 2018.

United Nations (2017), World population prospects: The 2017 revision, Department of Economic and Social Affairs, Population Division, https://population.un.org/wpp/Download/Standard/Population/, accessed 16 October 2018.

USEPA (United States Environmental Protection Agency). (2017), 'Effects of acid rain', www.epa.gov/acidrain/effects-acid-rain, accessed 2 November 2017.

Zhang, X.Y., Zhong, T.Y., Liu, L., and Ouyang, X.Y. (2015), 'Impact of soil heavy metal pollution on food safety in China', *PLOS ONE*, http://journals.plos.org/plosone/article?id=10.1371%2Fjournal.pone.0135182, accessed 14 March 2016.

Further reading and resources

FAO. (2018), 'FAO AQUASTAT database', www.fao.org/nr/water/aquastat/data/query/index.html?lang=en. From this database, one can find all statistics related to water since 1960 at the global, continental, sub-continental and country levels.

FAO. (2018), 'FAOSTAT database', www.fao.org/faostat/en/#data. This database provides a barrage of valuable statistics related to food and agriculture since 1961 at the global, continental, sub-continental and country levels, including: production, trade, food balance, food security, prices, inputs, population, investment, macro-statistics, agri-environmental indicators, emissions (agriculture, land use), forestry, and R&D indicators.

Chapter 7

Technological progress and food supply

Summary

This chapter explains the influence of technological progress on food security. Section 7.1 establishes that technological progress is responsible for the expansion of global food supply in recent human history. The pace of technological progress depends greatly on the availability of new technologies. Adequate investment in agricultural research and development (R&D), extension, and education helps the invention and adoption of new technologies. The status of such investment in different parts of the world is examined in Section 7.2. Section 7.3 addresses issues concerning policy measures required to secure resources for investment in agricultural R&D, extension and education.

After studying this chapter, you should be able to:
- Explain the importance of technological progress in boosting the supply of food.
- Form a broad picture of global investment in agricultural R&D and explain where investment gaps exist.
- Enumerate major resources that can be mobilised for R&D investment.

7.1 Food supply expansion: the role of technological progress

Technological progress is another major supply shifter. Each time there is a major technological breakthrough, the yields of food crops are raised and food supply curve shifts to the right. One example is the advent of the Haber–Bosch process. All organisms must have nitrogen to live and nitrogen fertiliser promotes the healthy growth of food crops. In the first decade of the 20th century, the German chemists Fritz Haber and Carl Bosch developed the Haber–Bosch process. It converts atmospheric nitrogen (N_2) to ammonia (NH_3). Until the advent of this process, ammonia had been difficult to produce on an industrial scale. Today, this process is the main industrial procedure for the production of ammonia. Ammonia is the most common nitrogen fertiliser. The other typical example is the development of high-yielding varieties (HYV). High-yielding varieties of rice and wheat made the Green Revolution possible in the 1960s. This helped to boost food output in many parts of the globe, especially in India and Mexico. Both of the breakthroughs shifted the global supply of food to the right as demonstrated in Figure 7.1.

Indeed, in recent human history, the impressive expansion of food supply has been chiefly due to technological progress. As shown in Figure 7.2, world cereal output has increased significantly since the 1960s. Arable land used for cereal production, however, did not increase much, only by 11% between 1961 and 2016. Thus, the expansion of cereal output was mainly due to the impressive improvement in yield (193% between 1961 and 2016), derived from technological progress.

At the sub-continental level, the expansion of cereal output, or lack of it, is also chiefly due to yield. In Western Europe, the area sown to cereal crops actually dropped by 6% between 1961 and 2016. Yet, its total cereal output increased by 147%. This increase can be

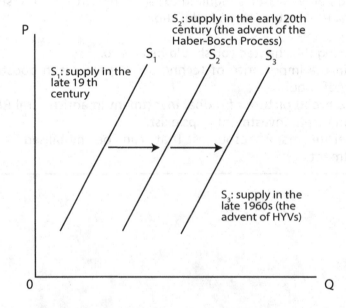

Figure 7.1 Supply curve shifts to the right due to technological progress.

attributed to the 161% increase in yield (Figure 7.2). On the contrary, in Middle Africa, its increase in total output of 295% was largely due to the expansion of arable land to cereal crops, by 169%. Had its yield improvement been comparable to the world level, the total cereal output in Middle Africa would have been much higher. Instead, its yield only increased by 47% between 1961 and 2016 (Figure 7.2).

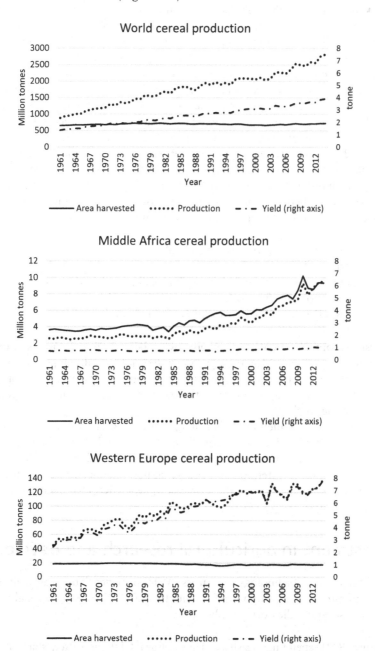

Figure 7.2 Global cereal production (1961–2016).
Source: Based on FAOSTAT (2018).

Crop output is the product of yield and area sown to the crop. Either expanding the sown area or raising yield or both will help increase total crop output. Globally, the ability to further expand areas sown to crop is limited as shown in Chapter 6. However, there is still scope to improve yield in many parts of the world, especially in developing countries (Nin-Pratt and Fan 2010).

Yield can be improved through factor accumulation and technological progress. The contribution of factor accumulation (i.e., increased use of factors such as fertiliser, water, or labour) is, however, limited (Solow 1956; Swan 1956). This is dictated by the law of diminishing marginal returns, which states that in all productive processes, adding more of one factor of production, while holding all others constant, will at some point produce lower incremental per-unit returns. Consequently, technological progress holds the key to improving yields.

Given that technological progress is the key to expanding food output in the long run, it is crucial to induce an adequate pace of technological progress. For technological progress to occur, two conditions are essential: (1) availability of new technologies that are profitable for farmers to adopt; and (2) institutional environments that are conducive to facilitating technological progress to take place including allocating adequate funds to develop new technologies.

Technology includes: (1) techniques that make use of production inputs more efficiently; and (2) management methods that manage and use production inputs more efficiently. Technology can be acquired through one of, or a combination of, the following ways:

1. Learning from other countries as a result of spill-ins (new technologies developed in other countries will have spill-overs that benefit others, especially new management methods and other more embodied technologies like improved seeds).
2. Buying new technologies from other countries.
3. Investing in R&D to produce new technologies at home.

With the first two options, a country is likely always behind other countries in the adoption and use of new technologies. Moreover, such new technologies developed overseas may not always suit local conditions. As such, investment in agricultural R&D at home is always necessary. In the next section, we examine the status of investment in agricultural R&D in different parts of the world.

It must be noted that while investment in agricultural R&D is important, investment in agricultural extension and education is equally important. Only through matching efforts in extension and education, can farmers become aware of and adopt new technologies from R&D. Lack of attention to extension and education may significantly discount the potential benefits from R&D. In the rest of the discussion, when R&D is mentioned, it includes 'extension and education'.

7.2 Investment in agricultural research and development

Agricultural Science and Technology Indicators (ASTI) provides data on agricultural research spending (from public sources only) (ASTI Initiative 2018). To reflect agricultural research intensity, it uses several indicators including:

● Agricultural R&D spending as a share of agricultural GDP (hereafter, 'share of agricultural GDP', SAG, is used to refer to this share).
● Agricultural R&D spending per 100,000 farmers.
● Agricultural R&D spending per million population.

- Number of agricultural researchers per 100,000 farmers.
- Number of agricultural researchers per million population.

Presented in Figure 7.3 is agricultural research intensity expressed using SAG for countries of different income groups and developing countries in different regions. Detailed data at the country level on all the above five intensity indicators are available from the ASTI website (see 'Further reading and resources' in this chapter).

It is generally accepted that developing countries significantly underinvest in agricultural R&D. Figure 7.3 supports this observation. In high-income countries, SAG in 1981 was

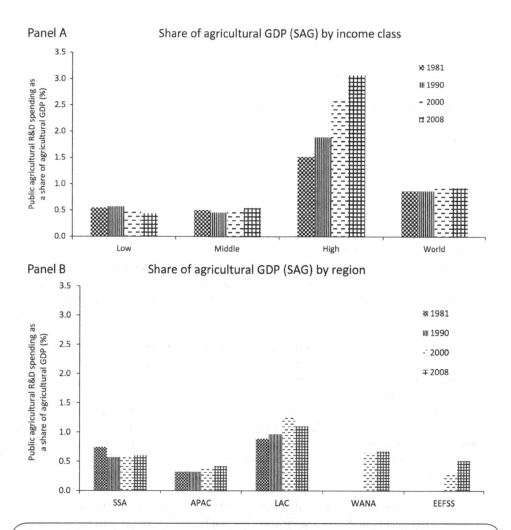

Figure 7.3 Agricultural research investment intensity, ASTI assessment.

Notes: SSA: Africa south of the Sahara; APAC: Asia–Pacific countries; LAC: Latin America and the Caribbean; WANA: West Asia and North Africa; EEFSS: Eastern Europe and former Soviet States. Intensity ratios by income group include estimated spending trends for WANA and EEFSS. Regional growth rates exclude high-income countries within that region (for example, Japan and South Korea in the APAC region). Data for 1981 and 1990 were not available for WANA and EEFSS.

Source: based on ASTI Initiative (2018).

1.52%, about three times that of low- and middle-income countries. It has also steadily increased and by 2008, it was 3.07%, around 6 times that of low- and middle-income countries. In low- and middle-income countries, SAG has fluctuated at around 0.5% over the period 1981–2008. At the regional level, Asia-Pacific has the lowest SAG though it has been increasing slightly from 2000 (Figure 7.3, Panel B). Underinvesting in agricultural R&D chiefly occurs in developing countries and regions.

However, the intensity indicators supplied by ASTI are believed to be inadequate in reflecting the adequacy of a country's agricultural R&D spending. They give no consideration to R&D investment from private sources. It is especially inappropriate to use them to compare the adequacy of investment levels between countries (Nin-Pratt 2016).

In their article on 'Agriculture R&D is on the move', Pardey, Chan-Kang, Dehmer, and Beddow (2016) use a very comprehensive dataset to reveal global agricultural R&D trends. Their data include (1) new and revised estimates of the amount of agricultural R&D spending from public sources for 158 countries from 1960 to 2011 and (2) new global estimates of the amount of such R&D spending by private firms from 1980 to 2011. Pardey et al. (2016) reveal three broad trends concerning agricultural R&D.

1. **For the first time in modern history, the governments of middle-income nations are investing more in public-sector agricultural R&D than those of high-income ones:** In 1980, global gross domestic public expenditures on agricultural R&D totalled $17.8 billion (in PPP dollars). It was $38.1 billion in 2011. The share invested by rich countries dropped from 60.9% in 1980 to 47.3% in 2011. The share invested by middle-income countries, however, increased from 35.8% in 1980 to 49.8% in 2011, surpassing high-income countries. The share invested by low-income countries remained low and dropped from 3.3% in 1980 to 2.9% in 2011.

2. **Globally, private-sector spending on agricultural R&D is catching up with public-sector spending:** Global total public and private expenditure on agricultural R&D was $27.4 billion in 1980 and US$69.3 billion in 2011. Expenditure by the private sector increased from $9.6 billion to $31.2 billion during the same time period. The share spent by the private sector increased from 35% in 1980 to 45% in 2011.

3. **The gap in spending on agricultural R&D by high-income and low-income countries remains large and is widening:** Per capita expenditure on agricultural R&D from both public and private sources are given in Table 7.1 for countries of all income groups. In 1980, high-income countries invested $13.25 per person in public agricultural R&D. The same investment in low-income countries was $1.73 per person. The difference is 7.7-fold. By 2011, this difference had widened to 11.7-fold: high-income countries invested $17.73 per person, whereas low-income countries invested just $1.51. For private-sector spending, the same observations are made and the gaps are even larger.

The trends discovered by Pardey et al. (2016) are of great significance for the future of food production. Investments in R&D are inextricably intertwined with growth in agricultural productivity and food supplies. More importantly, it takes decades for the consequences of such investments to be fully realised. Today's R&D investment decisions will cast shadows forward to 2050 and beyond.

The rising trend of investments in agricultural R&D by middle-income countries and by the private sector is certainly most welcome. However, the still very low investment in low-income countries is of grave concern. It is in those low-income countries where more food

Table 7.1 Per capita expenditure on agricultural R&D, 1980–2011 (2009 PPP dollars per person)

	Public expenditure						Private expenditure				
	1980	1990	2000	2005	2010	2011	1980	1990	2000	2005	2010
High income	**13.25**	**15.78**	**17.56**	**17.39**	**17.91**	**17.73**	**9.75**	**13.72**	**16.44**	**18.71**	**19.19**
United States	12.41	14.44	15.25	15.85	14.09	13.98	13.69	16.56	19.95	22.55	23.61
Japan	18.84	22.01	24.41	26.22	27.14	27.22	11.46	23.19	25.49	31.48	29.06
Germany	7.76	10.29	11.80	11.63	15.25	14.35	11.24	12.91	13.90	14.87	17.15
France	11.74	12.67	14.92	14.73	17.08	17.03	3.66	7.13	9.18	9.77	12.32
Republic of Korea	4.93	7.59	13.20	12.02	19.62	19.74	2.37	3.61	6.90	10.88	14.38
Spain	4.19	10.80	15.57	17.69	20.61	19.45	1.61	4.60	8.63	13.61	11.99
Upper middle	**2.69**	**2.81**	**3.09**	**3.55**	**5.22**	**5.32**	**0.71**	**0.79**	**1.01**	**1.75**	**3.08**
China	0.41	0.50	0.86	1.63	3.54	3.45	0.00	0.00	0.24	0.97	2.96
Brazil	8.56	8.91	7.77	7.22	9.24	9.34	5.34	5.59	4.83	5.78	7.46
Iran	6.67	9.22	10.05	10.00	11.65	12.25	1.13	1.58	1.75	1.60	1.85
Malaysia	14.75	16.43	19.66	20.86	20.31	23.89	5.75	6.67	7.44	12.04	9.39
Lower middle	**1.85**	**1.98**	**2.20**	**2.30**	**2.93**	**3.04**	**0.35**	**0.32**	**0.40**	**0.50**	**0.77**
India	0.94	1.29	2.06	2.15	3.02	3.09	0.26	0.31	0.54	0.55	1.08
Indonesia	2.55	2.49	1.48	1.66	2.34	2.37	0.45	0.41	0.22	0.24	0.46
Egypt	3.29	4.32	4.29	4.98	6.04	6.28	0.51	0.68	0.71	0.92	1.16
Nigeria	4.13	1.81	2.30	2.49	2.41	2.95	0.57	0.09	0.30	0.31	0.29
Low income	**1.73**	**1.68**	**1.49**	**1.30**	**1.51**	**1.51**	**0.17**	**0.22**	**0.21**	**0.20**	**0.19**
Kenya	6.90	7.41	6.62	5.17	6.00	6.11	0.90	0.99	0.88	0.73	0.80
Bangladesh	0.86	1.17	1.51	1.11	1.23	1.28	0.14	0.23	0.29	0.19	0.27
Uganda	1.10	1.15	1.89	2.96	3.58	3.56	0.00	0.05	0.01	0.04	0.72
Tanzania	2.85	1.11	1.39	0.89	2.52	2.04	0.25	0.19	0.21	0.11	0.28
World	**4.53**	**4.81**	**5.07**	**5.14**	**5.99**	**6.02**	**2.47**	**2.99**	**3.33**	**3.96**	**4.51**

Notes: Eastern European and Former Soviet Union countries are excluded. Countries are grouped into income classes using 2015 World Bank schema. High-income countries are those with 2013 GNI (gross national income) per capita of $12,746 or more; upper-middle-income countries had 2013 GNI per capita between $4,126 and $12,745; lower-middle-income countries had 2013 GNI per capita between $1,046 and $4,125; and low-income countries had 2013 GNI per capita less than or equal to $1,045.
Source: based on Pardey et al. (2016), Tables A2 and A5.

needs to be produced. Their population has expanded very rapidly in the past and is expected to continue to expand at a high rate into the future (see Chapter 3). Also of concern is the retreat of high-income countries from public agricultural R&D (Pardey et al. 2016).

Research has repeatedly shown that the rates of return on agricultural R&D investment have been one of the highest compared with returns on other investments. All countries need to ensure they have an adequate level of agricultural R&D investment (Fan et al. 2005; Pardey, Alston, and Piggott 2006; Nin-Pratt and Fan 2010; Guimón and Agapitova 2013). It is especially important for low-income countries to increase their investment to agricultural R&D.

7.3 Mobilising resources for agricultural research and development

To induce an adequate pace of agricultural technological progress, it is essential to have resources available to support research, development, extension, and education activities. In addition to public funding, investment by the private sector and contribution from farmers should be further mobilised to boost agricultural R&D.

7.3.1 Private investment

Agricultural R&D has characteristics of non-rivalry (a product is non-rival when it is consumed by one consumer without preventing simultaneous consumption by others, e.g., visits to national parks) and non-excludability (a product is non-excludable if non-paying consumers cannot be prevented from accessing it, e.g., a nation's defence system that protects everyone including those paying no tax). These characteristics make some degree of market failure inevitable; that is, the level of investment in agricultural R&D by private firms will be less. Often, private investors will just not be interested in agricultural R&D investment that will also benefit many others. Further, private investments are made in the pursuit of profits. Some agricultural R&D activities may not generate immediate and measurable benefits and thus do not attract the private sector although they are of long-term significance.

Both rich and poor countries face challenges in attracting private investment in agricultural R&D. In high-income countries, however, private investment in R&D tends to be higher because they have better intellectual property protection. For many developing countries, more policy efforts are needed to create an environment to encourage private investment (Naseem, Spielman, and Omamo 2010).

7.3.2 Contribution from farmers

Farmers can be convinced to partially contribute to agricultural R&D. Australia has pioneered this practice. In Australia, levies are collected from producers specifically for agricultural R&D purposes. The Australian Government contributes to agricultural R&D by matching the amount of funds collected from producers (up to a limit of 0.5% of industry's gross value of production). This co-investment model has existed in Australia for many decades and has been very successful. The funds from both industry and government sources are administered through a number of rural research and development corporations (RDCs). These rural RDCs provide an industry-driven, market-responsive approach to agricultural R&D. Zhou (2013, Chapter 7: Proactive R&D Investments) is a useful introduction to this unique Australian model.

Australia's RDC model can be of relevance to other countries; perhaps more so to countries where the use of public funds is adequately governed. Good governance is a pre-condition and must exist if the Australian model is to be successfully used in a country. That is, mechanisms must exist to prevent the levies collected from producers from becoming the prey of corrupt officials, or being misused or abused by fund-managing staff and researchers. Many developing countries do not have strong institutions in governing the use of public money. Caution would have to be exercised should they contemplate the adoption of such a co-investment model.

7.4 Public investment still essential

While it is useful to develop policy initiatives to encourage other sources to contribute to agricultural R&D, public spending in agricultural R&D is still essential in both developed and developing countries. The importance for public investment should never be overlooked (Sheng, Gray, and Mullen 2011). This is simply due to the characteristics of agricultural R&D: non-rivalry and non-excludability.

For developed countries, the share of private investment in agricultural R&D is likely higher, compared to developing countries. However, some degree of market failure due to the characteristics of agricultural R&D is still inevitable. In developing countries, such market failure is likely to be more serious. Hence, public investment has to be made available to mitigate problems resulting from the market failure in both developed and developing countries (Mullen 2011; Guimón and Agapitova 2013; Pardey et al. 2016).

Review questions

1. What evidence can you provide to argue that technological progress must be responsible for the recent expansion of world food supply?
2. Can you discover any examples to show that your country's food production has benefited from R&D spill-ins? Did your country actually provide R&D spill-overs to benefit other countries' food production?
3. Is your country's investment in agricultural R&D adequate? Why do you say so?
4. Which sector, the public or the private, is the major investor in your country's agricultural R&D? Are you able to determine the rough share of each sector in the total investment? Is there a single private enterprise that is a notable major investor in your country and why?
5. In recent decades, did technological progress play an adequate role in boosting your country's food production? Why yes or why not?

Discussion questions

1. Explain whether you would agree or not that R&D is the fundamental force that has driven the impressive expansion of food production in the past centuries.
2. If R&D is crucial in increasing a country's food output, how should the national government of a country promote the creation or adoption of new technologies?
3. In your judgement, what is the role played by the private sector in investing in agricultural R&D in your country? If great or small, why?
4. Can you provide a list of policy options that can be used to incentivise the private sector to increase their investment in agricultural R&D? Make sure you explain how they work.
5. What kind of trends do you foresee in investment in agricultural R&D in your country? For example, will the investment be made mainly by the public or private sector? Will the investment be adequate or insufficient? Will the focus be more on invention of techniques or more on improvements to management approaches? Are there any other aspects that you are able to observe?

6. Given that technological progress is a source of growth in the supply of food, it would be logical for poor countries with a low level of food security to strategically allocate their resources, with priority given to agricultural R&D activities that will help boost their food supply. In reality, more often than not, this is not the case. Why? Are they short of financial resources? If so, then, why do their rulers allocate much of their limited resources to military purposes or for the extravagant consumption of the elite few?

7. Genetically modified crops have been in existence for some decades. This has been a major technological breakthrough in increasing crop output. Yet, its impact on human health is still uncertain and this has prevented wide adoption. What is your view on the role of GM crops in increasing food supply in the future? In the absence of any other better alternatives, should human beings adopt this technology? Why?

References

ASTI Initiative. (2018), 'Agricultural science and technology indicators', www.asti.cgiar.org/data, and www.asti.cgiar.org/pdf/GlobalAssessmentDataTables.pdf, accessed 6 January 2018.

Fan, S.G., Chan-Kang, C., Qian, K.M., and Krishnaiah, K. (2005), 'National and international agricultural research and rural poverty: The case of rice research in India and China', *Agricultural Economics*, Vol. 33, pp. 369–379.

Guimón, J. and Agapitova, N. (2013), 'Why should governments of developing countries invest in R&D and innovation?', *African Journal of Business Management*, Vol. 7, pp. 899–905.

Mullen, J. (2011), 'Public investment in agricultural research and development in Australia remains a sensible policy option', *AFBM Journal*, Vol. 8, pp. 1–12.

Naseem, A., Spielman, D.J., and Omamo, S.W. (2010), 'Private-sector investment in R&D: A review of policy options to promote its growth in developing-country agriculture', *Agribusiness*, Vol. 26, pp. 143–173.

Nin-Pratt, A. (2016), 'Comparing apples to apples: A new indicator of research and development investment intensity in agriculture', IFPRI Discussion Paper, www.ifpri.org/publication/comparing-apples-apples-new-indicator-research-and-development-investment-intensity, accessed 9 November 2017.

Nin-Pratt, A. and Fan, S.G. (2010), 'R&D investment in national and international agricultural research', IFPRI discussion papers 986, IFPRI, Washington, DC.

Pardey, P.G., Alston, J.M., and Piggott, R.R. (2006), *Agricultural R&D in the Developing World: Too Little, Too Late?* IFPRI, Washington, DC.

Pardey, P.G., Chan-Kang, C., Dehmer, S.P., and Beddow, J.M. (2016), 'Agricultural R&D is on the move', *Nature*, Vol. 537, pp. 301–303.

Sheng, Y., Gray, E.M., and Mullen, J.D. (2011), 'Public investment in agricultural R&D and extension: An analysis of the static and dynamic effects on Australian broadacre productivity', ABARES Research Report 11.7, www.agriculture.gov.au/abares/publications/display?url=143.188.17.20/anrdl/DAFFService/display.php?fid=pe_abares20110914.01_11a.xml accessed 29 October 2018.

Solow, R. (1956), 'A contribution to the theory of economic growth', *Quarterly Journal of Economics*, Vol. 70, Issue 1, pp. 65–94.

Swan, T. (1956), 'Economic growth and capital accumulation', *Economic Record*, Vol. 32, Issue 2, pp. 334–361.

Zhou, Z.Y. (2013), *Developing Successful Agriculture: An Australian Case Study*, CAB International, Oxfordshire.

Further reading and resources

The Agricultural Science and Technology Indicators (ASTI) Initiative consists of a network of national, regional, and international agricultural R&D agencies. The initiative compiles, processes, and makes internationally available comparable data on investments in public and private agricultural R&D worldwide. Data can be downloaded from the ASTI website at: www.asti.cgiar.org/.

Keogh, M., Heath, R., Henry, M., and Darragh, L. (2017), 'Enhancing private-sector investment in agricultural research development and extension (R, D&E) in Australia', Research Report, Australian Farm Institute. The report provides a valuable information base about private-sector agricultural R, D&E investment, using Australia as a case study. It helps find ways to incentivise such investment, with the longer-term goal of optimising agricultural productivity growth. It is available at: www.farminstitute.org.au/publications/research_report/rde-private-sector-investment-in-agriculture (accessed 29 October 2018).

OECD. (2012), *Improving Agricultural Knowledge and Innovation Systems: OECD Conference Proceedings*, OECD Publishing. These are the proceedings of an OECD Conference on Agricultural Knowledge Systems (AKS), held in Paris, on 15–17 June 2011. They discuss a range of experiences and approaches to AKS and explore how to foster development and adoption of innovation to meet global food security and climate change challenges. Also considered in the proceedings are developments in institutional frameworks, public and private roles and partnerships, regulatory frameworks conducive to innovation, the adoption of innovations and technology transfers, and the responsiveness of AKS to broader policy objectives. It is available at: www.oecd.org/australia/improvingagriculturalknowledgeandinnovationsystemsoecdconferenceproceedings.htm, accessed 17 November 2017.

Sheng, Y., Gray, E.M., and Mullen, J.D. (2011), 'Public investment in agricultural R&D and extension: an analysis of the static and dynamic effects on Australian broadacre productivity', ABARES Research Report 11.7. This report provides evidence of the important contribution of public R&D and extension to broadacre total factor productivity in Australia. It offers a range of insights into the effects of R&D policies on farm performance. In particular, it helps those tasked with strategically balancing agricultural R&D and extension portfolios and underscores the importance of making strategic investment decisions that have long-term payoffs. It is available at: www.agriculture.gov.au/abares/publications/display?url=143.188.17.20/anrdl/DAFFService/display.php?fid=pe_abares20110914.01_11a.xml (accessed 29 October 2018).

Chapter 8

Other determinants of food supply

Summary

In this chapter, we discuss the impact of other important supply shifters, such as input costs, weather conditions, and other emerging forces, on food supply.

After studying this chapter, you should be able to:
- Explain and demonstrate how costs of production inputs, prices of related products, and weather conditions affect food supply.
- Provide your opinion on how some other special or emerging forces may affect food supply.

8.1 Other conventional determinants of food supply

8.1.1 Costs of production inputs

To produce food, production inputs, such as water, soil (land), labour, seeds, agricultural chemicals, electricity or fuel, and financial capital, are essential. Acquiring these resources costs money. Costs of such resources differ between countries.

In countries that are well endowed with natural resources, land and water costs could be relatively lower. Labour and capital costs differ between developed and developing countries. Generally, in developed countries, labour cost is higher but capital cost is lower. In developing countries, labour cost is lower but capital cost is higher. Commercial inputs such as chemicals, fuel and electricity can be relatively more expensive in developing countries than in developed countries.

Reducing the prices of production inputs is crucially important for farmers in both developed and developing countries. This can be achieved through two major approaches: (1) government subsidies on the use of production inputs (e.g., subsidies in the form of lower prices for commercial factors of production or lower interest rates for loans. Some such subsidies, however, may cause market distortions and are generally not encouraged; further discussion on potential distortions will be provided in Chapter 9); and (2) more efficient use of production factors (e.g., through improved management methods of input use, or by adopting better models of production – with the aid of agricultural R&D, extension and education as discussed in Chapter 7).

The prices of inputs can also be affected by changes in other sectors of the economy. For example, if the mining industry of a country is booming, more labour force may be attracted away from food production and labour costs become higher. Otherwise, more labour may become available to farming and labour costs become lower. Another example is the changes in fuel prices due to increased or reduced oil output.

Generally, with a given level of resources, if the cost of using them can be reduced, *ceteris paribus*, food supply will increase; that is, the supply curve will shift to the right.

8.1.2 Prices of related produce

The supply of a particular food item can be affected by the prices of other farm products because the resources to produce that particular food item can also be used to produce other farm products. If two products, say Product A and Product B, are substitutes, then if the price of Product B becomes more lucrative, the production of Product A will decline; there will be a shift in the supply curve of Product A to the left. For example, wheat and canola are substitutes in production. If the price of canola rises, less wheat will be produced. More resources will be devoted to the production of canola. The supply curve of wheat will shift to the left. Similarly, if farmers are attracted to produce more tobacco leaves due to relatively higher prices, they will produce less cocoa beans.

If two food items have to be produced jointly (that is, one of them cannot be produced without producing the other, e.g., eggs and meat from hens, milk and meat from dairy cows), then the supply of both will increase if the price for one of them becomes more lucrative. That is, if the prices of eggs and milk are very profitable, we would expect the supply of meat from hens and cows to also increase.

8.1.3 Weather conditions

Weather can have a significant impact on food supply. Favourable weather conditions can significantly boost output level; extreme adverse conditions can dramatically reduce the output or even wipe out the crops altogether. Little can be done to alter weather conditions. It is possible, however, to do things, e.g., irrigation, to mitigate its adverse impacts on food production.

It is noted that weather is different from climate. They differ in the measure of time. Weather is what conditions of the atmosphere are over a short period of time. Climate is how the atmosphere 'behaves' over relatively long periods of time. If the climate does change, weather conditions can be affected. Discussion on climate change is given in the next section.

8.2 Special factors and food supply

8.2.1 Climate change

Climate is the average of weather variables over a considerable number of years. It is much more stable than the short-run fluctuations in the weather. Climate should not be confused with weather or used in the place of weather although they are related. Climate changes may result in more erratic weather conditions, which then can adversely affect crop production, thus reducing food supply.

Scientific evidence has shown that global warming, or climate change, is happening. Global warming is the observed century-scale rise in the average temperature of the Earth's climate system and its related effects. It is largely caused by the increasing amount of greenhouse gases (GHG) released into the atmosphere (Australian Department of the Environment and Energy 2017). GHG includes water vapour, carbon dioxide (CO_2), methane (CH_4), nitrous oxide (N_2O), ozone (O_3) and some artificial chemicals such as chlorofluorocarbons (CFCs) (NASA 2018).

When the sun's energy reaches the Earth's atmosphere, some of it is reflected back to space and the rest is absorbed by the land and the oceans, hence heating the Earth. Heat radiates from the Earth towards space. Some of this heat is trapped by greenhouse gases in the atmosphere, keeping the Earth warm. Such a natural process that warms the Earth's surface is called the greenhouse effect (Lallanilla 2015; NASA 2018). This process maintains the Earth's temperature at around 33°C warmer than it would otherwise be, allowing life on the Earth to exist.

However, if too much GHG is released into the atmosphere, it will then trap extra heat and cause the Earth's temperature to rise. This is the problem we are facing now. From the mid-19th century, GHG emissions generated by human activities started to increase. This increase has sped up significantly since the mid-20th century. The fast increase in GHG emission caused by human activities has been regarded by many people as the major cause of global warming (for example, Scientific American 2009; Gerlach 2010; IPCC 2014; Scott and Lindsey 2016; NASA 2018; USGS 2018).

There are, however, disagreements about whether GHG emissions from human activities are the major source of global warming. It has been argued that natural events such as earthquakes and volcanic eruptions also release enormous amount of GHG. Some argue that the GHG released from such events is far greater than that caused by human beings (for example, Plimer 2009, 2017; Collomb 2014 document American climate change deniers and investigates what drives climate change denial in the United States).

Nonetheless, given that GHG emissions from human activities have recently increased enormously, curtailing these emissions is urgent. Efforts must be made to reduce emissions to slow down global warming and thus lessen damage to future food production.

Global warming affects food production in various ways. (1) A higher Earth surface temperature affects the growth of some plants, which may result in low output. (2) A higher temperature leads to higher sea levels, which leads to the loss of arable land in low areas. One of the countries facing the threat of rising sea levels is Bangladesh. By the 2080s, it is projected that 40% of productive land will be lost in the southern region of Bangladesh due to a 65cm sea-level rise (World Bank 2013). (3) Global warming will cause erratic weather, which in turn adversely affects food production.

While global warming affects agriculture, agricultural activities also contribute to global warming. GHG emissions from agriculture consist of non-CO_2 gases, namely methane (CH_4) and nitrous oxide (N_2O), produced by aerobic and anaerobic decomposition processes in crop and livestock production and management activities.

Sub-domains of total agricultural emissions include:

- Enteric fermentation (CH_4): methane gas produced in digestive systems of ruminants and to a lesser extent of non-ruminants.
- Manure management (CH_4, N_2O): methane and nitrous oxide gases from aerobic and anaerobic manure decomposition processes.
- Rice cultivation (CH_4): methane gas from the anaerobic decomposition of organic matter in paddy fields.
- Synthetic fertilisers (N_2O): nitrous oxide gas from synthetic nitrogen additions to managed soils.
- Manure applied to soils (N_2O): direct and indirect nitrous oxide emissions from manure nitrogen (N) added to agricultural soils.
- Manure left on pastures (N_2O): direct and indirect nitrous oxide emissions from manure nitrogen (N) left on pastures by grazing livestock.
- Crop residues (N_2O): direct and indirect nitrous oxide emissions from nitrogen (N) in crop residues and forage/pasture renewal left on agricultural fields.
- Cultivation of organic soils (N_2O): nitrous oxide gas from cultivated organic soils under cropland and grassland.
- Burning – crop residues (CH_4, N_2O): methane and nitrous oxide gases produced by the combustion of a percentage of crop residues burnt on-site.

The amount of total GHG emissions from agriculture is available from the Database on 'Emissions – Agriculture' in FAOSTAT (2017). It covers the period 1961 to present with annual updates. Projections for 2030 and 2050 are also provided. The emissions are expressed as Gg CO_2 and CO_2 equivalent (from CH_4 and N_2O).

From 1961 to 2014, total GHG emission from agriculture increased from 2.75 million gigagrams (m Gg) to 5.25 m Gg, an increase of 91% or an annual growth rate of 1.23%. The annual growth is expected to slow down. By 2030 and 2050, it is forecast that the total emission will increase to 5.80 m Gg (annual growth of 0.64%) and 6.38 m Gg (annual growth of 0.47%), respectively.

Out of the total emission, livestock raising has contributed an overwhelming share. In 1961, this share was about 80%. This share has reduced in recent years as a result of efforts by the livestock industry to reduce its emission. Nonetheless, it still stands at about 70%.

Globally, emission from agricultural activities is responsible for roughly a quarter of total GHG emissions (agriculture: 24%; industry: 21%; transportation: 14%; buildings: 6%; other energy: 10%; and electricity and heat production: 25%) (IPCC 2014). Given that around 80% of total agricultural emission is from animal husbandry, the livestock industry alone contributes about 1/5 or 20% to total GHG emissions. Among the domesticated animals, beef production is by far the largest GHG emitter.

It is pertinent for the agricultural sector to reduce its total GHG emission, given its relatively large share (24%) in total global emission. While various initiatives have been developed, the agricultural sector is yet to do more to reduce its total emission. Such efforts will help lessen global warming which, in turn, will help the agricultural sector itself to achieve better output.

Some indirect measures have also been promoted to reduce agricultural GHG emissions, such as eating less meat, especially beef and lamb (Harvey 2016; Carrington 2017). Meat production generates far more GHG emissions than that of vegetal foods (Box 8.1). Beef and lamb have the highest emission intensities (the emission rate of a given pollutant relative to per unit activity; e.g., grams of carbon dioxide released per kg of food produced).

8.2.2 Loss and waste reduction

According to the FAO, roughly one-third of food produced for human consumption is lost or wasted globally, which amounts to about 1.3 billion tonnes per year (FAO 2011). Food can be wasted either in the consumption process or in the production, processing, and retailing processes.

In Chapter 5, we briefly touched on the issue of food waste from the consumption side, i.e., food waste in the consumption process cause unnecessary higher demand for food. If such waste can be avoided, more food then becomes available in the food systems. In poorer countries, food loss and waste during consumption is generally lower. In richer countries, however, the loss and waste is much higher.

A large amount of food is also lost and wasted during the production, processing, and retailing stages. This is the case especially in developing countries, due to lack of adequate harvesting equipment, storage, or chilling transportation and retailing facilities. In higher-income countries, a relatively large share of food is wasted at the retailing stage, often due to excessive emphasis on the size, shape, or colour of foods that do not match cosmetic standards.

BOX 8.1

GHG emission by meats and vegetal foods

Meat production generates far more GHG emissions than that of vegetal foods. Post-production emissions by meats are also higher in absolute terms.

In Figure 8.1, the lifecycle total of greenhouse gas emissions for common protein foods and vegetables are expressed as kilograms (kg) of carbon dioxide equivalents (CO_2e) per kg of consumed product.

Lamb has the highest emission intensity (the emission rate of a given pollutant relative to per unit activity; e.g., grams of carbon dioxide released per kg of food produced). Beef has the next highest emission intensity. Indeed, all foods of animal origin, with the exception of yogurt and milk, have emission intensities higher than those of vegetal foods.

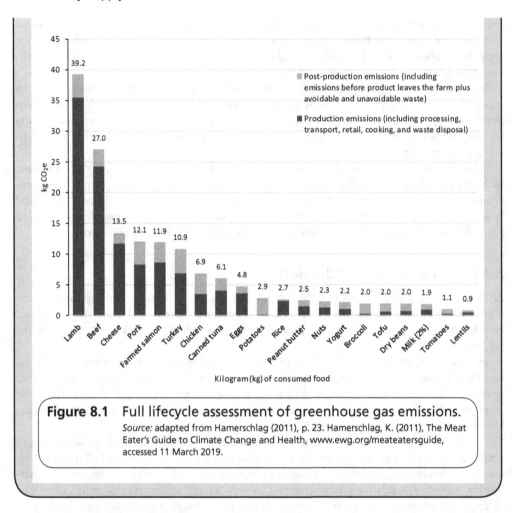

Figure 8.1 Full lifecycle assessment of greenhouse gas emissions.
Source: adapted from Hamerschlag (2011), p. 23. Hamerschlag, K. (2011), The Meat Eater's Guide to Climate Change and Health, www.ewg.org/meateatersguide, accessed 11 March 2019.

The loss and waste of 1.3 billion tonnes of food per year needs to be arrested. In all countries, efforts need to be made to curtail food loss and waste. To reduce food loss and waste is to increase food supply while benefitting the environment. Consumer education holds the key to reducing waste in consumption. Advancement in food storage, processing, and transportation technologies can help reduce waste in other stages.

8.2.3 Bio-security

The world has become increasingly globalised. It has become ever easier for a large number of human beings, vessels, and other kinds of transport to move across national boundaries. This, subsequently, has made it ever easier for plants and animals and their diseases and pests to spread. If not handled in time and thoroughly, output of crop and animal production can be seriously affected. Continuous vigilance needs to be exercised to prevent breaches of bio-security.

8.2.4 Discovery of new foods or sources for the production of conventional foods

Some organisms have been consumed by human beings due to their protein content. Though on a small scale and rarely known to the majority of the human race, the knowledge of their edibility may lead to wide acceptance. For example, in China, scorpions and ants are consumed as delicacies.

Some organisms may not be readily accepted for direct human consumption. They can, however, be used as inputs to produce conventional foods. For example, the larvae of the black soldier fly may be used to transform organic waste into animal feed. Not only does this process generate valuable feed, it also has great potential in organic waste management. Using the larvae to turn waste into feed for animals such as pigs and chicken has become more widely accepted and practised (Veldkamp and Bosch 2015; Nyakeri et al. 2017; Claughton and Bryant 2018). Such practices may lower feed costs in these animal industries shifting the supply curve to the right.

8.2.5 Bio-fuel production

In recent decades, cereals and other edible organics have been used for producing bio-fuel. Although these resources are renewable, the use of them for producing fuel does reduce the supply of food. Bio-fuel production normally takes place in countries where food availability is not a major issue. Nonetheless, this does pose a moral question: how could the food be used to produce fuel while people elsewhere are suffering from starvation?

8.2.6 Trade liberalisation

Trade liberalisation can help increase global food supply. This encourages production in countries that have an advantage in food production. If trade is restricted, then such countries cannot produce more as there is no place for them to sell. It is beneficial for countries to engage in trade liberalisation and collectively foster a global trade institution that is conducive to free trade.

8.2.7 Industrialisation and urbanisation

Increased industrialisation and urbanisation which alienates agricultural land will generally deplete food production resources. If not planned carefully, such a reduction in resources can have very adverse impact on food production. Smart planning and design will reduce such impact. One area that tends to be overlooked by many developing countries is the neglect of the reuse of the top soil when urban development takes place or when arable land is used for industrial purposes. Measures should be in place to guide the relocation of such top soil to land where the soil is less developed.

8.3 Further discussion

In the very short run, the price of food often has limited impact on the quantity of food supplied because production cycles in agriculture range from months to years. In the medium and long term, however, this factor has a very important impact on the amount of food supplied. If the price is kept low with government interventions, it will significantly discourage farmers. In countries where central planning is exercised and the supply price is kept low in favour of consumers, often food supply shortages occur. This has happened, with few exceptions, in communist countries since World War II. Unfortunately, it is still happening in some countries today in the early 21st century, such as in Venezuela and Zimbabwe.

Land and water are two very important inputs for food production. Some countries are short of land, or water, or both. As technologies further advance, it may be expected that it will become more and more economically viable to desalinise seawater and recycle waste water to help mitigate water shortage and to adopt vertical farming to 'expand' land area. Vertical farming has been heralded as having great potential in feeding the world in the 21st century (Despommier 2010). It is an area that deserves close attention. This is the reason why a vertical farming illustration has been used for the cover of this book.

Another issue worth further discussion is the role of smallholders in a nation's quest for improved food security. There are strong beliefs that small farms are important in achieving a country's food security. There is no shortage of published opinions with titles such as 'Smallholder farmers key to food security', 'Smallholder farmers essential to achieve food security' (for example, Lewandowsky 2011; Lewis 2013; Maritim 2018). This, however, is a fantasy.

Small-scale operations often generate limited marketable surplus food. A large number of small farms are needed to feed the growing non-farming population in many food-insecure developing countries. Often these small operators are also poor. When many small poor farmers have to produce food, whether the country can achieve a high level of food security remains a question to be answered. Global experiences have so far shown that the share of population working in agriculture is negatively associated with a country's level of food security (correlation coefficient = -0.77; based on FAO (2018) that has data for 39 countries). The share of population working in agriculture and the associated GFSI of selected countries are shown in Table 8.1.

Table 8.1 Share of population working in agriculture and the level of food security

	Share of population working in agriculture (%)	Global Food Security Index (score)		Share of population working in agriculture (%)	Global Food Security Index (score)
United Kingdom	0.6	84.2	South Korea	2.8	74.7
United States	0.7	84.6	Bulgaria	2.9	62.9
Germany	0.7	82.5	Russia	3.3	66.2
Canada	0.8	82.2	Greece	4.4	71.9
Sweden	0.9	81.7	Malaysia	5.3	66.2
Netherlands	1.0	82.8	Turkey	6.8	61.1
France	1.1	82.3	Philippines	11.0	47.3
Norway	1.1	81.4	Sri Lanka	11.2	53.0
Denmark	1.2	80.3	Romania	12.5	67.7
Australia	1.3	83.3	Indonesia	15.1	51.3
Switzerland	1.9	81.6	Thailand	18.5	58.3
Finland	1.9	81.0	Vietnam	25.9	54.0

Source: FAO (2018); share of population working in agriculture: employment in agriculture/population.

In the future, it is important for researchers and policy makers to distinguish between family farms and small farms. Small farms are small but family farms do not have to be small and can be large in operation. Encouraging family-based farming is fine but not small farming.

Overstating the role of small-scale farming in a country's quest for food security is, at best, maintaining the status quo; at worst, it would mean leading the country towards worsened food security. Confining the farming population to rural areas will only make the already small farms even smaller. Farmers need to be helped to exit farming in an orderly way. This needs to take place fast enough to allow more able farmers to operate at a larger scale, reaping gains of higher productivity. Over-populated but resource-scarce developing countries are no exception. It is important for their governments to understand the long-run limitations of small-scale farming.

We often also hear that there may be not enough farmers working in agriculture. Such concerns are not necessary. So long as farming income is comparable to the income in other sectors of the economy, there will be always people who are willing to work on farms. What is important is to ensure that resources including labour can move freely between farm and non-farm sectors in response to economic incentives.

Review questions

1. Draw a diagram similar to Figure 3A.7; the market is in equilibrium with the equilibrium price being $0.8 per kg, and the corresponding quantity traded is 120 kt. Then, show how the supply curve of rice may shift, *ceteris paribus*:
   1) A new rice variety has been adopted that is pest- and disease-resistant and its yield is 10% higher than the one it has replaced;
   2) The Rasian government provides a 50% subsidy for fertiliser purchase;
   3) An extreme adverse weather condition damaged the rice crops very badly.

   For each situation, point out whether the resulting quantity of rice traded and the price of rice will be higher or lower.
2. Draw a diagram similar to Figure 3A.7; the market is in equilibrium with the equilibrium price being $0.8 per kg, and the corresponding quantity traded is 120 kt. Then, show how the supply curve of rice may shift, *ceteris paribus*:
   1. The price of sugar has dropped sharply (sugar is made out of sugar cane); and
   2. The price of watermelons has become more lucrative.
3. Can you think of any factors other than those discussed so far that may greatly affect the amount of food supplied? Explain how.

Discussion questions

1. In your country of residence, what is the current situation of food waste from harvesting to kitchen? In your opinion, what should be done in order to reduce such waste by one tenth?
2. Would you regard food production in your country as small farm dominated or large farm dominated? If the former, do you think smallholders hold the key to your country's food security? If the latter, do you think they are playing an adequate role in facilitating the country's food security? In either case, explain why.

References

Australian Department of the Environment and Energy. (2017), 'Greenhouse effect', www.environment.gov.au/climate-change/climate-science-data/climate-science/greenhouse-effect, accessed 23 November 2017.

Carrington, D. (2017), 'Want to fight climate change? Have fewer children', *The Guardian*, www.theguardian.com/environment/2017/jul/12/want-to-fight-climate-change-have-fewer-children, accessed 24 November 2017.

Claughton, D. and Bryant, S. (2018), 'Could insects munch their way through the world's waste?', www.abc.net.au/news/rural/2018-05-10/insects-could-solve-the-worlds-waste-problems/9714190, accessed 11 March 2019.

Collomb, J.D. (2014), 'The ideology of climate change denial in the United States', *European Journal of American Studies*, https://journals.openedition.org/ejas/10305, accessed 6 November 2018.

Despommier, D. (2010), *The Vertical Farm: Feeding the World in the 21st Century*, Picador, New York.

FAO. (2011), *Global Food Losses and Food Waste – Extent, Causes and Prevention*, Food and Agriculture Organization, Rome.

FAO. (2018), 'Employment in agriculture', www.fao.org/faostat/en/#data/OE, accessed 30 November 2018.

FAOSTAT. (2017), 'Emissions – agriculture', www.fao.org/faostat/en/#data, accessed 21 November 2017.

Gerlach, T. (2010), 'Comment: Volcanic versus anthropogenic carbon dioxide: The missing science', www.earthmagazine.org/article/comment-volcanic-versus-anthropogenic-carbon-dioxide-missing-science, accessed 31 October 2018.

Harvey, F. (2016), 'Eat less meat to avoid dangerous global warming', *The Guardian*, www.theguardian.com/environment/2016/mar/21/eat-less-meat-vegetarianism-dangerous-global-warming, accessed 24 November 2017.

IPCC (Intergovernmental Panel on Climate Change). (2014), 'Climate change 2014: Mitigation of climate change', www.ipcc.ch/report/ar5/wg3/, accessed 23 November 2017.

Lallanilla, M. (2015), 'Greenhouse gas emissions: Causes & sources', www.livescience.com/37821-greenhouse-gases.html, accessed 6 November 2018.

Lewandowsky, S. (2011), 'Smallholder farmers essential to achieve food security', www.shapingtomorrowsworld.org/fansmallholder.html, accessed 16 October 2018.

Lewis, K. (2013), 'Smallholder farmers key to food security', www.voanews.com/a/smallholder-farmers-actionaid-agriculture-food-security-/1780613.html, accessed 28 October 2018.

Maritim, N. (2018), 'Smallholder farmers key to food security', www.nation.co.ke/oped/opinion/-Smallholder-farmers-key-to-food-security-/440808-4272544-hex9vtz/index.html, accessed 7 November 2018.

NASA (National Aeronautics and Space Administration) (2018), 'What is climate change: Evidence, causes, effects and solutions', https://climate.nasa.gov/, accessed 6 November 2018.

Nyakeri, E.M., Ogola, H.J., Ayieko, M.A., and Amimo, F.A. (2017), 'An open system for farming black soldier fly larvae as a source of proteins for smallscale poultry and fish production', *Journal of Insects as Food and Feed*, Vol. 3, pp. 51–56.

Plimer, I. (2009), *Heaven and Earth: Global Warming – the Missing Science*, Connor Court Publishing, Brisbane, Australia.

Plimer, I. (2017), *Climate Change Delusion and the Great Electricity Rip-Off*, Connor Court Publishing, Brisbane, Australia.

Scientific American. (2009), 'Are volcanoes or humans harder on the atmosphere?' www.scientificamerican.com/article/earthtalks-volcanoes-or-humans/, accessed 31 October 2018.

Scott, M. and Lindsey, R. (2016), 'Which emits more carbon dioxide: Volcanoes or human activities?' www.climate.gov/news-features/climate-qa/which-emits-more-carbon-dioxide-volcanoes-or-human-activities, accessed 30 October 2018.

USGS (US Geological Survey). (2018), 'Volcanoes can affect the Earth's climate', https://volcanoes.usgs.gov/vhp/gas_climate.html, accessed 31 October 2018.

Veldkamp, T. and Bosch, G. (2015), 'Insects: a protein-rich feed ingredient in pig and poultry diets', *Animal Frontiers*, Vol. 5, pp. 45–50.

World Bank. (2013), 'Warming climate to hit Bangladesh hard with sea level rise, more floods and cyclones', www.worldbank.org/en/news/press-release/2013/06/19/warming-climate-to-hit-bangladesh-hard-with-sea-level-rise-more-floods-and-cyclones-world-bank-report-says, accessed 21 November 2017.

Further reading

IFPRI (International Food Policy Research Institute) (2017), *2017 Global Food Policy Report*, www.ifpri.org/publication/2017-global-food-policy-report, accessed 3 March 2018. The Global Food Policy Reports by IFPRI focus on a distinct theme each year. The 2017 Report takes an in-depth look at how rapid urbanisation is reshaping food systems and its impact on food security and nutrition for rural and urban populations. The 2018 Report (www.ifpri.org/publication/2018-global-food-policy-report, accessed 8 October 2018) focuses on the impacts of globalisation and the challenge of growing anti-globalisation pressures on food security. This Report Series was first published in 2011 and all past reports can be obtained from http://gfpr.ifpri.info/past-reports.

Part 4

Coordinating demand and supply for food security

Contents

9 Balancing food demand and supply for food security: approaches used at the national level

10 Coordinating demand and supply for food security: collaboration at the international level

In the previous two parts, we have studied demand for and supply of food and key factors that affect them. Bringing together demand and supply establishes an equilibrium for the food market as shown in Figure 3A.7 in Appendix 3A. This equilibrium tells us the quantity of food traded in the market and the price.

Generally, the demand for food is relatively stable but the supply of food can fluctuate greatly. Thus sometimes, markets become very volatile and fail to deliver outcomes that are efficient and equitable to a society. In this part, we follow the demand–supply equilibrium framework to address how national governments and international organisations have tried to tame market volatilities and to balance food demand and supply nationally and globally in order to feed the ever-increasing world population. In Chapter 9, we first discuss approaches used at the national level to influence food demand and supply. Then, in Chapter 10, we highlight major international efforts to help coordinate food demand and supply at the national, regional, and global levels.

Balancing food demand and supply for food security

Approaches used at the national level

Summary

By now you understand the important forces affecting the demand for and supply of food in the market. When the demand and supply are brought together, a market equilibrium is determined. In Figure 9.1 the market equilibrium is shown as point E (which is based on Figure 3A.7 in Appendix 3A). Here the equilibrium price is $0.8 per kg and the equilibrium quantity is 120 kilo tonnes (kt).

It would be ideal if (1) the food market of a country is at equilibrium; (2) the equilibrium amount of food is adequate to meet the needs of all residents; and (3) the equilibrium price level is compatible with the level of disposable income of the country's residents.

Achieving such an ideal situation is desirable but has never been easy. Governments have tried many policy tools to this end. Not all such tools, however, are useful. In some cases, they have been counterproductive. In this chapter, we discuss some major approaches used by various national governments to coordinate their food demand and supply.

First, in Section 9.1, we argue that ensuring the food security of each and every citizen of a nation is the government's responsibility. In Section 9.2, we introduce a spectrum to categorise government policy tools according to their levels of administrative controls and market forces. The examination of various policy tools is carried out in Section 9.3. The best option for national governments to manage their food demand–supply balance is suggested in Section 9.4. Finally, in Section 9.5, the role of NGOs

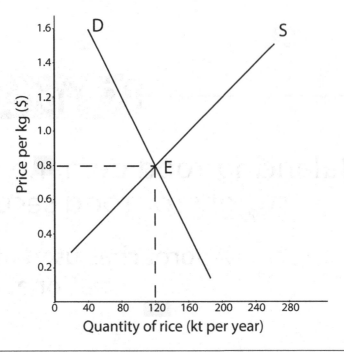

Figure 9.1 A market in equilibrium.

(non-governmental organisations) in complementing governments' efforts to improve food security is briefly discussed.

After studying this chapter, you should be able to:
- Argue whether the government of a country must assume the responsibility of ensuring the citizenry have a reasonable level of food security.
- List major policy tools that have been used by governments to coordinate their food demand and supply.
- Explain the impact of each of those policy tools on the welfare of consumers, producers, and society at large and say whether they are conducive or, in fact, counterproductive to improving a country's food security.
- Discuss the possible roles of NGOs in enhancing food security.

9.1 Ensuring food security: whose responsibility?

Ensuring that all residents have a reasonable level of food security must be the responsibility of the country's government. The food system (see Appendix 2A) has evolved dramatically since the start of human beings' permanent settlements. In the old days, it was possible for individuals, families, or small communities to produce foods for their own needs, although there were still times of feast and famine. This has become unrealistic in today's modern societies given the high level of division of labour. As such, governments are entrusted by the public with ensuring food security for each of their citizens. It is a government failure if a citizen does not have sustained food security.

While ensuring food security is a government's responsibility, the public also has an obligation to contribute to improving food security in their country. All individuals can and should contribute to their country's food security in the following ways:

- By not completely leaving food security solely in the hands of their government. Instead, the public should pay regular attention to the status of their country's food security and demand that their governments maintain a reasonable level of food security for everyone.
- By always consuming rationally and trying to avoid food waste.
- By helping protect the environment in order to sustain food production capacity.

9.2 Categorising food security managing approaches

There are diverse means at the disposal of a government to manage food security. The level of government control varies from full control to no control. If there is no control at all by the government, then it is left to the market to coordinate food demand and supply. At the other extreme, there is 100% control by the government. In between these two extremes, there are numerous combinations of varying levels of administrative controls and market forces.

A spectrum may be used to illustrate the above description (see Figure 9.2). Full administrative control and pure free market are at the two ends of the spectrum. In between the two extremes, the level of control and market varies. If the combination is closer to the free market end, food security management uses more market and less administrative control. The opposite is also true.

A fully controlled approach to managing a country's food security has been adopted by some countries. In such cases, food production and distribution and how much people can eat and what they eat are all decided by the government. A completely free market approach, however, rarely exists in today's societies. This is because in reality, some government intervention is always necessary. For example, intervention may be needed to ensure low-income residents have adequate access to food. Often this is done by supplementing their income.

9.3 Some commonly used policy tools

In this section, some policy measures that were or are still being commonly used by national governments to balance food demand and supply are explained and examined. Some such tools help to balance a country's food demand and supply; some actually create,

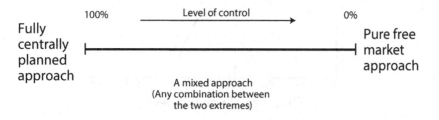

Figure 9.2 A spectrum denoting the level of control.

exacerbate, and perpetuate an imbalance. Some improve the welfare of consumers at the expense of producers, and *vice versa*. Some measures result in a net loss of welfare for the whole society – such a loss is called deadweight loss (DWL, a loss of economic efficiency that occurs when equilibrium for a good or a service is not achieved). Such a loss can never be recovered, hence the name deadweight loss. To help us evaluate policy effectiveness, it is useful to first introduce the concepts of consumer surplus and producer surplus.

Consumer surplus is defined as the difference between the total amount that consumers are willing and able to pay for a good or service and the total amount that they actually do pay. In Figure 9.3 (which is based on Figure 3A.1), the market price is $0.80 per kg, but at all quantities less than 120 kg, John is prepared to pay more than $0.80 per kg. For example, he is prepared to pay $1.20 for the 80th kg, a surplus of $0.40. John's total consumer surplus is $72 when he purchases 120 kg of rice at $0.8 per kg. This total surplus is calculated as follows. John's total cost of purchase is $96 (120 kg × $0.8 per kg, which is represented by the area of d + e). The total amount John is willing and able to pay is $168 (which is the area of a + b + c + d + e). The area of a + b + c is his consumer surplus, which is equal to $72, calculated by following the formula of (rise × run)/2 to calculate the area of a triangle (1.2 × 120)/2 = $72).

In Figure 9.3, had the price of rice gone up to $1.2 per kg, John would buy 80 kg of rice. His total consumer surplus would be reduced to area a only, which is $32. His total cost of purchasing the 80 kg of rice is the area b + d, being $96 (1.2 × 80 = 96). Hence, when the

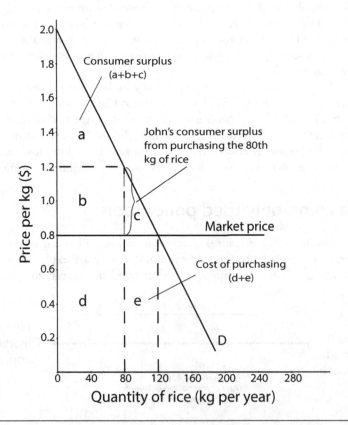

Figure 9.3 A consumer's demand and consumer surplus.

price of a product goes up, consumer surplus declines; when the price falls, consumer surplus increases, *ceteris paribus*.

Producer surplus is defined as the difference between the minimum amount of revenue producers must receive in order for them to be willing to supply a good or service and the total amount of revenue they actually receive. In Figure 9.4 (which is based on Figure 3A.4), the market price is $0.80 per kg. At all quantities less than 6000 kg, Sarah is willing to sell and receives a price of $0.80 per kg. The price she receives is higher than her cost of supply. For example, she is happy to sell the 4000th kg at a price of $0.80 per kg. Her cost of supplying that kg is $0.60, a surplus of $0.20. Sarah's total producer surplus is $1800 when she sells 6000 kg of rice at $0.8 per kg. It is calculated as follows. Sarah's total revenue from supplying the rice is $4800 (6000 kg × $0.8 per kg, which is represented by the area of a + b + c + d + e). Her total cost of supply is $3000 (which is the area of d + e). Thus, the difference between her total revenue and her total cost of supply is $1800 ($4800 - $3000 = $1800 which is her producer surplus; a + b + c + d + e minus d + e, which equals a + b + c).

In Figure 9.4, had the price of rice dropped to $0.6 per kg, Sarah would be only willing to supply 4000 kg of rice to the market. Her total producer surplus will be reduced to area c only, which is $800 (Her total cost of supplying the 4000th kg of rice is area d, being $1600. Her total revenue is $2400, the area of c + d). Hence, when the price of a product drops, producer surplus declines; and when the price rises, producer surplus increases, *ceteris paribus*.

Consumer surplus measures the welfare that people gain from purchasing and consuming goods and services. Producer surplus measures producer welfare in supplying goods and services. Based on Figure 3A.7, we can work out consumer surplus and producer surplus for

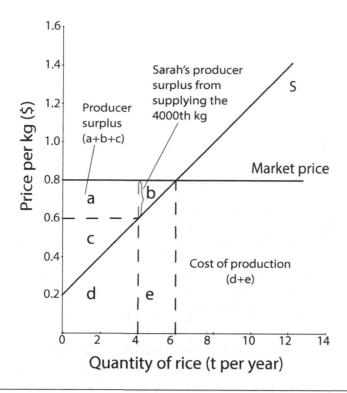

Figure 9.4 A producer's supply and producer surplus.

all consumers and producers in the whole country of Rasia (see Figure 9.5). At the price of $0.8 per kg with 120 kilo tonnes of rice produced/consumed, total consumer surplus (area a) is $72 million and total producer surplus (area b) is $36 million. Their sum (a + b) is $108 million. This sum is the highest. No other quantities or price levels can generate a sum greater than this. When this sum is maximised, resources are used most efficiently.

As we saw in earlier chapters, there are many factors that cause demand and supply to shift, and hence the market equilibrium to change also. For example, new technology shifts the supply curve to the right with a new lower equilibrium price, a larger equilibrium quantity and gains in both producer and consumer surplus. Generally, such shifts do not call for government intervention in the operation of markets.

However, governments may choose to intervene in markets for a number of reasons (some of which are political in nature):

- Because market prices are too volatile perhaps because of weather conditions or because of volatile international markets.
- Because they would prefer producers to get a higher price than the market delivers.
- Because they would prefer consumers to get a lower price than the market delivers.

Developed economies often try to induce the price to be above the market equilibrium to ensure farmers receive higher incomes. Developing countries often try to depress the price to be below the market equilibrium to ensure urban consumers pay lower prices for their food.

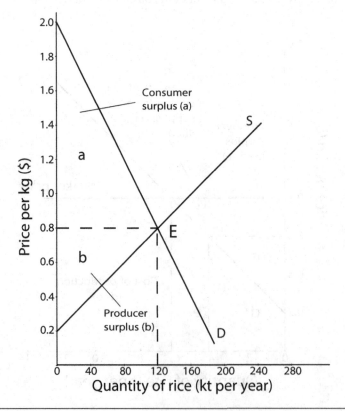

Figure 9.5 Consumer surplus and producer surplus.

When governments intervene, very often some consumer surplus is transferred to become producer surplus, or part of the producer surplus is transferred to become consumer surplus. Such transfers are also often associated with losses of efficiency in the economy, i.e., the creation of DWLs.

Some examples of policy tools used to intervene in the food market are examined below. We examine them for their impact on price and quantity, the extent to which economic surplus is transferred between consumers and producers, and the welfare losses to the country as a whole.

9.3.1 Price ceiling

A price ceiling is a government-imposed price control, or limit, on the price charged for a product. If this ceiling is above the market equilibrium price, it is not binding – producers are more than happy to sell their product at a price higher than the equilibrium price. If it is below the equilibrium price, it is then binding and production is limited.

When the price ceiling is set below the market equilibrium price, consumers find they now pay a lower price for the same product and subsequently they increase their purchases. In the meantime, producers find they are receiving a lower price than they were receiving before. They are not happy to produce as much as they used to. The combined effect is that there is now a supply shortage. This leads to surplus transfers and DWL.

A binding price ceiling prevents the market from moving towards the equilibrium (Figure 9A.1). The impacts of a binding price ceiling include (how these impacts arise is explained in Appendix 9A):

- Reduced quantity of food supplied, but increased quantity demanded at the ceiling price, leading to a shortage.
- A transfer of surplus from producers to consumers, resulting in higher consumer surplus but reduced producer surplus.
- A deadweight loss.

Clearly, this policy tool is counterproductive in boosting a country's food supply and does not help a country to balance its food demand and supply. Its adoption works against a country's effort to improve food security. It is often used in low-income and food-insecure countries to lower prices for non-farming consumers at the expense of producers. In the long run, it generally also works against the interest of consumers when food supply shortages become persistent.

Many countries have used this policy measure, which has always contributed to their food shortages. These countries include, for example, China, Vietnam, North Korea, and Venezuela. China and Vietnam have abandoned this policy tool, but others are still practising this policy (North Korea) or have recently introduced it (Venezuela).

9.3.2 Price floor

A price floor is a government-imposed price control, or limit, on the minimum price paid to farmers. In order to be effective (binding), a price floor must be higher than the equilibrium price.

When the price floor is set above the market equilibrium price, consumers find they are now paying a higher price for the same product and subsequently they reduce their purchases. In the meantime, suppliers find they are guaranteed a new, higher price than they were receiving before and they are happy to increase production. The combined effect is that there is now an excess supply. This then leads to surplus transfers and DWL.

What does a government do with the excess supply? There are two common approaches a government can use. (1) The government buys the excess to store, destroy, or export. (2) It makes a deficiency payment to producers.

9.3.2.1 Binding, excess supply purchased by government
When a government purchases the excess supply, the following changes take place in the market compared to what happens without a price floor (Figure 9A.2, Table 9A.2):

- There is excess supply which is bought by the government.
- Consumers purchase less and at higher prices.
- Consumer surplus drops but producer surplus increases.
- Tax revenues are diverted from other uses to the purchase and to the storage and disposal of the purchase.
- There is DWL which may be very large.

9.3.2.2 Binding, with a government deficiency payment plan
In this case, the excess supply is not purchased by the government. The total supply is sold in the market at a lower price determined by the demand curve (Figure 9A.3, Table 9A.3). The government covers the gap between the binding floor price and the price received by producers, hence, the so-called deficiency payment. The following changes take place in the market compared to what happens without a price floor:

- The supply is sold at a lower price.
- Consumers purchase more at lower prices; higher consumer surplus.
- Producers produce more with the guaranteed floor price and receive higher producer surplus.
- Tax revenues are diverted from other uses.
- There is DWL, which is generally smaller compared to government purchase of excess supply.

Binding price floors are generally used in high income countries such as the US, Europe, Canada, and Australia. In the EU, if the price of a targeted food fell below an intervention price, the European government would purchase tonnes of the surplus agricultural produce. Such protective floor prices have created so-called 'milk lakes', 'butter mountains', or 'beef mountains'.

Price floors induce over-supply and hence cause resource waste. They also cause trade distortions and hurt farmers in other countries. If the excess supply is exported, the world price is generally depressed. It is even worse if the excess supply is exported at subsidised prices; the world price would be much more depressed. Many farmers in developing (and some developed) countries may find it difficult to compete and survive even though they have a comparative advantage.

9.3.2.3 Non-binding, excess supply purchased by government
It is also possible for governments to use non-binding price floors to provide limited income protection to producers when there is a supply glut (Figure 9A.4) or when demand is volatile. If there is an oversupply in the market, without any price floor, the price received by producers can be very low. Some producers may not even be able to cover their cost. This will cause the

producers enormous hardship and also affect their ability to produce in the future. When a price floor is instigated, though not binding, it can help producers to some extent to reduce their loss (Table 9A.4). Major impacts of a non-binding price floor include:

- Consumers buy less and consumer surplus reduces.
- Producer surplus increases.
- Producer loss is reduced.
- The government purchases any surplus in the market at the floor price.
- There will be DWL but it may be small in size.
- The surplus has to be stored and sold when normal market conditions return.

A non-binding price floor is chiefly used by governments of developing countries such as China and India to partially protect the interests of farmers. It can help mitigate farmers' loss. The extent of the mitigation depends on the level of the price floor. In most cases, despite the existence of such a floor price, farmers are still unable to cover their cost of production, causing them financial hardship.

In the short run, this policy tool is generally effective in rendering farmers some temporary relief. In the long run, however, governments need to evaluate whether there are too many farmers in the industry. If so, encouraging some producers who are less efficient to leave the industry should be considered.

9.3.3 Production subsidy

Subsidies can be provided to either outputs or inputs. The deficiency payment discussed above is a kind of output subsidy. An export subsidy, which will be discussed later in this section, is also an output subsidy.

When a subsidy is provided to inputs, it reduces the cost of production. The supply curve then shifts to the right. With increased supply, the equilibrium price declines but the equilibrium quantity increases (Figure 9A.5).

Major impacts of input subsidy include:

- Increased food supply at a lower price.
- Consumer surplus increases.
- Producer surplus generally also increases.
- Less tax revenue is available for use in other sectors of the economy.

Both developed and developing countries use input subsidies. In the former, it is chiefly to boost farmers' income. For example, prior to the early 1990s when wide-ranging reductions in assistance to Australian rural industries occurred, subsidies were provided to a small, but significant number of inputs used by many farmers, in a wide range of industries, to increase production and exports (Zhou 2013, p. 81). In the latter, the major purpose is to increase food supply. For example, in India, the subsidy on fertiliser use has been substantial. The use of electricity and water is also subsidised but to a much smaller extent. (These subsidies, however, do not automatically imply that farmers in India are better off; they can still be worse off if the distortions on the output price or the trade restrictions outweigh the benefits of subsidised input use; which is generally the case). In China, an increasing amount of subsidy has been provided to farm inputs (such as farming tools and machinery, improved seeds) and the production of grains. China's subsidy to the production of grains has increased dramatically since 2006 and accounts for a major share of the total subsidy.

While input subsidies can help farmers to reduce their production costs and boost food supply, not all such subsidies are legitimate according to WTO rules. Some subsidies, both input and output, are deemed to be distorting and are not allowed. Details about which subsidies are allowed and which are not can be found at the WTO website (WTO 2018).

9.3.4 Output quota

An output quota is used to limit the supply of food to the market. With an output quota in place that is binding, consumers lose and producers gain (Figure 9A.6). This policy tool is used to guarantee higher income for producers through transfers of consumer surplus to producers.

Key impacts of a binding output quota are as follows:

- Less food is made available to the market.
- Consumers pay a higher price.
- Part of consumer surplus is transferred to become producer surplus.
- Producers receive a higher price and generally earn a higher income.
- There is a DWL.

This tool is mainly used in high-income countries. For example, there were quotas for the number of eggs to be produced in Australia. New South Wales was the first state to remove the egg quota in 1989. By 2005, all egg quotas were abolished in Australia (Zhou 2013, p. 85). This approach is rarely used nowadays.

9.3.5 Procurement quota

A procurement quota is set by a government to enforce how much of a crop a producer has to deliver to the government. If a producer's output is roughly divided into farm use (e.g., human consumption, feed, seed, etc.) and marketable surplus, the quota generally is a percentage of the marketable surplus. If the quota is below the marketable surplus, the producer may trade the rest of the marketable surplus (after quota delivery) in the market. If the quota is very close to or equal to the marketable surplus, little would be left for the farmer to trade. The price at which the government procures the food may be set at a level equal to or below the market price. Generally, the latter is the case (Figure 9A.7).

Impacts of a procurement quota with a price below the equilibrium price include:

- Producer surplus reduces.
- Reduced incentives for farmers to produce.
- Consumer surplus (or government revenue) may or may not increase depending on at which price level the government resells the procured food.
- If sold at the market equilibrium price, consumer surplus does not change but government revenue increases (assuming zero transaction costs).
- If sold at the procurement price, consumer surplus increase but government gains no extra revenue.
- If sold between the equilibrium price and the procurement price, the sizes of consumer surplus and government revenue vary according to the price level.
- Over time, the total amount supplied to the market generally drops below the equilibrium quantity, aggravating the food shortage of a country.

Such a measure may be used in food emergencies. When South Korea and Japan had severe food shortages after World War II, both countries used such quotas to procure food from farmers and then distributed the food to non-farming people. As soon as the food situations improved, they moved away from this practice towards the market approach.

Procurement quotas have also been used in countries where the intention is to deliberately milk the farming community in favour of non-farming population. For example, China and North Korea's compulsory food procurement was institutionalised for many decades starting from the early 1950s. Both countries experienced prolonged severe food shortages culminating in famines. China started to remove this approach in 1985, and by the early 1990s such procurement quotas had largely disappeared. China has not suffered any food shortages since. But this kind of procurement quota is still in use in North Korea and food shortage there has continued.

9.3.6 Food trade

Some countries may be well endowed with food production resources and there are food surpluses. Others may be poorly endowed, not being able to produce enough. (Or, actually, in terms of food production resources, some countries may have been well endowed but they cannot produce enough food, purely because the institutions they adopt discourage food production, such as in Venezuela and Zimbabwe.) Food trade is an important option to balance domestic food demand and supply. Exporting food will reduce the supply of a nation while importing food will increase food supply.

Many countries, both developed and developing, intervene in food trade in various ways. Generally, developed countries subsidise their food exports to make them easier and cheaper while developing countries impose restrictions on imports to make them harder and dearer.

Measures to intervene in trade are generally placed into two major categories: tariff trade barriers and non-tariff trade barriers (NTBs). Tariffs are duties collected by a government when trade takes place between nations. They can be imposed either on imports (import tariff) or exports (export tariff). NTBs are any measures that are used to restrict trade other than a tariff. There are many kinds of NTBs used by various countries, such as quotas, embargoes, sanctions, technical requirements, or hygiene standards. The number of NTBs is in the hundreds and is increasing.

9.3.6.1 Import tariff
An import tariff will make imports more expensive to domestic consumers. When a tariff is imposed on food imports, less is imported. Consumers pay a higher price for their food and their surplus is reduced. Domestic producers produce more and receive a higher price and their surplus increases. This tariff results in DWL. For full analyses of the welfare changes, see Figure 9A.8 and associated explanations.

9.3.6.2 Export tariff
An export tariff will make the exports more expensive to foreign consumers. When an export tariff is imposed, the price at which the food is exported becomes higher by the amount of the tariff. This makes the export less competitive and less may be exported to the world market. *Ceteris paribus*, this reduces the supply available in the world market and the world supply curve shifts to the left. This results in a lower quantity of food traded in the world market but at a higher price.

Because export tariffs discourage exports, more food will be sold in the domestic market, which will have a downward pressure on price. Domestic consumers are likely to benefit from the imposition of an export tariff.

Export tariffs are rarely used. Some developing countries may use them for revenue collection purposes. In some extreme cases, countries may use them to restrict food exports when there are fears of domestic shortages. This indeed happened during the 2006–2008 crisis of global food price hikes (FAO 2011, pp. 22–24). See Box 9.1 for the price hikes and possible causes responsible for the hikes.

Abrupt imposition of food export tariffs and the subsequent reduction in the availability of food in the world market can cause serious damage to the world food trading regime – food import-dependent countries may lose their faith in the trading system. Thus they devote more resources to home production of food. This will force them to move away from more efficient uses of their resources and to sacrifice gains from trade.

9.3.6.3 Import quota

When an import quota is set on food imports, it has similar effect to an import tariff. Less food is imported. Consumers pay a higher price for their food and their consumer surplus is reduced. Domestic producers produce more and receive a higher price and their surplus increases. There is also DWL resulting from the quota. The only major difference between an import tariff and an import quota is in the amount that can be imported. With a tariff, the total amount of imports is not limited – you can import as much as you wish so long as you are happy to pay the tariff. With a quota, the amount that can be imported is fixed. Hence a tariff partially restricts the role of the market but the quota completely restricts the role of the market.

Import quotas are used in both developed and developing countries. For example, quotas were used on sugar imports to the USA. In some developing countries, quotas may be set for food imports. After the WTO came into being, more countries shifted to the use of tariff-rate quotas (see the discussion below).

9.3.6.4 Export quota

Occasionally, food export quotas may be used to restrict exports, as happened during the 2006–2008 food price hikes (FAO 2011, pp. 22–24). Like export tariffs, export quotas are rarely used. An export quota burdens domestic producers. More food has to be sold on domestic market at lower prices. Domestic consumers benefit from export quotas at the expense of producers.

9.3.6.5 Tariff-rate quotas (TRQ)

These are a combination of the tariff and quota. They allow a specified number of goods (the quota) to be imported at one tariff rate (the within-quota rate) and any imports above the quota at a higher tariff rate (the above-quota rate). The within-quota rate is generally very low. The above-quota rate is often, however, prohibitively high. Hence, although it does not completely stop imports after the quota is filled, the very high above-quota rate generally makes the trade less financially warranted. Nonetheless, unlike import quotas, they do not completely stop trade after the quota is reached so long as one is prepared to pay the higher duties.

When TRQ are used, less food is imported. Consumers pay a higher price for their food and their consumer surplus is reduced. Domestic producers produce more and receive a higher price and their producer surplus also increases. There will be DWL.

BOX 9.1

Global Food Price Crisis of 2006–2008

World food prices increased dramatically in late 2007 and the first two quarters of 2008 (see Figure 9.6). Maize initially led the spike in late 2006. This was followed by wheat and then rice.

It is believed that the initial causes of price spikes in late 2006 included droughts in grain-exporting nations and rising oil prices. Higher oil prices resulted in general escalations in the costs of fertilisers, food transportation, and industrial agriculture. Other factors include the falling world-food stockpiles and the lack of R&D investment in many developing countries since the 1980s (Nin-Pratt and Fan 2010). Some people argue that the root causes are the increasing use of biofuels in developed countries and the rising demand for more food across the expanding middle-class populations of Asia.

All these explanations may be valid and those forces might have contributed to the rising prices. However, they cannot explain one important fact. That is, why had the prices increased so fast and also dropped so fast? In the world food market, it is impossible for a supplier to unilaterally choose to increase or reduce its price so as to lead to a sharp price rise and drop. So, according to our demand–supply analysis in Appendix A3, for the prices to escalate and then dive so rapidly, there must be forces that had resulted in the sharp shift of the demand curve to the right or the supply curve to the left. None of the above mentioned factors were observed to undergo drastic changes and thereby cause the sharp shift in the demand or supply curve.

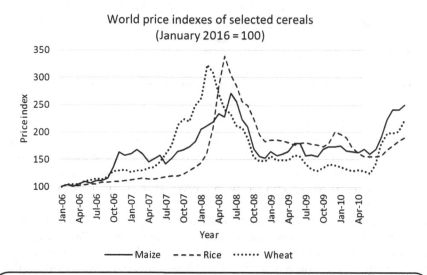

Figure 9.6 World price indexes of selected cereals (Jan 2016 = 100).
Source: International Grains Council (IGC) (2019), IGC Price Indices, www. amis-outlook.org/indicators/en/, accessed 8 March 2019.

So, the factor that caused the sudden sharp increase and then decrease must be found elsewhere. FAO and OECD expressed concerns about the role of hedge funds speculating on prices leading to major shifts (FAO 2010; OECD and FAO 2011, p. 20). In a Policy Brief, FAO points out that apart from actual changes in supply and demand, the upward swing in the world market might have been amplified by speculation in organised futures markets (FAO 2010).

Exploring the causes for the sudden and worldwide increases in food prices during 2007 and 2008 has attracted enormous interest. Some of the findings so far are widely accepted but others continue to be the subject of debate.

Whatever the factors responsible are, the food price hike during 2007–2008 caused serious political and economic instability and social unrest in many developing countries. Countries particularly severely affected are Burkina Faso, Cameroon, Senegal, Mauritania, Côte d'Ivoire, Egypt, and Morocco. In these countries, severe protests and riots broke out in late 2007 and early 2008 over the unavailability of basic food staples. Food-related unrest also occurred in other countries such as Mexico, Bolivia, Yemen, Uzbekistan, Bangladesh, Pakistan, Sri Lanka, and South Africa.

References

FAO (2010), 'Price surges in food markets – How should organized futures markets be regulated?' Policy Brief No. 9, Department of Economic and Social Perspectives, www.fao.org/3/al296e/al296e00.pdf, accessed 7 March 2019.

FAO (2011), *The State of Food Insecurity in the World 2011*, www.fao.org/publications/sofi/en/, accessed 4 October 2018.

Nin-Pratt, A. and Fan, S.G. (2010), 'R&D investment in national and international agricultural research', IFPRI Discussion Papers No. 986, IFPRI, Washington, D.C.

OECD and FAO (2011), 'OECD-FAO Agricultural Outlook 2011–2020', www.oecd-ilibrary.org/docserver/agr_outlook-2011-en.pdf?expires=1551925440&id=id&accname=ocid53019574&checksum=16981E79F0725679992A139A11F0837B, accessed 7 March 2019.

9.3.6.6 Export subsidies

Many developed countries are able to produce more than domestic demand. Their governments often help export the surplus by providing subsidies to make exports cheaper. This helps their farmers maintain higher income but at the expense of consumer surplus because domestic prices rise. It also results in a DWL. The effects of food export subsidies are shown in Figure 9A.9.

This practice, however, distorts the international food market. While the price drop in the world market is beneficial to consumers of importing countries in the short run, it hurts their farmers, especially in many less-developed countries. This is because the artificial lower price, caused by the extra supply which otherwise would have not been produced without the export subsidy, makes it difficult for the farmers of importing countries to compete and their survival may become difficult. Developed countries' export subsidies artificially reduce the comparative advantage of farmers in importing countries. In the long run, importing countries' food production will be hurt and their consumers will also suffer from reduced domestic ability to produce food.

Because of the distorting impacts of export subsidies on food production in importing countries, they are not allowed according to WTO rules (WTO 2018).

9.3.6.7 No trade, or with severe trade restrictions

We have demonstrated that with the use of any of the above trade intervention measures, trade volumes are either discouraged or encouraged, at lower or higher world prices, but trade is still possible. When trade is not allowed or severely restricted, then the domestic market is completely or partially separated from the world market. Consequently, producers will suffer if the domestic price is lower than the world price, and consumers will suffer if the domestic price is higher than the world price. Government expenditure for managing the food economy also increases. Basically, when the world price is higher than the domestic price and trade is not allowed, there will be welfare loss (see Table 9A.6 and related discussions in the Appendix to this chapter).

Some countries do restrict food trade. One example is India (see the section on India in Chapter 11 for more details). India exercises some restrictions to discourage food exports. The Indian government instead spends money to set floor prices and to provide input subsidies to farmers. In this way, domestic prices remain subdued so that more consumers, especially poorer ones, can afford to buy food. Because floor prices are offered as a protection or input subsidies are provided, farmers have the illusion of protection and their voices can be easily muted.

Another example is China (see the section on China in Chapter 11 for more details). Prior to 1976, food imports were severely restricted. The justification was that China was a socialist country and the people of a socialist country should not eat food produced by capitalist countries (Zhao and Qi 1988, p. 153, p. 163). China abandoned this kind of mentality in 1980 (Zhao and Qi 1988, pp. 176–177).

9.3.7 Reserve stocks

Many countries maintain reserve food stocks. These stocks are designated for handling unpredictable and non-continuing food crises or emergencies. Hence, their usage is strictly controlled by governments. Such reserve stocks should not be confused with a country's operational food stocks, which are used for handling generally predictable seasonal variations in food supply.

For many food-deficit countries, while imports are essential in balancing demand and supply, having food reserves is also important. Having a reserve stock generally makes the public feel secure. It is especially valuable in dealing with any abrupt and unforeseen short-lived supply shortages in the market.

Loosely, both the strategic reserve stocks and common operational stocks can be regarded as parts of a country's buffer stock. The existence of a buffer stock helps maintain price stability. This, however, comes at a cost. Sometimes the cost can be very large, depending on the size of the stocks maintained and the efficiency with which the stocks are managed.

The target size of a food reserve was traditionally determined by the cereal requirements of the vulnerable population for the time from the recognition of an imminent food emergency until additional supplies could be made available for distribution, i.e., the lead time. It was typically assumed that the cereal requirement was equivalent to 160–175 kg per person per year and that a lead time of three months would be required to organise and receive additional supplies (FAO 1997). The size for the reserve can be substantially smaller in countries where the market functions well, especially if the import channels are well maintained. Smaller reserves lead to huge financial savings.

9.3.8 Other policies

There are various other policy tools that governments can use to affect food demand or supply and thus the balance between them. Some of these policy measures have been touched on elsewhere. For example, investment in infrastructure (reducing the cost of food production, transportation, processing, and retailing), agricultural R&D investment (new techniques and management methods resulting in higher productivity), adjustments to industry policies (thus affecting their rates of return), and government control of food marketing and distribution (affecting how people access food and how much they can eat).

9.4 What is the best option to manage a country's food demand–supply balance?

During peacetime, fully controlled approaches to managing a country's food security have rarely been successful. Many communist countries, influenced by the former USSR, adopted full control of their food production and distribution. All failed miserably. Two typical examples are China and North Korea. Their adoption of a full control approach contributed to the advent of famines in their countries, resulting in millions of deaths. After China abandoned full control in the early 1980s, its food supply and food security started to improve. North Korea is still largely following a high control approach and its people have continuously suffered from lack of food. The recent limited relaxation of control in North Korea, by permitting some markets to exist, has brought improvements in food availability, especially in rural areas (Silberstein 2017).

In reality, some level of government intervention is often necessary. Hence, a completely free market approach is unlikely to exist. However, it has generally been the case that a system that is close to the free market end of the spectrum has always enjoyed more success in achieving a high level of food security. Reviewing those countries with a high GFSI as given in the 'Food security and related variables' table, it is clear that very few of them exercise high levels of government control over their markets. This is reflected by their high 'index of economic freedom'; for example, Australia, New Zealand, Singapore, and Switzerland.

This is not to completely discount the applicability of high levels of control in some situations. It may be highly relevant and useful to adopt such an approach in cases of emergency. Concentrated management of limited food resources in order for them to be distributed to the people in an orderly way can be very powerful to help overcome food crises, helping to avoid or reduce large numbers of human casualties. What must be noted, however, is that the use of such emergency measures should be discarded in favour of the market approach when the food situation starts to improve. Prolonged use of emergency approaches is most likely to jeopardise a country's effort to recover from a food crisis.

The experiences of South Korea and Japan provide strong endorsement (see the case studies of Japan and South Korea in Chapter 12 for details). After World War II, to handle food shortages, both countries used government controls to procure and distribute food. Despite limited success, the controls did help them to overcome the severe food shortage. Recognising the limitations of controls, both countries abandoned them and moved towards the market approach as soon as the food situation started to improve. North Korea also used the control approach to manage its food emergency after the Korean War. But the control was gradually institutionalised and is still in place, preventing the country from improving its food security.

All the cases provided in Part 5 tend to support the argument that a food management system that is close to full control is more prone to failure in balancing food demand and supply, while a system that is close to a free market is more likely to succeed. It should be beneficial for countries that still practise high levels of control to shift to using more market mechanisms in coordinating their food demand and supply.

In addition to fostering the fundamentals – institutions that facilitate the market coordinating food demand and supply – the following three aspects also deserve close attention from governments of food-deficit and import-dependent countries, no matter whether they are food-secure or insecure, developing or developed:

- Boost food production as much as their comparative advantages justify, both at home and in other countries (i.e., through foreign direct investment).
- Maintain mutually beneficial relationships with trading partners, especially major food exporters by being a responsible food importer.
- Keep a strategic food reserve stock with its size adequately and regularly reviewed.

The efficacy of these measures will be repeatedly borne out in Part 5 where country experiences in managing food demand and supply are shown. Highlighting them here in this chapter is admittedly pre-emptive but follows what we have been discussing.

One other trend worth noting is the diversification of food import sources. Today, many countries rely on imports to ensure domestic food supply. Stable import sources are crucial for them to achieve and sustain their food security; especially for those with very low food self-sufficiency ratios (SSRs). By diversifying import sources, it is unlikely that all trading partners will simultaneously be unable to supply food at the time of need.

9.5 The role of NGOs

In Section 9.1, we pointed out that (1) governments must assume the ultimate responsibility of ensuring food security and (2) individual citizens should also do their share to help their countries to achieve a high level of food security. In today's modern society, there is another force that can and has played an important role in improving food security: non-governmental organisations (NGOs).

NGOs help improve food security in various ways: (1) they appeal to governments to improve food security and to monitor progress; (2) they raise resources (financial and food in kind) and channel food to those in need in society; and (3) they contribute to initiatives that can better help less fortunate and disadvantaged members of the population to receive food assistance.

As an example, Leket Israel plays an important role in delivering food to those who are in need in Israel. It sources food primarily by rescuing good quality, edible, surplus food that would otherwise have been discarded (Leket Israel 2018).

For NGOs to be able to contribute to improving food security, they must be allowed to exist and to operate without undue government interventions. In the past two decades, NGOs' operations have been increasingly restricted in more and more countries (Vernon 2009; UN 2012; Dupuy, Ron and Prakash 2014; Sriskandarajah 2014; Wong 2016; Berry 2017; Kumar 2019). This tendency has not been arrested; instead it has become stronger.

Review questions

1. In today's modern society, would you agree that a country's government has the ultimate responsibility to ensure each and every citizen of the country has a reasonable level of food security? Explain why.
2. Identify major policy tools that are used in your country to coordinate food demand and supply balance. Would you classify them as being more towards the free market end or the administrative control end?
3. Evaluate the impacts of each of the major policy tools as identified in Review Question 2 by following the consumer surplus and producer surplus framework. Point out any changes in the size of consumer surplus, producer surpluses, and DWL if any. (Information about the slopes of demand and supply curves may not be readily available. Based on your understanding of the chosen food market, i.e., rice or wheat, make your best assumption about the likely slopes. You should be able to discover the volume of the food traded and at what price from your country's statistical bureau).
4. If the policy tools used in your country are closer to the control end, do you believe changes should be made to make them more towards the free market end? Why?
5. In your opinion, how can NGOs play a role in helping improve the food security of needy people in your country? Are there currently any such NGOs that are helping needy people? If not, why not? If so, is their work limited in any way by the government and, if yes, why?

Discussion questions

1. Continuing from Review Question 2. The policy tools used in your country to coordinate food demand and supply balance may be either more towards the free market end or the administrative control end. Can you find out why such policies have been adopted (or, in other words, against what backgrounds they have been adopted)?
2. If you were the decision-maker in your country, would you adopt the policy tools that are currently in use in your country? Why?
3. Some foods are substitutes, such as foods made out of rice and wheat flour. Let us call the two related foods A and B. In your view, is it possible to manage the price of B in order to achieve better balance between the demand for and supply of A? Why?
4. Refer to Figure 9A.9. Rice is exported but no subsidy is provided. What would be the size of consumer surplus, producer surplus, and the DWL if no export subsidy is provided? In terms of total welfare, would Rasia be better off or worse off if no subsidy is provided to the producers?

References

Berry, A. (2017), 'Egyptian President signs law to restrict operations of foreign-funded NGOs', *Nonprofit Quarterly*, https://nonprofitquarterly.org/2017/06/02/egyptian-president-signs-law-restrict-operations-foreign-funded-ngos/, accessed 29 November 2017.

Dupuy, K., Ron, J., and Prakash, A. (2014), 'Stop meddling in my country! Governments' restrictions on foreign aid to non-governmental organizations', SSRN, https://papers.ssrn.com/sol3/papers.cfm?abstract_id=2529620, accessed 29 November 2017.

FAO. (1997), 'Strategic grain reserves - Guidelines for their establishment, management and operation', FAO Agricultural Services Bulletin – 126, www.fao.org/docrep/w4979e/w4979e00.htm#Contents, accessed 13 December 2017.

FAO. (2011), *The State of Food Insecurity in the World 2011*, www.fao.org/publications/sofi/en/, accessed 4 October 2018.

Kumar, S. (2019), 'India: decades of hostility against NGOs have worsened under Narendra Modi', https://theconversation.com/india-decades-of-hostility-against-ngos-have-worsened-under-narendra-modi-113300, accessed 4 May 2019.

Leket Israel. (2018), 'Rescuing healthy food for Israel's needy', www.leket.org/en/on-food-rescue/, accessed 28 November 2018.

Silberstein, B.K. (2017), 'Sanctions, and the weakness of North Korean food security', www.nkeconwatch.com/2017/10/18/sanctions-and-the-weakness-of-north-korean-food-security/, accessed 27 May 2019.

Sriskandarajah, D. (2014), 'Why restricting foreign funding of NGOs is wrongheaded', www.huffingtonpost.com/danny-sriskandarajah/why-restricting-foreign-ngos_b_5036049.html, accessed 28 November 2017.

UN. (2012), 'Restrictions on NGOs worldwide undermining human rights', www.un.org/apps/news/story.asp?NewsID=41858#.Wh0FqaLjGQh, accessed 28 November 2017.

Vernon, R.B. (2009), 'Restrictions on foreign funding of civil society: Closing the door on aid', *The International Journal of Not-for-Profit Law*, Vol. 11, Issue 4, www.icnl.org/research/journal/vol11iss4/special_1.htm, accessed 28 November 2017.

Wong, E. (2016), 'Clampdown in China restricts 7,000 foreign organizations', *The New York Times*, www.nytimes.com/2016/04/29/world/asia/china-foreign-ngo-law.html, accessed 29 November 2017.

WTO. (2018), 'Domestic support in agriculture: The boxes', www.wto.org/english/tratop_e/agric_e/agboxes_e.htm, accessed 28 November 2018.

Zhao, F.S. and Qi, X.Q. (eds) (1988), *Grain in Contemporary China*, Chinese Social Sciences Press, Beijing.

Zhou, Z.Y. (2013), *Developing Successful Agriculture: An Australian Case Study*, CAB International, Oxfordshire.

Appendix 9A

Welfare analyses of policy tools

9A.1 Price ceiling

When a binding price ceiling of $0.6 per kg is imposed in Rasia, the total amount of rice supplied is reduced from 120 kilo tonnes (kt) to 80 kt, a reduction of 40 kt per year (Figure 9A.1). Due to the lower price, the total quantity of rice demanded increases from 120 kt to 140 kt, an increase of 20 kt. This results in a shortage of 60 kt (140 kt – 80 kt) per year.

A binding price ceiling also brings about inequity and welfare loss. Without the price control, total consumer surplus is a + b and total producer surplus is c + d + e. With the control, total consumer surplus is a + c and total producer surplus is e. Consumers lose b but gain c. The gain in c ($16 m) is greater than the loss in b ($8 m). Thus, consumer surplus increases by $8 million (= c – b = 16 – 8). However, producer surplus decreases by $20 million (c + d), of which $16 million, c, is transferred to consumers to become consumer surplus. The other $4 million, d, becomes the dead-weight loss (DWL). The area b ($8 million) is also DWL resulting from the price control. Hence the total welfare loss to Rasia is $12 million (b + d). The calculation of consumer and producer surpluses and the DWL under a price ceiling is given in Table 9A.1.

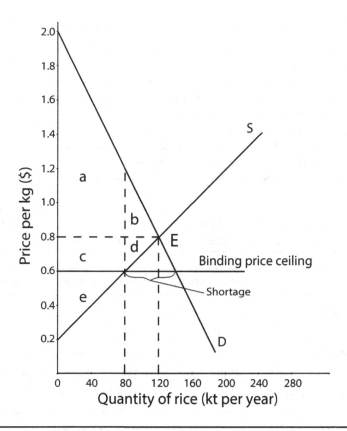

Figure 9A.1 A binding price ceiling and its effect on food supply.

Table 9A.1 Calculation of consumer and producer surpluses and the DWL – price ceiling, binding

	Before price ceiling	After price ceiling	Change
Consumer surplus (CS)	a + b	a + c	c – b
	$72 m	$80 m	+$8 m
Producer surplus (PS)	c + d + e	e	– c – d
	$36 m	$16 m	-$20 m
Government (taxpayers, G)	zero	zero	zero
	$0 m	$0 m	$0 m
Total welfare (CS + PS – G)	a + b + c + d + e	a + c + e	– b – d
	$108 m	$96 m	– $12 m

9A.2 Price floor

9A.2.1 Binding, excess supply purchased by government

When the binding price floor is set at $1.0 per kg, the quantity supplied increases to 160 kt and the quantity demanded reduces to 100 kt – thus an excess supply of 60 kt. Consumer surplus reduces to a only from a + b + c without the floor. Producer surplus increases to b + c + d + e + f from e + f without the floor. The government has to spend c + d + f + h + g + i to buy the 60 kt of rice at a price of $1.0 per kg (Figure 9A.2).

The purchased rice may be destroyed, exported, or stored. Assuming the rice was destroyed and cost no extra money, then the majority of the rice purchase spending, which is taxpayers' money, becomes the DWL resulting from the floor (except d which is captured as producer surplus). Table 9A.2 shows the calculation of consumer and producer surpluses and the DWL.

Table 9A.2 Calculation of consumer and producer surpluses and the DWL – price floor with government purchase, binding

	Before price floor	After price floor	Change
Consumer surplus (CS)	a + b + c	a	– b – c
	$72 m	$50 m	– $22 m
Producer surplus (PS)	e + f	b + c + d + e + f	b + c + d
	$36 m	$64 m	$28 m
Government (taxpayers, G)	zero	– c – d – f – h – g – i	– c – d – f – h – g – i
	$0 m	– $60 m	– $60 m
Total welfare (CS + PS – G)	a + b + c + e + f	a + b + e – g – h – i	– c – f – h – g – i
	$108 m	$50 m	– $54 m

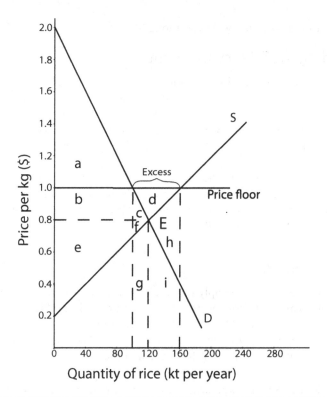

Figure 9A.2 A binding price floor when government buys the excess.

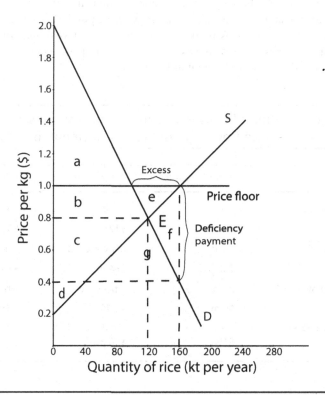

Figure 9A.3 A binding price floor with a deficiency payment plan.

9A.2.2 Binding, deficiency payment

Figure 9A.3 shows the changes in consumer and producer surpluses and the DWL from making a deficiency payment when a price floor is imposed. In this case, the government does not buy the 60 kt of excess supply. Instead, it provides the producers with a deficiency payment, which is the vertical distance between the floor price ($1.0 per kg) and the price the producers receive ($0.4 per kg). The total deficiency payment is the area b + e + c + f + g.

Part of the money used for the deficiency payment has been captured as consumer surplus or producer surplus. A deficiency payment plan results in a much smaller DWL compared to that under government purchase of excess supply. Calculations of consumer and producer surpluses and the DWL are given in Table 9A.3.

9A.2.3 Non-binding

This is the case where there is a supply glut (price falls to $0.40) and the government sets a floor price ($0.60) which is below the normal market price ($0.8) (Figure 9A.4). There is an excess supply of rice of 40 kt (160 kt – 120 kt) in relation to the equilibrium quantity. The price would need to be $1.0 per kg for farmers to recover their costs. At this price, however, the farmers cannot sell all their rice. If they have no other alternative but to sell the rice, the price would be $0.4 per kg. Farmers would be facing a huge loss.

With a price floor at $0.6 per kg, farmers can sell their rice at $0.6 per kg rather than $0.4 per kg, up to 140 kt in the market. The government then spends a total of j + i + n to buy the remaining 20 kt at the floor price.

Determining the size of the DWL is a bit complicated. It depends on what caused the supply glut and also what the government will do with the purchased 20 kt at the floor price. Generally, the rice so purchased is unlikely to be wasted in developing countries, as it can be stored for future domestic use or for export. Hence, the spending of j + i + n may well be recovered, reducing the size of the potential DWL.

Table 9A.3 Calculation of consumer and producer surpluses and the DWL – price floor with deficiency payment, binding

	Before price floor	After price floor	Change
Consumer surplus (CS)	a + b	a + b + c + g	c + g
	$72 m	$128 m	$56 m
Producer surplus (PS)	c + d	b + e + c + d	b + e
	$36 m	$64 m	$28 m
Government (taxpayers, G)	zero	– b – e – c – g – f	– b – e – c – g – f
	$0 m	– $96 m	– $96 m
Total welfare (CS + PS – G)	a + b + c + d	a + b + c + d – f	– f
	$108 m	$96 m	– $12 m

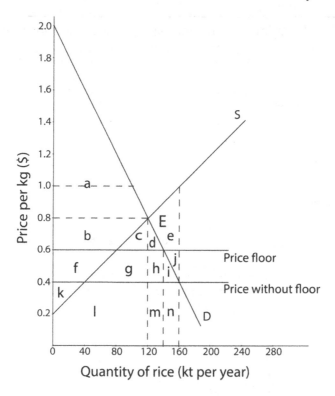

Figure 9A.4 A non-binding price floor with government purchase.

If the glut was caused by favourable weather conditions, the actual DWL may be relatively smaller because the extra output was not brought about by using extra inputs. If the glut was caused by farmers' response to a favourable price signal from the previous season, then the DWL will be e + j.

A glut caused by weather is extremely hard to avoid. One caused by a price signal is also hard to avoid in many developing countries due to (1) many small farmers tending to respond in the same direction simultaneously, and (2) market intelligence services being generally weak.

The welfare changes with and without the price floor are shown in Table 9A.4, assuming that the excess supply was due to farmers' response to a favourable price signal (hence the use of extra inputs), and that it is bought by the government, will be sold at the price the government bought it for, and there are no storage costs or other transaction costs.

9A.3 Production subsidy

Impacts of input subsidy are shown in Figure 9A.5. A certain amount of input subsidy by the government reduces the cost of rice production in Rasia and thus results in the shift of the supply curve from Supply 1 to Supply 2. Consequently, consumer surplus increases from a

Table 9A.4 Calculation of consumer and producer surpluses and the DWL – price floor with government purchase, non-binding

	Before price floor	After price floor	Change
Consumer surplus (CS)	$a + b + c + d + f + g + h + i$	$a + b + c + d$	$-f - g - h - i$
	$128 m	$98 m	$- $30 m
Producer surplus (PS)	k	$k + f$	f
	$4 m	$16 m	$12 m
Government (taxpayers, G)	zero	$-j - i - n$	$-j - i - n$
	$0 m	$- $24 m	$- $24 m
Total welfare (CS + PS − G)	$a + b + c + d + f + g + h + i + k$	$a + b + c + d + k + f - j - i - n$	$-g - h - 2i - j - n$
	$132 m	$90 m	$- $42 m

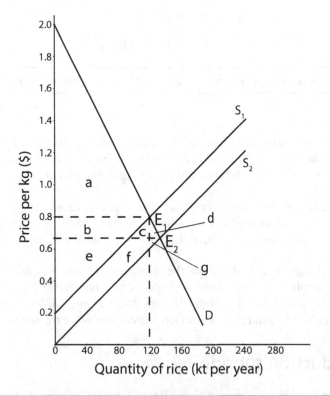

Figure 9A.5 Input subsidy and food supply.

to a + b + c + d. Producer surplus changes from b + e to e + f + g. Because the area of f + g is greater than the area of b, producer surplus also increases. The cost to Rasia is the amount of input subsidy.

9A.4 Output quota

In Figure 9A.6, the government does not allow farmers to produce more than 80 kt. This output quota is binding. Consequently, the amount of rice traded in the market is limited to 80 kt at a price of $1.2 per kg.

Without the output quota, consumer surplus is a + b + c and producer surplus d + e. After the imposition of the quota, consumer surplus is reduced to a. b is transferred to producers and c becomes the DWL. e now is no longer part of producer surplus but becomes DWL. Total DWL is c + e. Because b is far greater than e, producers are much better off as a result of the output quota.

9A.5 Procurement quota

When a procurement quota is used, the price at which the government procures food is generally below the market price. Assume in this case, the marketable surplus in Rasia is 120 kt with an equilibrium price being $0.8 per kg. The government sets a procurement quota

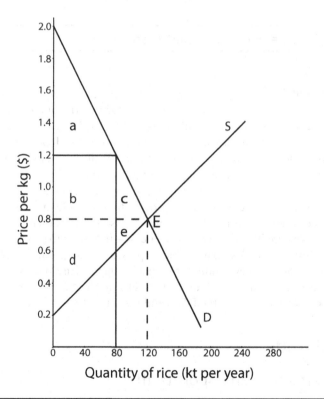

Figure 9A.6 Output quota and food supply.

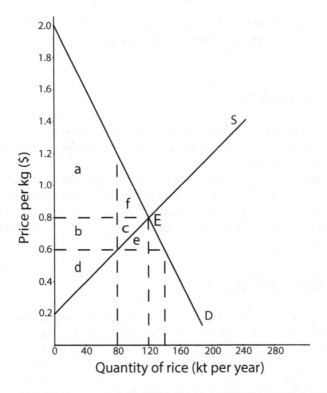

Figure 9A.7 Procurement quota and food supply.

at 80 kt at a price of $0.6 per kg. As a result, producer surplus reduces from b + c + d to c + d only (Figure 9A.7). If the government sells the procured rice at a price of $0.8 per kg, b becomes government revenue (assuming all transaction costs being zero), or is the equivalent of a kind of tax collected from the farmers by the government. If sold at $0.6 per kg, b is transferred to consumers to become consumer surplus. At this price, the total quantity of rice demanded will increase to 140 kt, causing a shortage of 20 kt.

It is also possible for the government to set its procurement quota to equal the total marketable surplus, i.e., 120 kt. Then, if the procured food is sold at $0.6 per kg, a shortage of 20 kt will also emerge. If that is the case, farmers also lose c as their producer surplus. In addition, they are now unable to even cover their cost – they have to incur a loss of e. Farmers would be better off producing less marketable surplus, say, only producing 80 kt to supply to the market. That is, the less they produce, the smaller their financial losses.

If farmers had only produced 80 kt marketable surplus, consumer surplus would be reduced by the area of f. f becomes the DWL and the total DWL is f + c.

9A.6 Food trade

9A.6.1 The effects of an import tariff

Now assume the equilibrium price in Rasia ($0.8 per kg) is much higher than the world price ($0.4 per kg) (see Figure 9A.8). It is cheaper to import rice. Rasia's import quantity is small

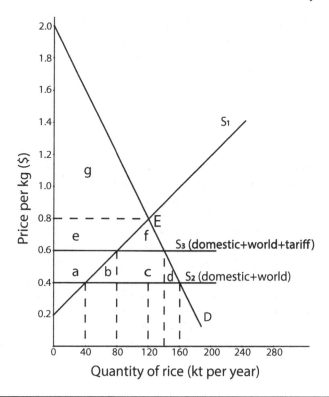

Figure 9A.8 Effects of an import tariff.

compared to total world trade and its rice import will have little impact on the world price. As a price taker, it faces a constant world price level for its import. This is not rare; many nations are not important enough to influence the prices at which they import.

In Figure 9A.8, the autarky (which means a country has no trade at all with any other countries) equilibrium is at point E. Now suppose that Rasia is opened to trade and the world rice price is $0.4 per kg. The highest price that domestic producers can receive now is $0.4 per kg. At this price, they will only supply 40 kt. The rest of the demand is met by the supply from the world market. The world market supply is very large and can supply an unlimited quantity of rice to Rasia at the price of $0.4 per kg. Hence, the world supply curve (from 40 kt onwards) is a horizontal line (i.e., perfectly elastic).

With free trade, the amount of rice demanded is 160 kt, whereas domestic production is 40 kt. The import of 120 kt fulfils the excess domestic demand. Consumers are now better off but domestic producers sell less at a lower price.

Suppose the Rasian government decides to help producers by levying a protective tariff of $0.2 per kg on rice imports. Now, the overall supply curve shifts upward by the amount of the tariff, from the supply curve (domestic + world) to the supply curve (domestic + world + tariff).

With the protective tariff, domestic production increases by 40 kt to 80 kt while domestic consumption falls by 20 kt. Imports decrease from 120 kt to 60 kt. The tariff impedes imports and protects domestic producers.

Without a tariff, consumer surplus is the area of a + b + c + d + e + f + g. With the tariff, consumer surplus falls to the area e + f + g. The loss of consumer surplus is equal to a + b + c + d.

Out of the consumer surplus loss, a is transferred to producers to become producer surplus. c is collected by the government to become its revenue. The resultant DWL is b + d. b is the loss to the economy resulting from resources used to produce additional rice at higher costs. The loss of d arises from the decrease in consumption resulting from the tariff which resulted in the price increase from $0.4 per kg to $0.6 per kg.

9A.6.2 The effects of an export subsidy

In Figure 9A.9, the equilibrium price is $0.8 per kg without trade. This equilibrium price is also equal to world price. Rasia produces more than domestic needs at 160 kt. If Rasian farmers export to the world market, they incur a loss. If they do not export and just sell in the domestic market, the loss is even greater. Suppose that the Rasian government makes a payment of $0.2 for each kg of rice exported to help farmers. Assume Rasia is a relatively small producer of rice and its export to the world market does not affect the world price. With the export subsidy, farmers will export 60 kt to the world market at the world price of $0.80 per kg. They receive $1.00 for each kg they export (the world price of $0.80 per kg + the subsidy of $0.20 per kg). Domestic consumers now have to pay $1.00 per kg to purchase their rice because this is what the farmers can receive by exporting (Figure 9A.9).

The export subsidy results in a decrease in consumer surplus by the area of b + c and an increase in producer surplus by the area of b + c + d. The cost of the export subsidy, which the taxpayers cover, equals the per-unit subsidy ($0.2) times the quantity of rice exported (60 kt),

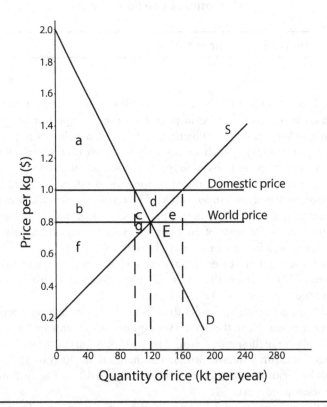

Figure 9A.9 Effects of an export subsidy.

174

> **Table 9A.5** Calculation of consumer and producer surpluses and the DWL – if export was subsidised

	Without subsidy	With subsidy	Change
Consumer surplus (CS)	a + b + c	a	− b − c
	$72 m	$50 m	− $22 m
Producer surplus (PS)	f + g	f + g + b + c + d	b + c + d
	$36 m	$64 m	$28 m
Government (taxpayers, G)	zero	− c − d − e	− c − d − e
	$0 m	− $12 m	− $12 m
Total welfare (CS + PS − G)	a + b + c + f + g	a + f + g + b − e	− c − e
	$108 m	$102 m	− $6 m

which is the area of c + d + e. Thus, Rasian rice producers gain at the expense of the Rasian consumers and taxpayers (Table 9A.5).

The export subsidy also results in a DWL to the Rasian economy. The DWL consists of the area of c + e. c is a DWL due to lost consumer surplus because the price has increased. e is a DWL due to the increasing domestic cost of producing additional rice.

9A.6.3 No trade

Recall Figures 9A.4 and 9A.5. Figure 9A.4 shows how a non-binding price floor is used to partially help farmers. Figure 9A.5 indicates how an input subsidy may help farmers. Such measures seemingly provide support to farmers. They often in fact do more harm than good to farmers in developing countries. In both cases, it was implied that trade was not allowed or that the world price was below domestic price before intervention – which is often unlikely – otherwise, if the world price was above domestic prices, the food would have been exported to the world market for a higher price.

Based on Figure 9A.4, let us assume there are three world prices: (1) $0.6 per kg, which is equal to the price floor; (2) $0.8 per kg, equal to the market equilibrium price; and (3) $1.0 per kg, above domestic equilibrium price. Rasia trades with other countries. As a result, consumer surplus, producer surplus, and government spending will all change with farmers gaining the most (see Figure 9A.10).

If the world price is $0.6, $0.8, and $1.0 per kg, the amount of rice exported is 20 kt (160 kt − 140 kt), 40 kt (160 kt − 120 kt) and 60 kt (160 kt − 100 kt), respectively. In Table 9A.6, consumer surplus, producer surplus, and government spending are all calculated for different world prices. In terms of total national welfare, Rasia is better off allowing export. The government spends no money on protective purchase. Producers gain higher producer surplus as the world price goes higher. The consumer surplus does decline when the world price increases. However, the whole nation is better off.

The above delineations are based on if trade was allowed. However, if trade was not allowed, all the possible welfare gains are foregone.

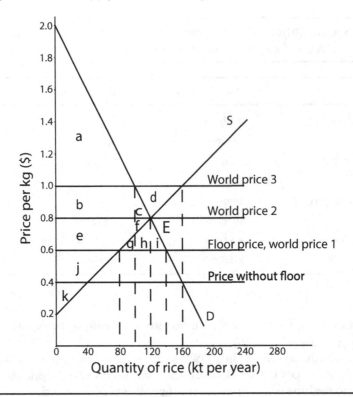

Figure 9A.10 When trade is allowed.

Table 9A.6 Calculation of consumer and producer surpluses and the DWL – if trade was allowed

	World price = $0.6 per kg	World price = $0.8 per kg	World price = $1.0 per kg
Consumer surplus (CS)	a + b + c + e + f + g + h + i	a + b + c	a
	$98 m	$72 m	$50 m
Producer surplus (PS)	j + k	e + f + j + k	b + c + d + e + f + j + k
	$16 m	$36 m	$64 m
Government (taxpayers, G)	zero	zero	zero
	$0 m	$0 m	$0 m
Total welfare (CS + PS – G)	a + b + c + e + f + g + h + i + j + k	a + b + c + e + f + j + k	a + b + c + d + e + f + j + k
	$114 m	$108 m	$114 m

Chapter 10

Coordinating demand and supply for food security

Collaboration at the international level

Summary

Having discussed the approaches used at the national level to coordinate food demand and supply, in this chapter we highlight collaborative efforts at the regional and global levels. Some individual countries or regions may have limited capacity to achieve an adequate level of food security. Sometimes, certain events (e.g., natural disasters) may temporarily hinder a country or a region's ability to maintain an adequate level of food security. Hence, collaborative efforts at the regional and global levels are needed. In Section 10.1, we outline major events that have taken place in recent history to promote international collaboration and coordination for better global food security. In Section 10.2, some current key international arrangements and initiatives for improving global food security are presented. Finally, in Section 10.3, we shed some light on prospects and challenges for future international collaboration and coordination.

After studying this chapter, you should be able to:
- List chronologically major events of international cooperation to improve global food security since World War I.
- Explain how each of the current major global and regional institutions of collaboration and coordination helps improve global food security.
- Discuss potential challenges to future international efforts for global food security.

10.1 Collaboration and coordination: key milestones

After World War I, it was recognised that multilateral arrangements at the international level were needed to coordinate food production and trade, in order to reap gains from trade and to respond to famines and other food crises. Since then there have been continued efforts to set up mechanisms at the international level to coordinate global food demand and supply. Some of these efforts have been mentioned in Section 1.3 in Chapter 1 when addressing the history and evolution of the concept of food security. Below we highlight some key events since World War I (Shaw 2007; Gibson 2012).

- It was recognised by the League of Nations (an intergovernmental organisation founded in January 1920 after World War I to provide a forum for resolving international disputes) that there was the need for a multilateral world food security arrangement to coordinate food production and exchange for the benefit of both consumers and producers. Food security was perceived as a universal issue for the first time.
- The League of Nations disseminated world hunger statistics for the first time in the 1930s. Subsequently, the Health Division of the League of Nations produced a report on nutrition and public health in poor countries. This report contributed to the start of international collaboration on nutrition policies. Since then, hunger and nutrition issues have been perceived as global issues.
- In 1945, the FAO was formed under the United Nations, an end product of a series of food security related conferences held during World War II.
- In 1946, the FAO produced its first *World Food Survey* report. The report revealed that at least one-third of the world population was starving, showing that world hunger did not improve even after establishing the FAO.
- The then Director-General of the FAO, John Boyd Orr, proposed the establishment of the World Food Board (WFB) in 1946. The WFB proposal was not successful due to lack of support.
- In 1954, a resolution passed by the UN General Assembly requested that the FAO conduct an in-depth study of the then popular concept of a 'world food reserve' (WFR). Concerned about food price instabilities, some national governments did not accept the WFR proposal.
- Following the lack of acceptance of the WFB and WFR proposals, in 1955, the concept of a World Food Bank was contemplated. But it did not lead anywhere.
- In 1961, the World Food Programme (WFP) was established. WFP is the food-assistance branch of the United Nations.
- In the early 1970s, world food supply fell. In response to the international food crisis, the first World Food Conference was organised to review the food deficit conditions and decide on possible solutions (5–16 November 1974, Rome). The term 'food security' was put forward to a wider audience at this Conference.
- The first International Conference on Nutrition was held in Rome, 1–3 December 1992, to discuss ways to eradicate hunger and malnutrition.
- The World Food Summit (WFS) was held in Rome, 13–17 November 1996. At the Summit, leaders of 185 participating countries agreed to 'pledge our political will and our common and national commitment to achieving food security for all and to an ongoing effort to eradicate hunger in all countries, with an immediate view to reducing the number of undernourished people to half their present level no later than 2015'.

- On 8 September 2000, following a three-day Millennium Summit of world leaders at the headquarters of the United Nations, the General Assembly adopted the Millennium Declaration. These leaders committed their nations to a new global partnership to reduce extreme poverty and set out a series of time-bound targets – with a deadline of 2015 – that have become known as the Millennium Development Goals (MDG). One of the three targets of MDG1 was to halve the proportion of individuals suffering from hunger in the period between 1990 and 2015.
- During 1–13 June 2002 the FAO held a world meeting in Rome, 'World Food Summit: Five Years Later', to track progress made since the summit of 1996 and consider ways to accelerate these efforts. Data at the time showed that the fall in the number of undernourished people in the world was well below the yearly target.
- The World Summit on Food Security took place in Rome, between 16 and 18 November 2009. Participating countries unanimously adopted a declaration pledging renewed commitment to eradicate hunger from the Earth at the earliest possible date.

10.2 Collaboration and coordination: major institutions

Globally and at the regional level, some organisations are entrusted to help in coordinating or assisting the balance of food demand and supply.

10.2.1 At the global level

The Food and Agriculture Organization (FAO)

The FAO is a specialised agency of the United Nations that leads international efforts to defeat hunger (FAO 2018). It was formed on 16 October 1945 in Quebec City, Canada. Washington, DC was designated as temporary FAO headquarters.

Following the fifth session of the General Conference in 1949, Member States decided to move the offices of the FAO to Rome. Two ships, Saturnia and Vulcania, set sail from Washington in the early spring of 1951 with 76 families on board.

After the FAO moved to Rome, the assets and mandate of the International Institute of Agriculture (IIA) were handed over to the FAO. IIA was founded in Rome in 1905 with the intent of creating a clearinghouse for the collection of agricultural statistics.

The FAO's goal is to achieve food security for all and make sure that people have regular access to enough high-quality food to lead active, healthy lives.

Serving both developed and developing countries, the FAO acts as a neutral forum where all nations meet as equals for negotiations and policy debate and development. It is a useful source of knowledge and information, thanks to its maintenance of a large number of databases that are freely available to the public. It has carried out many programs to help developing countries modernise and improve their agriculture, forestry and fisheries practices for improved nutrition and food security.

Since its inception, FAO has played an important role in fighting hunger. Major activities carried out by FAO can be found on its website at: www.fao.org/about/en/.

The World Food Programme (WFP)

The WFP is the food-assistance branch of the United Nations and the world's largest humanitarian organisation addressing hunger and promoting food security. It was first established in 1961 after George McGovern, director of the US Food for Peace Programmes, proposed in 1960 to establish a multilateral food aid program. The WFP was formally established in 1963 by the FAO and the United Nations General Assembly on a three-year experimental basis. In 1965, it was extended to a continuing basis.

The WFP focuses its food assistance on those who cannot produce or obtain enough food for themselves and their families. In particular, it has played a major role in emergency relief around the globe since its inception. Emergencies are described as:

> urgent situations in which there is clear evidence that an event, or series of events, has occurred which causes human suffering or imminently threatens lives or livelihoods, and which the government concerned has not the means to remedy; and it is a demonstrably abnormal event, or series of events, which produces dislocation in the life of a community on an exceptional scale.
>
> (WFP 2018)

Significant emergency relief activities carried out by the WFP over the past decades can be found at www1.wfp.org/history.

Each year, the WFP assists some 80 million people in around 80 countries. Currently, it has about 14,000 staff worldwide, of whom over 90% are based in the countries where the agency provides assistance. It works closely with its two Rome-based sister organisations, the FAO and the IFAD (International Fund for Agricultural Development). It also partners with more than 1,000 national and international NGOs to provide food assistance and tackle the underlying causes of hunger.

The WFP chiefly works on the supply side to help balance the demand and supply of recipient countries. In recent years, while providing food assistance, it has tended to also move to help recipient countries build their own resilience and capacity to supply food to their people – a function that is also integral to some other international bodies such as the FAO.

The International Food Policy Research Institute (IFPRI)

The IFPRI is an international agricultural research centre founded in 1975. It is not directly involved in balancing food demand and supply but helps indirectly through its research work to improve the understanding and formation of national agricultural and food policies. Its mission is to provide research-based policy solutions that sustainably reduce poverty and end hunger and malnutrition (IFPRI 2018).

Based in Washington, DC, the IFPRI has offices in several developing countries, including China, Ethiopia, and India. It also has research staff working in over 50 countries around the world. Most of the research takes place in developing countries in Central America, South America, Africa, and Asia.

Research at the IFPRI focuses on six strategic areas:

- Ensuring sustainable food production.
- Promoting healthy food systems.
- Improving markets and trade.
- Transforming agriculture.
- Building resilience.
- Strengthening institutions and governance.

The Global Food Policy Report is one of its flagship publications. The report offers an overview of food policy developments that have contributed to or hindered progress in reducing hunger and improving nutrition. It reviews what has happened in food policy and why, examines key challenges and opportunities, shares new evidence and knowledge, updates key food policy indicators, and highlights emerging issues. The IFPRI has also produced a Global Hunger Index (GHI) yearly since 2006, measuring the progress and failure of individual countries and regions in the fight against hunger.

The IFPRI is part of a network of international research institutes funded in part by the CGIAR (Consultative Group on International Agricultural Research), which in turn is funded by governments, private businesses and foundations, and the World Bank. CGIAR is a global partnership that unites organisations engaged in research for a food-secured future. The IFPRI is one of the 15 CGIAR research centres.

The World Trade Organization (WTO)

The WTO officially commenced on 1 January 1995. Its predecessor is the General Agreement on Tariffs and Trade (GATT), which commenced in 1948. GATT was established after World War II in the wake of other new multilateral institutions dedicated to international economic cooperation – such as the World Bank and the International Monetary Fund. The WTO is headquartered in Geneva, Switzerland.

The WTO is the international organisation that deals with the global rules of trade between nations. Its main function is to ensure that trade flows as smoothly, predictably, and freely as possible (WTO 2018). The WTO deals with rules concerning the trade of all goods and services, with food trade being part of that. As a result of the international trade institutions maintained by the WTO, food trade has been greatly facilitated between countries. This has helped many countries to balance their food demand and supply through trade.

In addition to the above major international bodies, there are also others that help countries improve their food security. For example, the World Bank provides loans to countries to build their food storage capacities. This helps such countries to smooth out gluts or severe shortages of food supply.

Many international NGOs also play an important role in helping those countries in need of improved access to food. Some important NGOs operating globally include Oxfam, Save the Children, Catholic Relief Services, and World Vision.

10.2.2 At the regional level

The ASEAN Plus Three Emergency Rice Reserve (APTERR)

The APTERR is a major initiative in the east Asian region. The objective of the APTERR is to help the members of ASEAN (Brunei Darussalam, Cambodia, Indonesia, Lao PDR, Malaysia, Myanmar, Philippines, Singapore, Thailand, and Vietnam) plus China, Japan, and South Korea in food emergencies. Its primary function is to provide rice assistance to help member countries to build confidence in dealing with temporary food shortages (APTERR 2018). The APTERR is based on the ASEAN Emergency Rice Reserve (AERR) which was established in 1979. The office of the APTERR is located in Bangkok, Thailand.

The South Asian Association for Regional Cooperation (SAARC) Food Bank

In the south Asian region, states of the SAARC (comprising Afghanistan, Bangladesh, Bhutan, India, the Maldives, Nepal, Pakistan, and Sri Lanka) signed an agreement in 2007 to establish a SAARC Food Bank. The Food Bank is to supplement national efforts to provide food security to the people of the region. It would have a reserve of food grains to be maintained by each member state consisting of either wheat or rice, or a combination of both (SAARC 2018).

The Economic Community of West African States (ECOWAS) Regional Food Security Reserve

The ECOWAS Regional Food Security Reserve is a regional cooperation initiative in the Western African region. The ECOWAS is made up of fifteen member countries – Benin, Burkina Faso, Cabo Verde, Côte d'Ivoire, The Gambia, Ghana, Guinea, Guinea Bissau, Liberia, Mali, Niger, Nigeria, Senegal, Sierra Leone, and Togo (SWAC and OECD 2016).

Adopted in early 2013, this reserve has become an important instrument of regional solidarity. The European Union, among others, provides major financial support for this reserve. Part of the financing is supposed to come from ECOWAS resources. The four major objectives of the Reserve are to:

● Improve crisis response by enhancing capacity and responsiveness at different levels using various lines of defence.
● Promote regional solidarity and reduce dependence on international assistance.
● Promote a storage system specifically targeted for emergency response.
● Reduce price volatility and its impact on producers and consumers.

Following a request from the Nigerian government, in August 2017, the ECOWAS delivered some 1800 tonnes of cereals to help vulnerable populations that were subject to a food crisis in northeast Nigeria. This was the first test case for the Reserve (SWAC 2018).

At the regional level, some organisations like the Asian Development Bank (ADB) also indirectly help balance food demand and supply through providing loans to countries for building food storage facilities or other food production or handling capacities. The ADB also provides funds to support research into policy measures to improve the food security of individual countries in Asia.

10.3 Collaboration and coordination: prospects and challenges

Collaboration and coordination at the international level have played a very important role in combating food insecurity around the globe. Such efforts have made our world a much better place since World War II.

Areas of global cooperation that seem to have been relatively more beneficial to improving global food security include:

● Consultative and cooperative international agricultural research and development.
● Multilateral food aid programs dealing with international food crises.
● Trade institutions more conducive to trade flows under multilateral arrangements.
● Availability of essential data and information on individual countries from databases coordinated and maintained by international bodies.

Such collaboration and coordination should be continued and expanded in the future (Ministry of Foreign Affairs 2013; Page 2013; Bouët and Laborde 2017; Committee on World Food Security 2017; Hogan 2017; ICD 2018). In the meantime, increased efforts are needed to extend such cooperation into emerging or new areas including, for example, joint efforts to lessen the impact of likely climate change on food production and personnel training for food-insecure countries to help them govern better.

At the regional level, cooperation is yet to receive more substantial endorsement. Member countries in the current regional food reserves need to make strong commitments so that member countries can rely upon the reserves when in need. Countries in South America, Africa and Asia that are not yet members of any reserve may embrace such a regional approach to help them deal with food emergencies.

While international collaboration and coordination have helped the human race to improve food security enormously over more than 70 years since World War II, some recent developments in various parts of the globe present cause for concern. Since the mid-2010s, the world has seen worrying rises in populism, nationalism, anti-globalisation sentiment, and trade protectionism. Their rise is of grave concern because they are destructive to international cooperation and can lead to instability at the country, regional, and global levels. Such instability is detrimental to basic food availability and can inflict food insecurity on a wide scale.

Should food security worsen as a result of the rise of such sentiments, the victims will be the ordinary general public. Individuals who support such sentiments are likely to be unaware of the consequences in terms of food security, particularly for those in poor countries.

Given the current prevalence of these ill sentiments, it may take the world some time to curtail their rise. Nonetheless, it is utterly crucial for the public to discard rather than prop up such sentiments. Each of us has an obligation to reject those sentiments; instead, we should make our contributions to foster a more harmonious world.

International cooperation benefits all countries' food security, no matter whether they are food exporting or importing, rich or poor. However, it must be pointed out that there are no grounds for any country to rely on international assistance to manage its food security in the long-term (prolonged food aid may lead to unintended consequences (FAO 2006)). Ultimately, each nation has to develop a food security framework that suits its own peculiar circumstance to help the country achieve resilient and sustainable food security.

Any country can achieve a high level of food security for its citizens. In the next part, we look into the experiences and lessons of some selected countries in managing their food security. We endeavour to discover why some countries have been successful in achieving a high level of food security and why others failed.

Review questions

1. In your view, what are the five most important events of international cooperation since World War I that helped to shape today's collaboration and coordination for better global food security? Why?
2. Using your own words, explain how each of the current major global and regional institutions of collaboration and coordination helps to improve global food security.
3. Do you see any challenges that may derail the efforts of international cooperation for improving global food security? What and in which way?

Discussion questions

1. Having studied this chapter, summarise major approaches the human race has so far used to collaboratively combat global food insecurity (find such approaches both from the chapter and from other sources, e.g., through a Google search).
2. Can you briefly comment on the efficacy of each as identified in Discussion Question 1?
3. How much do you know about the FAO and the WFP? What is your understanding of their performance in helping the human race to fight hunger? Are there any criticisms of their performance?

References

APTERR. (2018), 'What is APTERR', www.apterr.org/about-us/what-is-apterr, accessed 17 March 2018.
Bouët, A. and Laborde, D. (2017), 'Building food security through international trade agreements', www.ifpri.org/blog/building-food-security-through-international-trade-agreements, accessed 4 December 2018.
Committee on World Food Security. (2017), 'Global strategic framework for food security & nutrition (GSF), Section 5: Uniting and organizing to fight hunger', www.fao.org/cfs/home/products/onlinegsf/5/en/, accessed 4 December 2018.
FAO. (2006), 'Food aid for food security?', in *The State of Food and Agriculture 2006*, FAO, Rome, pp. 1–80.
FAO. (2018), 'About FAO', www.fao.org/about/en/, accessed 7 January 2018.
Gibson, M. (2012), *The Feeding of Nations: Redefining Food Security for the 21st Century*, CRC Press, Boca Raton, FL.
Hogan, P. (2017), 'Fighting food insecurity through global cooperation', *EU Commissioner for Agriculture, European Union*, www.openaccessgovernment.org/fighting-food-insecurity-global-cooperation/34748/, accessed 4 December 2018.
ICD (International Cooperation and Development, European Commission). (2018), 'ACP - multi-country cooperation - Food security and nutrition', https://ec.europa.eu/europeaid/regions/african-caribbean-and-pacific-acp-region/acp-multi-country-cooperation/food-security-and_en, accessed 4 December 2018.
IFPRI. (2018), 'About IFPRI', www.ifpri.org/about, accessed 11 January 2018.
Ministry of Foreign Affairs (The Netherlands). (2013), 'Zero hunger, zero malnutrition: New inroads towards food and nutrition security', www.government.nl/documents/leaflets/2014/02/07/zero-hunger-zero-malnutrition, accessed 4 December 2018.
Page, H. (2013), 'Global governance and food security as global public good', https://cic.nyu.edu/sites/default/files/page_global_governance_public_good.pdf, accessed 4 December 2018.
SAARC. (2018), 'Agreement on establishing the SAARC Food Bank', http://saarc-sec.org/digital_library/detail_menu/agreement-on-establishing-the-saarc-food-bank, accessed 11 March 2018.
Shaw, D.J. (2007), *World Food Security: A History since 1945*, Houndsmill, Basingstoke, Palgrave Macmillan, UK.

SWAC. (2018), 'The regional food security reserve is taking shape', www.west-africa-brief. org/content/en/regional-food-security-reserve-taking-shape, accessed 3 December 2018.

SWAC and OECD (Sahel and West Africa Club; Organisation for Economic Co-operation and Development). (2016), 'Maps & Facts, No. 41', www.oecd.org/swac/maps/41-regional-food-security-reserve.pdf, accessed 3 December 2018.

WFP. (2018), 'Emergency relief', www1.wfp.org/emergency-relief, accessed 9 January 2018.

WTO. (2018), 'The WTO', www.wto.org/english/thewto_e/thewto_e.htm, accessed 15 January 2018.

Further reading

Gibson, M. (2012), *The Feeding of Nations: Redefining Food Security for the 21st Century*, CRC Press, Boca Raton, FL. Gibson offers his examination of how the aspiration of global food security has evolved and unfolded.

Shaw, D.J. (2007), *World Food Security: A History since 1945*, Houndsmill, Basingstoke, Palgrave Macmillan, UK. This is a comprehensive volume that surveys international organisations' attempts to develop world food policies from the 1930s through to the early 21st century within the framework of evolving development paradigms.

Part 5

Quest for food security

Country experiences

Contents

11 Country cases: low and medium level of food security

12 Country cases: high level of food security

13 Why countries' food security levels differ

At the national level, the status of food security varies enormously. For example, the current proportion of undernourished people in North Korea and Zimbabwe is over 40%. The proportion is about 15% in India. Some other countries, such as Japan, Singapore, and the Netherlands, have done exceptionally well in improving their food security, with the proportion of undernourished people being less than 5%.

In this part, we look into how some countries have managed to balance their food demand and supply to improve their food security. When selecting countries, consideration has been given to their population, resource endowment, income levels, and geographical locations. Consequently, China, Fiji, India, North Korea, Venezuela, and Zimbabwe are selected to represent countries with low or medium levels of food security. Israel, Japan, the Netherlands, Singapore, and South Korea represent countries with a high level of food security. It is hoped that the examination of such diverse countries will reveal valuable lessons and experiences that may help improve future food security elsewhere.

As was made clear earlier, food availability is the most important dimension of food security. The FAO also positions food availability as the first indicator in the first dimension of its suite of food security indicators (Table 1.1 in Chapter 1). In our discussion, emphasis will be given to the approaches used by national governments to balance their food demand and supply to ensure adequate food availability.

It is again noted that, while we emphasise the importance of food availability, this by no means implies other dimensions are not also very important. Indeed, when we examine country experiences, we will make references to all five dimensions of food security, as shown in Section 1.2, and the suite of food security indicators adopted by the FAO, as shown in Table 1.1.

A similar point needs to be made about energy, protein, and fats and various micro nutrients. For many food-insecure countries, energy supply is fundamentally important. Without an adequate intake of dietary energy, it is hardly possible that the intake of other nutrients can be adequate. It is generally the case that only after an adequate energy intake is achieved will people devote more attention to securing other nutrients.

In this part, we first examine food security practices in countries with low or medium levels of food security in Chapter 11 and those with a high level of food security in Chapter 12. In Chapter 13, we compare these countries' food security practices and examine why their food security levels differ.

We will chiefly use the FAO's 'average dietary energy supply adequacy' (ADESA) in our discussion. This indicator is adequate to show to what extent a country has balanced its food demand and supply at the national level.

Chapter 11

Country cases

Low and medium level of food security

Summary

In this chapter, we examine food security practices in countries where the levels of food security are low or medium. Countries included in the examination are, in the following order, China, Fiji, India, North Korea, Venezuela, and Zimbabwe.

After studying this chapter, you should be able to:
- Form your own judgement about the status of food security in each of the countries examined.
- List and discuss major forces that are responsible for shaping each of the countries' current food security.
- Share your view on the most important issue each of the countries needs to deal with in order to make notable improvements to their current food security.

11.1 China

China, officially the People's Republic of China (PRC), is a country in East Asia and the world's most populous country. It has a population of around 1.4 billion. The total land area is approximately 9.6 million km², the third-largest country by area in the world.

Over China's long history, food shortage and famine were common. It was referred to as the land of famine (Mallory 1926; Becker 1996, pp. 9–23). In the first half of the 20th century, the country suffered from frequent wars: civil wars and wars with foreigners. In 1949, the civil war came to an end with the Communist Party of China (CPC) defeating the Kuomintang (KMT). The CPC established the People's Republic of China in 1949.

After years of wars, food was in short supply all over the country and many people were starving. Grain was the major type of food and the supply of non-grain food was minimal. While the supply was very low, some merchants hoarded grain for profit. Various measures were used by the new government, including force, to boost food supply, but with limited success. However, population growth was recovering and fast. In late 1953, the government introduced a 'unified grain procurement and sale system'.

This unified system was to procure grains from farmers and sell it to consumers through ration (the ration varied according to age, sex, and labour strength). The state grain agencies were the sole buyers and sellers in the market. A compulsory procurement quota and a government-set procurement price were two major instruments in this system. Under this scheme, a grain procurement quota was assigned to each individual farm household with surplus grain. Surplus grain is the quantity left over after a farmer retains grain for home consumption, seed, and feed according to standards set by the local governments, and after the farmer pays agricultural tax. The quota generally accounted for 80–90% of the surplus amount (Zhao and Qi 1988, p. 75).

The imposed quota with government-set prices which were often low did not stimulate food output. Making things worse, very soon, various politically-motivated campaigns followed, one after another (Zhou 2017, pp. 38–66). A brief account of the endless campaigns follows.

During 1953–1957, farmers were initially persuaded and then forced to join agricultural cooperatives. By the end of 1957, the majority of the farmers had surrendered their land, which they had just received during the land reform campaign of 1949–1952, to the state. In 1957, an 'anti-rightists campaign' cruelly suppressed many intellectuals and others who were keen to contribute to the country's reconstruction. This campaign virtually shut any voices that criticised or commented on the doings of the new government.

In 1958, farmers were coerced to join the highly collectivised people's communes. In the same year, the Great Leap Forward campaign was launched. It was based on the political whim of Mao Zedong, the leader of the Communist Party of China. The harvest of 1958 was only marginally higher than that of 1957 (but the input use in 1958 was much higher). Population, however, had increased rapidly since 1951 at an annual rate of 2% or higher. Food shortages started to emerge in late 1958, marking the beginning of the long-lasting large-scale famine (1958–1962).

In the next two years, grain output slid by huge margins, from 200 mt in 1958 to 170 mt in 1959 and then to 143 mt in 1960. With limited availability of other foods, food availability was dire. Instead of importing grains to combat the supply shortage, the government exported 4.16 mt of grains in 1959 and 2.65 mt in 1960. Famine became widespread and lasted till mid-1962. Some 37 million people died of hunger (Ding 1996; Dikötter 2010).

Starting from 1960, various measures were used to increase grain output. They include a price increase for grains procured under the unified purchase, higher prices to farmers who sold grains to the government above their quota, providing farmers with coupons to buy industrial goods as incentives if they sold grains to the government, and reopening rural fairs and allowing farmers to sell grains in the market (Zhao and Qi 1988). In the meantime, each year, grain was imported in the order of 4–5 mt.

Nonetheless, the supply was still seriously short due to the slow recovery of grain output. By 1965, grain output grew to 195 mt and was still below the 1958 level. Population levels, however, had recovered very rapidly since 1962 when the famine ended, growing at 2.7–3.3% per annum during 1962 and 1965. By 1966, grain output surpassed the 1958 level, reaching 214 mt. In this year, Mao launched the Cultural Revolution, another nation-wide political campaign that lasted ten years till 1976.

During the Cultural Revolution, grain output increased slowly while the population increased fast. There were grain imports but the quantity was small and erratic, between 0.5 mt and 4.5 mt. Consequently, food availability remained very poor with little improvement (per capita grain: 292 kg in 1966; 306 kg in 1976). Data from FAO show that the average per capita daily energy intake was 1426 kcal in 1961 and 1894 kcal in 1976, way below the average dietary energy requirement (ADER) for the Chinese, being 2350 kcal/capita/day.

Mao died in 1976 and the Cultural Revolution came to an end in the same year. The government became less stringent in controlling what farmers could do. Farmers tried various methods to link their individual efforts more closely to the rewards they got. These trials generated the momentum to reverse highly collectivised farming back to household-based farming – leading to nationwide adoption of the widely acclaimed 'household production responsibility system'.

The impact of reversion back to household-based operations on farmers' enthusiasm to work the land harder and smarter was enormous. It significantly boosted China's grain output. By 1984, grain had become abundant in the country. Per capita grain availability increased rapidly, reaching 397 kg per capita, a record.

In 1985, the procurement side of the 'unified grain procurement and sale system,' which had been in place since 1953, was abolished and replaced with a contractual grain procurement system. This new approach reduced incentives for farmers who produced and sold more grains to the government and led to an overall drop in grain output, from 407 mt in 1984 to 379 mt in 1985 (Carter and Zhong 1988; Zhou 1997). Various modifications were subsequently made to the contractual system over the following years. By 1993, grain procurement through contracts was abandoned in many parts of the country. Also in 1993, the 'unified grain sale system' was abolished.

From 1994 onwards, China moved to a market approach for domestic grain trade, with some occasional administrative interventions. Government grain procurement (for reserve purposes) was also done at market prices. Starting in 1997, guaranteed procurement of grains at state-set floor prices was introduced for major cereals (such as rice, wheat, and maize) in order to encourage farmers to stay in grain production while still receiving a reasonable remuneration. In 1998, grain harvest was at a record high of 512 mt. Grain was easily available in the market at a stable price. In the meantime, the output of non-grain foods also increased.

Key indicators of food security for China in Table 11.1 show that its improvements in food security in the past three decades have been impressive. The supply of dietary energy, protein, and fat has become more than adequate. By 2015, it had met both the international hunger reduction targets. For the WFS (World Food Summit) goal, China reduced the number of people undernourished from 289 million in 1990–1992 to 133.8 million in 2014–2016, a reduction of 53.7%, being 3.7% over the target. For the MDG1 goal (the Millennium Development Goals), the reduction was 60.9%, again over the target (from 23.9% in 1990–1992 to 9.3% in 2014–2016) (FAO, IFAD, and WFP 2015, p. 46). The rates of wasting,

Table 11.1 Key indicators of food security in China (five-year average)

	1991–1995	1996–2000	2001–2005	2006–2010	2011–2015
Dietary energy supply (DES) (kcal/capita/day)	2,561	2,760	2,847	2,967	3,114
Average dietary energy requirement (ADER) (kcal/capita/day)	2,345	2,391	2,439	2,459	2,451
Average dietary energy supply adequacy (ADESA) (%)	109.2	115.2	116.8	120.6	127.0
Average protein supply (g/capita/day)	70.2	80.4	85.2	91.2	na
Average fat supply (g/capita/day)	60.0	70.8	79.4	89.4	na
Prevalence of undernourishment (%)	22.8	17.1	15.8	14.0	10.4
Number of people undernourished (millions)	281.5	221.6	211.3	192.0	147.6
Political stability and absence of violence (index)	na	–0.3	–0.4	–0.5	–0.6
Domestic food price volatility (index)	na	na	10.3	11.6	9.5
Percentage of children under five years of age affected by wasting (%)	4.1	3.7	2.8	3.0	2.3
Percentage of children under five years of age who are stunted (%)	35.2	25.5	19.8	12.7	9.4
Percentage of children under five years of age who are underweight (%)	13.4	8.8	7.1	4.7	3.4
GDP per capita (in PPP) (constant 2011 international $)	1,990	3,093	4,440	7,219	10,632

kcal = kilocalorie, g = gram, GDP = gross domestic product, PPP = purchasing power parity, na = not available.
Source: based on FAO (2019).

stunting, and being underweight for children under five years of age have also dropped significantly (Table 11.1).

The above discussion shows that before the 1980s, Chinese people were starving. Since the early 1980s, food available to the Chinese people has improved, and today, food is abundant. One would wonder why the Chinese people did not have enough food to eat before the 1980s, when China had less people but relatively more natural resources, and why they have plenty to eat today, when there are more people but fewer resources. To fully answer these questions is complex but the most influential factors responsible for China's lack of food security before the 1980s include:

● **Forced collectivisation:** This is one of the major factors responsible for China's food shortage before the 1980s. Farmers had no incentives to work hard under such arrangements.
● **Totalitarian system:** By 1958, through various campaigns, the new government had become a totalitarian regime. The totalitarian government monopolised all production

resources, controlling the production, circulation, and distribution of all goods and services, leading to severe shortages in the supply of virtually all essential goods and services and, of course, foods (Yang 2008, pp. 1066–1067).

- **Lack of error-correcting mechanisms:** Under the totalitarian regime, there was no mechanism by which the government could be informed of the consequences of ill-perceived policies and many wrong or unsuitable policies remained unchecked, causing serious damage to agricultural production.
- **Government officials not accountable to the people:** In China, government officials were appointed by their superiors and not elected by the citizens. They were not held accountable to the citizens.
- **Lack of economic management capabilities:** Many officials in the new government were from a group of military generals or officers from the People's Liberation Army. They may have been good at fighting battles but had very little knowledge of and expertise on how to manage a country's economy, let alone a large one like China's.

Major factors that led to the improvement in China's food security include:

- **Reverting back to household-based farming:** This was most fundamental to, and instrumental in, bringing about improvements in China's food security in the 1980s.
- **Reintroducing the market mechanism into the economy:** Highly centralised planning is ineffective and inefficient. Allowing the market to coordinate food demand and supply has helped China enormously in improving its food security.
- **Reopening the doors of the country:** The benefits of the open-door policy have been multiple, including food trade. Food trade has enabled China to secure food from more sources and secure diverse foods to meet its growing demand for food.
- **Government emphasis on ensuring food supply:** Since the 1980s, China's government has paid increasing attention to ensuring that an adequate amount of food is available to the country's huge population.
- **Policy efforts for improved food security:** Efforts that have contributed to improving food security since the early 1980s include:
  - Enhancing China's domestic food production.
  - Facilitating food market development and food processing.
  - Increasing support and subsidy to food production and marketing.
  - Establishing and maintaining grain reserve stocks when more grains became available.
  - Investing to build new or expand existing rural infrastructure such as roads, irrigation facilities, electricity networks, mobile phone coverage, and internet access.
  - Investing in agricultural research and development.
  - Shifting from food subsidy to income subsidy for low-income consumers.
  - Making use of world food markets.

In recent years, the Chinese government has also gradually started developing a longer-term vision for a more secure food supply for the country. This is reflected in the conceptualisation of three major documents aimed at securing food supply: (1) the first medium- and long-term national grain security plan (2008–2020) issued in 2008; (2) a national plan for beef and lamb production (2013–2020) developed in 2013; and (3) the attempt in 2015 to develop a 'Grains Act' – the first in China's history to ensure the provision of staple food to its citizens through legislation (still in draft and not yet legislated).

Currently, China's food availability is comfortable. There has been improvement in its level of food security. Its GFSI (Global Food Security Index) by the EIU (The Economist

Intelligence Unit) has steadily increased from 62.5 in 2012 (first available) to 65.1 in 2018. Its GHI (Global Hunger Index) by the IFPRI (International Food Policy Research Institute) has declined from 25.1 (hunger is serious) in 1990 to 7.6 (hunger is low) in 2018.

There are, however, weaknesses in some dimensions of its food security:

- The widespread prevalence of unsafe and low quality foods.
- Serious environmental pollution and degradation, which undermine food production sustainability.
- Large and increasing income inequalities, which affect social stability.

China has to overcome these challenges in order to further improve its food security. In addition, it also needs to deal with some other challenges and obstacles:

- Reducing and avoiding food wastage – the wastage in China is enormous between post-harvest and prior to consumption and at the consumption stage.
- Carrying out innovative reforms to institutions – most fundamentally, to ensure governments and their officials at various levels are accountable to the people under their jurisdiction.

The current comfortable food availability status provides no grounds for complacency concerning China's food security in the years to come. How China's food security will evolve is yet to be seen and deserves close attention. In addition to the above remaining and emerging challenges, which are not easy to overcome, the major cause of concern is the recent political developments. Following Mao's death in 1976, China gradually moved away from totalitarianism to authoritarianism. However, signs since the mid-2010s have shown that the country is now moving backwards to totalitarianism. This is most concerning as the totalitarianism made the catastrophic famine of 1958–1962 possible.

11.2 Fiji

Fiji, officially the Republic of Fiji, is an island country in Melanesia in the South Pacific Ocean. It is an archipelago of more than 330 islands, of which 110 are permanently inhabited, and more than 500 islets, amounting to a total land area of about 18,300 km². The two major islands, Viti Levu and Vanua Levu, account for 87% of the total population of 898,760 in 2016. The country's capital of Suva is on Viti Levu. About three quarters of Fijians live on Viti Levu's coasts.

Europeans started to visit Fiji from the 17th century. The British established the Colony of Fiji in 1874. It remained as a colony until 1970, when the British granted Fiji independence, as the Dominion of Fiji. Endowed with forest, mineral, and fish resources, Fiji experienced a period of rapid growth in the 1960s and 1970s. It is one of the better developed of the Pacific Island economies although it still has a large subsistence sector.

In the 1980s, the economy stagnated. Two military coups occurred in 1987 which interrupted democratic rules. The second 1987 coup saw both the Fijian monarchy and the Governor General replaced by a non-executive president and the name of the country changed from the Dominion of Fiji to the Republic of Fiji. The political turmoil in the 1980s, the 1990s, and the 2000s had severe impacts on the economy, resulting in frequent negative growth. Since 2010, the economy has been growing, though with some volatility (World Bank 2019).

In Fiji, hunger of the type seen in some Asian and African countries is uncommon although some low-income people do sometimes have less secure access to food. Table 11.2 shows that the prevalence of undernourishment has been typically low, below 5% since 2001. At the national level, the intake of all three macro nutrients is above the RDI (recommended daily intake).

Traditionally, the Fijians consume what they grow and catch on the land and in the water. The all-year-round warm climate in Fiji, coupled with other natural resource endowment, helps food production. Over the past several decades, however, the consumption of non-traditional foods and processed foods has become popular among the Fijians. Such foods are often imported. Limited foreign exchange is used to finance such imports. The consumption of such foods has been blamed for the increasing levels of food and nutrition related health problems among the local population, such as obesity, heart disease, and diabetes, which rarely existed in the past.

Overall, Fiji's food security status is commendable. The GFSI by the EIU does not include Fiji. However, the GHI by the IFPRI clearly shows that the level of hunger is very low – under 10% since 2000 (Figure 11.1 (IFPRI 2018)). Indeed, since the beginning of the 21st century, the share of the population that is undernourished in Fiji has been below 5%, an outcome that is often achieved mainly by developed economies.

Table 11.2 Key indicators of food security in Fiji (five-year average)

	1991–1995	1996–2000	2001–2005	2006–2010	2011–2015
Dietary energy supply (DES) (kcal/capita/day)	2,774	2,834	2,910	2,930	2,929
Average dietary energy requirement (ADER) (kcal/capita/day)	2,285	2,305	2,342	2,366	2,371
Average dietary energy supply adequacy (ADESA) (%)	121	123	124	124	124
Average protein supply (g/capita/day)	70	71	75	75	na
Average fat supply (g/capita/day)	100	98	96	94	na
Prevalence of undernourishment (%)	5.8	5.2	<5.0	<5.0	<5.0
Number of people undernourished (millions)	<0.1	<0.1	na	na	na
Political stability and absence of violence (index)	na	0.76	0.35	0.03	-0.07
Domestic food price volatility (index)	na	na	12.0	12.1	10.7
Percentage of children under five years of age affected by wasting (%)	9.80	na	6.30	na	na
Percentage of children under five years of age who are stunted (%)	4.30	na	7.50	na	na
Percentage of children under five years of age who are underweight (%)	6.90	na	5.30	na	na
GDP per capita (in PPP) (constant 2011 international $)	5,745	6,231	6,738	7,128	7,282

kcal = kilocalorie, g = gram, GDP = gross domestic product, PPP = purchasing power parity, na = not available.
Source: based on FAO (2019).

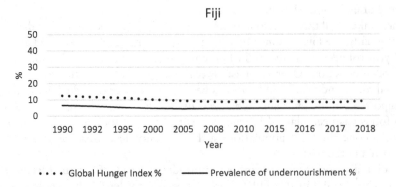

Figure 11.1 GHI and prevalence of undernourishment in Fiji.

GHI: Global Hunger Index, ranks countries on a 100-point scale. Hunger is low if the HGI ≤ 9.9; moderate if between 10.0–19.9; serious if between 20.0–34.9; alarming if between 35.0–49.9 and extremely alarming if ≥ 50. Prevalence of undernourishment: the share of the population that is undernourished (that is, whose caloric intake is insufficient).

Source: based on IFPRI GHI publications from 2015 to 2018.

To further improve Fiji's food security, there are some existing and emerging issues to which attention is warranted (Foraete 2001; Sharma 2006; FAO 2012):

- Inadequate domestic food production and productivity to meet food security and market demands for quality, consistency, and market competitiveness.
- Lack of consistent supplies of good quality fruit and vegetables to meet export market demands and opportunities, which is a major foreign currency earner for the imports of other foods for the country's food security.
- Rapidly rising levels of food and nutrition related non communicable diseases, which impact negatively on health system, families and the national economy.
- Inadequate/inefficient agricultural extension services and the lack of technologies responsive to local conditions.
- Lack of sustainable management for forest and fisheries resources.
- High rates of soil erosion and soil degradation.
- More importantly, weak policy analysis, formulation and coordination capacity in the country.

Corruption in Fiji also makes it hard for the country to achieve a higher level of food security. Similar to other Pacific Island Countries, political corruption and nepotism stand out as the main corruption risks in Fiji. To curtail corruption, there is a strong need to systematically strengthen the country's democratic institutions, increase civil society space, and enable the existence of opponents and free media.

Fiji is vulnerable to the threat posed by natural disasters. Extreme natural disasters cause problems for short-term food access in affected areas. They also affect food production, thus weakening food availability for a longer time. In this regard, cooperation with nations in the Pacific Islands to combat extreme conditions is most desirable. Indeed, other small island nations in the Pacific face similar threats (FAO 2012). The FAO and WFP (World Food Programme) have already started to assist Fiji and other island nations in the region with potential regional initiatives. In early 2017, the first-ever regional meeting on food security in disaster-prone Pacific Islands was held in Fiji (WFP 2017). The Australian Government has also provided assistance to support collaborative efforts for better food security in this region (Commonwealth of Australia 2011).

11.3 India

India, officially the Republic of India, is a country in South Asia. By total land area, it is the seventh largest country. It has a population of over 1.3 billion. The population is fast catching up with China's and is forecast to exceed China's in less than 10 years. Following market-based economic reforms in 1991, India is now one of the fastest-growing major economies. India is a federal republic governed under a parliamentary system.

The country was under the British colonial rule for nearly two centuries and gained independence in August 1947. In its history, famine was frequent. Prior to independence, food was often scarce. Grains were imported to remedy the shortages. Controls and interventions, such as price controls, grain procurement, and distribution through rations, were used in managing the country's food demand and supply.

Immediately after independence, the Government of India (GOI) started searching for measures to better manage the country's food demand and supply. From 1947 till the late 1970s, there were many policy changes and policy initiatives. The list below highlights some major ones.

- September 1947, the GOI introduced food control.
- December 1947, food controls were lifted.
- 1948, food controls were reintroduced.
- September 1948, as part of the re-control, relief-quota shops or fair price shops were introduced.
- In 1950, the GOI opted for a policy that was a combination of partial procurement, some statutory rationing, some informal rationing, and some degree of free market. This policy has been followed ever since, with some adjustments over time, depending on the demand and supply situations.
- 1955, many control measures were removed.
- 1957, a Foodgrains Enquiry Committee advised the GOI that the solution to the food problem lay somewhere between complete free trade and full control (GOI 1957). Hence, after about four years of decontrol (1953–1957), various measures of control were again introduced.
- During 1958–1964, crop output fluctuated and so did the level of control. Lower domestic production led to increased grain imports.
- 1965, two new agencies were established: the Food Corporation of India (FCI) and the Agricultural Prices Commission (APC, renamed as the Commission for Agricultural Costs and Prices, CACP, in 1985).
- 1967, the 'Green Revolution' began in India. It spread over the period from1967/68 to 1977/1978 and it significantly boosted India's food output.
- 1968, the name of the 'fair price shop' scheme was changed to the 'Public Distribution System' (PDS).
- 1971, for the first time, the dream of building up a buffer stock of targeted quantity was realised.
- 1973, the poor crop of 1971/1972 led to increased government procurement and later more market controls. Private traders were removed from the wholesale grain trade and only public agents would be engaged. The retailers were allowed to buy directly from producers.
- 1975, modifications were made to food controls: in addition to the procurement of wheat by public agencies, wholesalers, both private and cooperative societies, were allowed to operate under a system of licensing and control; movement of wheat within a state was allowed, but not across states.

- 1976, a production bonus scheme was used as an incentive to those states contributing a significant part of their surplus grain to the central government.
- 1977–1978, the good harvests of 1975–1976 resulted in significant improvements in government stocks with low imports. In 1977, the government encouraged the dispatch of grains from its stocks through the PDS and other possible outlets. In October 1978, all restrictions on grain movements via private traders were removed.

Hence, before 1978, policy measures used by the GOI to manage food supply and demand underwent many changes. These changes were sometimes significant ones, but more commonly were frequent 'switch-ons' or 'switch-offs' of, or modifications to, control measures.

Since 1978, policies have been relatively stable and the GOI was able to cope with occasional sharp drops in production (e.g., 1979/1980, 1986/1987 and 1987/1988) without introducing significant changes to its policies. In dealing with such sharp drops, buffer stocks played an important role. In addition, the assurance of a reasonably remunerative return to grain producers has been pivotal in securing a stable domestic food supply from farmers. The economic reforms started in mid-1991, according to the government, have further improved 'the relative profitability of agriculture as compared to industry' (GOI 1995, p. 12, 83).

While procurement prices were increased year by year from the early 1970s to ensure farmers a remunerative return, the prices at which the PDS dispatched the grains could not be raised correspondingly. This has led to increasing costs for the GOI to maintain the PDS. Despite periodical price revisions, prices were generally kept below costs in order to keep grains within the reach of vulnerable sections of society. The difference between the selling price and the cost is borne by central government by way of a food subsidy, which has increased enormously since the early 1970s. Two major factors that contributed to the increase in subsidy are (1) the high post-procurement cost due to low distribution efficiency or a surge in buffer stocks or both, and (2) leakages of grains into the open market by some corrupt PDS operators (Ahluwalia 1993; Pal, Bahl and Mruthyunjaya 1993).

Despite the lack of efficiency in managing its grain economy, India's improvement in food availability in the past three decades has been notable. During the past three decades, there have been no major food-related crises. In the late 1980s/early 1990s, India had managed to achieve adequacy in food calories at the national level (i.e., ADESA>100%; Table 11.3). India has also achieved self-sufficiency in food grains since the 1990s. Its self-sufficiency ratio has been over 100%. Indeed, India was a net food exporter in most of the recent years.

However, due to the vast poverty and large income inequalities, the improvement in ADESA and the achievement of self-sufficiency only made a limited contribution to improving the country's overall food security and especially the food security of those who are in desperate need. Consequently, the prevalence of undernourishment in India is still very high.

In fact, India has been unable to reduce the level of undernourishment to meet the two international hunger reduction targets. For the WFS goal, India only managed to reduce the number of people undernourished from 210.1 million in 1990–1992 to 194.6 million in 2014–2016, a reduction of a mere 7.4%. For the MDG1 goal, the reduction is 36% and is also short of the target (from 23.7% in 1990–1992 to 15.2% in 2014–2016) (FAO, IFAD, WFP 2015, p. 46).

The GFSI and GHI also suggest that India's current food security level is less satisfactory. Its GFSI in 2018 was 50.1, 15 points below China's (65.1). Its GHI, though declined over

Table 11.3 Key indicators of food security in India

	1991–1995	1996–2000	2001–2005	2006–2010	2011–2015
Dietary energy supply (DES) (kcal/capita/day)	2,298	2,366	2,292	2,400	2,455
Average dietary energy requirement (ADER) (kcal/capita/day)	2,176	2,200	2,226	2,252	2,272
Average dietary energy supply adequacy (ADESA) (%)	105.6	107.4	103.0	106.6	108.0
Average protein supply (g/capita/day)	55.8	56.4	54.8	57.8	na
Average fat supply (g/capita/day)	41.0	45.8	45.8	50.6	na
Prevalence of undernourishment (%)	22.4	18.4	19.6	17.7	15.4
Number of people undernourished (millions)	206.0	184.9	215.1	207.5	192.5
Political stability and absence of violence (index)	na	−1.0	−1.2	−1.1	−1.2
Domestic food price volatility (index)	na	na	5.1	6.6	5.3
Percentage of children under five years of age affected by wasting (%)	21.1	19.6	na	20.0	na
Percentage of children under five years of age who are stunted (%)	57.1	49.8	na	46.3	na
Percentage of children under five years of age who are underweight (%)	50.7	42.8	na	41.9	na
GDP per capita (in PPP) (constant 2011 international $)	1,838	2,263	2,748	3,732	4,886

kcal = kilocalorie, g = gram, GDP = gross domestic product, PPP = purchasing power parity, na = not available.
Source: based on FAO (2019).

years, is still very high; it dropped from 48.1 (hunger is alarming) in 1990 to 31.1 (hunger is serious) in 2018.

The major causes for the slow improvement in food security are:

● **Slow production but high population growth.** After independence, India's health services improved which in turn boosted population growth; however, food production failed to keep pace. Population growth has slowed down since the early 1980s but is still above 1% per annum (2.35% in 1982 and 1.24% in 2015).
● **Insufficient investment in agriculture.** Slow growth in food production was largely due to inadequate investment in agricultural R&D, extension and education, irrigation, and general rural infrastructure.
● **Slow progress in curtailing poverty.** The lack of economic growth before the 1990s and the lack of political will and action to effectively reduce poverty deprived many of the poor of economic access to food.
● **Slow in reforming policies.** Since the start of the economic reforms in the early 1990s, there have been many changes in society; notably, rising consumer incomes and the wide

adoption of information technologies. However, innovative food policies are yet to emerge in response to such changes to more effectively manage the country's food economy; such as moving to an income subsidy to the needy and reducing government intervention in grain markets.

- **Ineffective government operations:** Being a democratic country, India is expected to improve food security. Inefficient bureaucracy has resulted in difficulties in implementing many well-intended government policies.
- **Ineffective judicial systems:** Corruption in general and rent-seeking and corruption in the PDS in particular have hindered the country's ability to achieve a higher level of food security. The lack of efficiency in the country's judicial systems in dealing with such problems in a timely manner makes it difficult to reduce them.

Some forces have acted to help improve food availability. One such force is the government price support and buffer stock schemes. India's agricultural markets are undeveloped and imperfect. Bumper harvests or large market arrivals can easily result in market price collapse. Price support provides an assurance to encourage farmers. The maintenance of a buffer stock helps absorb any supply glut. Another force is the provision of input subsidies. The use of some major inputs such as fertilisers, electricity, and irrigation water by farmers has been subsidised. It must be pointed out, however, while the price support and input subsidy may help improve food availability in the short run, such measures are not necessarily helpful in the long run. This has been demonstrated in Chapter 9.

In recent years, India's per capita income has been rising following economic reforms. Improved disposable income together with accelerated urbanisation have resulted in changes in food consumption away from food grains towards more diverse foods. Future demand for more food and more diverse food is likely to be sizeable, considering the still fast-growing population (from 1.31 b in 2015 to 1.45 b or even more by 2030).

Major challenges in India's quest for future food security are:

- Large and still fast-growing population.
- Limited and declining quantity of food-producing resources with quality deteriorating.
- High levels of interventions in the food market and low efficiency in government operations of the PDS.
- Emerging and growing food safety problems.
- Still widespread poverty.

To deal with these and other emerging challenges, attention needs to be given to the following areas:

- Control population growth to be compatible with resource availability and sustainability.
- Increase investment in agriculture in general and in R&D, irrigation, and rural infrastructure in particular.
- Protect and rehabilitate the environment and natural resources for sustainable food production.
- Reduce government intervention in the management of the country's food security and move towards more use of private systems.
- Enhance the efficacy of the country's judicial systems to curtail corruption in general and rent-seeking and corruption in the PDS in particular.
- Reduce absolute poverty and narrow income inequalities.
- Safeguard the safety and quality of food for the public.
- Innovate new ways to handle 'old problems' in response to changing circumstances.

In 2013, the GOI promulgated the 'National Food Security Act' with a view to ensuring food security for the vast Indian population through legal frameworks. This is a great move towards protecting citizens' right to food security. Putting the Act into operation and evaluating implementation effectiveness is essential.

11.4 North Korea

North Korea (officially the Democratic People's Republic of Korea) and South Korea (the Republic of Korea) used to be the same country: Korea. Korea is a region in East Asia. In 1945, Korea gained its independence from Japanese colonial rule and was divided into two countries soon after. The 38th Parallel separated the two countries – North Korea (the northern part of the Korean Peninsula) and South Korea (the southern half of the Korean Peninsula). US Forces were stationed in South Korea, while Soviet Armed Forces were stationed in North Korea.

In 1950, the Korean War began, and a fierce battle continued for three years. On 27 July 1953, the two Koreas signed an armistice to make a new border with the Military Demarcation Line (MDL). The massively fortified strip (the Korean Demilitarised Zone) bisects the Korean peninsula and has been one of the world's most dangerous potential flash points throughout the Cold War until today. As a result, people in South Korea and North Korea have lived totally different lives under totally different regimes. South Korea chose to be a democratic market-based economy; North Korea was based on a centrally planned economy as a socialist state.

FAO data show that food supply has rarely been adequate at the aggregate level in North Korea. The intake of all the macro nutrients is below requirements. In the case of protein and fat, intake has been only about half of requirements in recent years. The sharp drop in 1991 in all three macro nutrients was followed by a severe famine in the following years, lasting until 1998, in which millions of North Koreans died from starvation or hunger-related illnesses (Song and Kwon 2017). Since the famine, the food situation has improved little and many North Koreans are still suffering from food insecurity (DailyNK 2017; Silberstein 2019).

Since the early 1990s, the prevalence of undernourishment has steadily increased in North Korea, from 27% in 1991–1995 to 42% in 2011–2015 (Table 11.4). During the same period, the number of people undernourished increased from 5.7 million to 10.4 million. Other key food security indicators in Table 11.4 also suggest an overall low level of food security in North Korea. The rates of wasting, stunting, and being underweight for children under five years of age were high in the late 1990s but have shown a sharp decline since the mid-2010s (It is not clear why there is such a big drop given that food has been in short supply in the country).

According to the FAO, North Korea is one of the 38 countries that need food support from other countries (FAO 2014). Among these countries, 29 are located in Africa, five countries including North Korea in Asia, and four in South America. The Assessment Capacities Project (ACAPS) operated by three private international relief organisations (Save the Children International, Action Contre la Faim, and the Norwegian Refugee Council) suggests that 16 million out of 24.6 million North Koreans experience a chronic unstable food supply (ACAPS 2015).

Before the 1990s, North Korea was able to obtain some assistance from various socialist states it was allied with. The collapse of many socialist states, starting from the late 1980s, has made it difficult for North Korea to obtain aid to help with its food supply. As one of the few socialist states refusing to carry out substantial reforms, its overall economy has suffered from lack of growth. Slow economic growth coupled with self-isolation has often resulted in inadequate food supply to its residents.

Table 11.4 Key indicators of food security in North Korea (five-year average)

	1991–1995	1996–2000	2001–2005	2006–2010	2011–2015
Dietary energy supply (DES) (kcal/capita/day)	2,241	2,117	2,172	2,108	2,102
Average dietary energy requirement (ADER) (kcal/capita/day)	2,345	2,344	2,357	2,375	2,395
Average dietary energy supply adequacy (ADESA) (%)	95.6	90.4	92.2	88.8	88.0
Average protein supply (g/capita/day)	67.0	58.6	60.2	56.8	na
Average fat supply (g/capita/day)	39.0	33.4	36.4	34.2	na
Prevalence of undernourishment (%)	26.9	36.9	35.8	39.1	41.8
Number of people undernourished (millions)	5.7	8.3	8.4	9.5	10.4
Political stability and absence of violence (index)	na	–0.5	0.2	0.2	–0.3
Domestic food price volatility (index)	na	na	na	na	na
Percentage of children under five years of age affected by wasting (%)	na	20.8	9.8	5.2	4.0
Percentage of children under five years of age who are stunted (%)	na	63.9	46.3	32.4	27.9
Percentage of children under five years of age who are underweight (%)	na	55.5	21.0	18.8	15.2
GDP per capita (in PPP) (constant 2011 international $)	na	na	na	na	na

kcal = kilocalorie, g = gram, GDP = gross domestic product, PPP = purchasing power parity, na = not available.
Source: based on FAO (2019).

North Korea is not included in the GFSI by the EIU. Available GHI since 1990 shows that the hunger situation in North Korea has been 'serious' or 'alarming' (Figure 11.2 (IFPRI 2018)). The prevalence of undernourishment has been trending upwards. Both the GHI and the undernourishment indicator for 2018 point to worsening food availability in North Korea.

Major causes for North Korea's lack of food supply are as follows:

- **Forced collective farming and lack of economic incentives:** The adoption and continuance of the model of forced collective farming is a major factor responsible for food shortage. Like many other previously socialist states, forced collective farming does not guarantee individual farming rights and is lacking in economic incentives for individuals in production, thus lowering agricultural productivity (Song and Kwon 2017). The collective system needs a major overhaul, but this is unlikely. This will continue to undermine the country's ability to boost its food output.
- **Lack of investment in agriculture, especially in agricultural R&D:** The adoption and subsequent failure of the 'heavy industries first approach', resulted in there being little to spare for investment in agriculture, especially in agricultural R&D. Another reason why

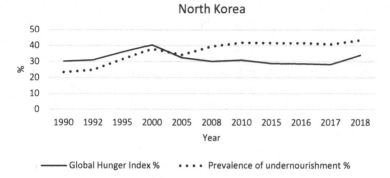

North Korea

——— Global Hunger Index %   • • • • Prevalence of undernourishment %

Figure 11.2 GHI and prevalence of undernourishment in North Korea.
GHI: Global Hunger Index, ranks countries on a 100-point scale. Hunger is low if the HGI ≤ 9.9; moderate if between 10.0–19.9; serious if between 20.0–34.9; alarming if between 35.0–49.9 and extremely alarming if ≥ 50. Prevalence of undernourishment: the share of the population that is undernourished (that is, whose caloric intake is insufficient).
Source: based on IFPRI GHI publications from 2015 to 2018.

North Korea has been short of funds to invest in agriculture is the 'military first' strategy – money has been used on military expenses.

- **Damages to natural resources:** Due to the pressure of producing more food over the past decades, serious damage has been done to natural resources. This affects current food output and, if left unattended for long, may lead to the country falling into a vicious cycle in its attempt to produce more food.
- **Lack of food imports and foreign food aid:** Lack of food from domestic production can be addressed by means of imported food or food aid. The North Korean government did not import adequate amounts of food, due to the lack of foreign currencies, which have been often used for purchasing foreign goods to maintain the lavish lifestyle of the elite and for military equipment to back the political agenda. Food aid to North Korea has also been declining in recent years. Some donors have become less willing to provide aid. The North Korean government has also become less willing to accept aid. For example, in early 2000, North Korea had the opportunity to secure some food aid. Yet, it refused the aid as the government did not want its people to know more about the outside world and raise any questions (Song and Kwon 2017).
- **Central planning and strict control over the economy:** Central planning and strict control over the economy of a nation has rarely proven to be successful. It also negatively affects a country's food security due to the resultant poor economic status. There is no sign that North Korea will move away from this approach.

In the most recent years, there have been attempts to bring about some changes in North Korea, including some relaxation of the control over food production and marketing. Collective farms have been allowed some flexibility in deciding what and how to produce, how to distribute output among team members, and where to sell. These changes, though small, have significantly altered farmers' motives, leading to higher output and increased grain availability in the market (Song and Kwon 2017; Silberstein 2019).

If further rural reforms can be allowed, North Korea's agricultural productivity and grain output can be further increased. If North Korea allows a family-based farming system, food production can be expected to be even higher in view of the experiences of China. This would have a positive impact on food security.

It is noted, however, that the North Korean government still insists on a 'military first' strategy (not people's livelihoods first). This will most likely jeopardise its capacity to produce more food and hence improve the status of its food security for the future due to resource misallocation and other related problems (Silberstein 2017). For example, the lack of a stable supply of essential agricultural inputs such as fertilisers, machinery, and pesticides may make food output expansion very difficult, even if a family-based farming system is allowed (Ah 2019).

Food security cannot be achieved by just increasing the production of grains. It is also essential to increase the availability of diverse foods, enhance accessibility to foods, and provide safe and quality foods. Food security can be better achieved through transparent and market-friendly policies. In this regard, the role of the market cannot be overstated. Recent changes in North Korea have also led to the growth of markets, to which North Koreans have enjoyed access (Silberstein 2019). The North Korean government is still trying to control the market whenever and wherever it can. In reality, it has become increasingly harder for the government to deny the existence and the role of markets. Revitalised markets in North Korea will have a positive impact on its food security.

There are uncertainties surrounding North Korea's future food supply and food security. It is hard to anticipate North Korea's longer-term food security status due to its political institutions, which can be responsible for either social stability or instability. For North Korea to achieve a stable food supply and thus enhanced long-term food security, institutional reforms to its political arrangements are necessary. The political arrangements need to be able to foster a government that places people's livelihoods first, is accountable to the people, has transparent policies, and has efficient administration.

11.5 Venezuela

Venezuela, officially the Bolivarian Republic of Venezuela, is a country on the northern coast of South America, consisting of a continental landmass and a large number of small islands and islets in the Caribbean Sea. It is well endowed with natural resources. It has rich oil reserves, initially discovered in the early 20th century. Today, Venezuela has the world's largest known oil reserves. It was once one of the world's leading exporters of oil.

Venezuela used to be an underdeveloped exporter of agricultural commodities such as coffee and cocoa. Since its discovery, oil has dominated exports and government revenues. Oil export revenues prompted an economic boom. By 1945, Venezuela's per capita GDP was the highest in South America.

During the long-lasting economic boom, the country did not save an adequate amount of funds for future economic hardships. In the 1970s, Venezuela's oil income was significantly boosted as a result of soaring oil prices following the 1973 oil crisis. Again, not much was saved from the funds. Instead, this resulted in massive increases in public spending and, in the meantime, increases in external debts. When the 1980s oil glut hit, the country suffered from an external debt crisis, followed by a long-running economic crisis.

The economic crises in the 1980s and then the 1990s led to political and social crises. Hundreds of people died in the Caracazo riots of 1989. Two attempted coups occurred in 1992. President Carlos Andrés Pérez was impeached for corruption in 1993. A collapse in confidence in the existing parties saw the 1998 election of Hugo Chávez as president, who had led the first of the 1992 coup attempts. Chávez took office in February 1999. After taking office, he launched the 'Bolivarian Revolution', a left-wing populist social movement and political process practising socialistic economic policies, most of which have been proven to be failures elsewhere. These included, for example, setting price ceilings on food, which then caused food shortages and hoarding.

The recovery of oil prices after 2001 helped to improve the Venezuelan economy and facilitate social spending. There was notable progress in social development in the early 2000s. The overspending on public works, however, was not sustainable. Soon, the policies of the Chávez government resulted in increasing economic issues. The 2008 global financial crisis caused a sharp downturn in the Venezuelan economy.

In March 2013, Nicolás Maduro became the president. He reinforced the majority of Chávez's economic policies. Growing shortages, including necessities such as milk, flour, and toilet paper, led to price inflation and the devaluation of the Venezuelan currency. The government then nationalised some activities such as food distribution. Maduro also decided to force stores and their warehouses to sell all of their products, which led to even more shortages in the following years (Anido and Daniel 2015). In 2016, consumer prices in Venezuela increased 800% and the economy declined by 18.6%.

Since the early 2000s, food security in Venezuela started to deteriorate. The averages of the macro nutrients as shown in Table 11.5 reveal limited details of the deterioration (because

Table 11.5 Key indicators of food security in Venezuela (five-year average)

	1991–1995	1996–2000	2001–2005	2006–2010	2011–2015
Dietary energy supply (DES) (kcal/capita/day)	2,447	2,393	2,450	2,790	2,962
Average dietary energy requirement (ADER) (kcal/capita/day)	2,292	2,315	2,330	2,340	na
Average dietary energy supply adequacy (ADESA) (%)	105	105	114	125	129
Average protein supply (g/capita/day)	64	65	68	80	na
Average fat supply (g/capita/day)	69	67	72	84	na
Prevalence of undernourishment (%)	14	17	14	8	<5.0
Number of people undernourished (millions)	3	2	na	na	na
Political stability and absence of violence (index)	na	-0.67	-1.33	-1.25	-1.06
Domestic food price volatility (index)	na	na	11.18	14.54	11.78
Percentage of children under five years of age affected by wasting (%)	4	4	5	5	na
Percentage of children under five years of age who are stunted (%)	18	19	17	15	na
Percentage of children under five years of age who are underweight (%)	5	4	4	4	na
GDP per capita (in PPP) (constant 2011 international $)	15,522	15,331	13,675	16,038	17,162

kcal = kilocalorie, g = gram, GDP = gross domestic product, PPP = purchasing power parity, na = not available.
Source: based on FAO (2019).

Table 11.6 GFSI and GHI in Venezuela since 2012

	GFSI score	Ranking	GHI score	Proportion of undernourished people in the population (%)	Total population (m)
2012	61.6	41	<5	7.0	29.89
2013	60.8	41	<5	2.7	30.32
2014	62.5	41	<5	2.1	30.74
2015	61.7	48	7.0	1.3	31.16
2016	56.9	60	7.0	1.3	31.57
2017	50.2	71	13.0	13.0	31.98
2018	47.4	78	11.4	11.7	32.38

Sources: GFSI score and ranking: EIU, various issues; GHI and the proportion of undernourished: IFPRI, various issues; population: UN Population Division.

the data were up until 2015). Other indicators do suggest rising problems in the country. In Table 11.5, the index of 'political stability and absence of violence' was -0.62 in 1996. It quickly dropped to -1.39 in 2004, indicating that the country is highly unstable politically and has high levels of violence.

The 'domestic food price volatility' index is also relatively high, which points to hardship experienced by residents in accessing food. During the 2000s, this index was as high as, or exceeding, 20 in some years (e.g., 20.9 in 2010). This is very high compared to many other countries. In fact, in early 2019, price inflation was over two million percent. Despite this very high inflation, food was not readily available for purchase.

There have been numerous reports of food insecurity experienced by an increasing number of Venezuelans since 2015. Several other indicators confirm this fast deterioration of its food security in the recent years. The GFSI for Venezuela has been sliding since 2015 at an alarming rate. Its overall ranking has dropped by more than 30 places between 2015 and 2018 (Table 11.6). The GHI and the proportion of undernourished people in the population have also pointed to the deterioration of its food security.

Some Venezuelans have chosen to escape from the situation and migrated to other countries. This helps reduce the total demand for food. However, the total population is still increasing (Table 11.6). There has been no notable improvement in Venezuela's total food supply. Access to an adequate amount of food may increasingly become an issue for more people. There has been no sign that the worsening food situation may be arrested any time soon as Maduro has another six years of presidency following the 2018 election. It is hard to expect him to radically discard the policies he has been following over the past years. Improvements to Venezuela's food security can happen only if some radical changes occur within the country's political settings and new measures are adopted that can lead the country to recovery.

11.6 Zimbabwe

Zimbabwe, officially the Republic of Zimbabwe, is a landlocked country located in southern Africa. White colonists arrived in Zimbabwe in the late 19th century. The British colonised it during 1888–1980. On 11 November 1965, the colony issued a Unilateral Declaration of

Independence (UDI) from the United Kingdom. The UK deemed this declaration an act of rebellion, but did not re-establish control by force. After the Declaration in 1965, there were continued guerrilla wars. On 21 December 1979, major forces involved in the guerrilla wars signed the Lancaster House Agreement to end the war.

The Agreement between the Rhodesian government and the liberation movements was facilitated and presided over by the British government. It paved the way for the first elections in 1980. Being a negotiated settlement, there were clauses in the Agreement such as preserving the land ownership system for at least ten years and a guaranteed minimum number of parliamentary seats for the white minority in the first parliament.

Following the elections in April 1980, Robert Mugabe, leader of the ZANU (Zimbabwe African National Union) party, became the country's first Prime Minister and Head of Government. Canaan Banana became Zimbabwe's first president (1980–1987, a mainly ceremonial role as Head of State) after its independence. In late 1987, through constitutional amendments, Mugabe became the country's executive president, and the post of prime minister was disbanded. Ideologically, he identified himself as a Marxist–Leninist during the 1970s and 1980s and later as a socialist.

The Lancaster House Agreement made it impossible for the ZANU government to make any major changes to the constitution for ten years from 1980. The government felt its hands had been tied in terms of delivering on one of its liberation struggle promises which was the redistribution of land to the black majority, relieving the land pressure in the less productive marginal lands where the majority of Africans had been placed by the colonial authorities. For the first ten years it could only carry out a 'willing-buyer-willing-seller' land reform program.

In 1990, the Agreement lapsed. The Zimbabwean general election in March 1990 resulted in a huge victory for Mugabe and the ZANU-PF party (in 1987, the Patriotic Front was merged with ZANU to become ZANU–PF). The government tried to put in place legislation to allow it to acquire and redistribute land. A number of political statements were made as the government tried to walk the fine tightrope of telling the black majority that it still intended to redistribute land to them while at the same time reassuring investors, particularly in agriculture that their investments were safe and property rights were enshrined. Thus, in the early 1990s the political message was that underutilised and derelict land as well as land with absentee landlords would be compulsorily acquired.

There was a lot of uncertainty in the agricultural sector and some inertia from the government about what course of action to take. Commercial white farmers were not sure whether to continue to invest or to pack up. The government was not sure of the full effects of a widespread land acquisition program (Makadho 2006; Moyo 2006). In 1994, a Commission of Inquiry into Appropriate Agricultural Land Tenure Systems was set up, chaired by an agricultural economist, Professor Mandivamba Rukuni of the University of Zimbabwe. The Commission's report had a number of recommendations on how a land reform program could be successfully implemented by minimising any anticipated negative effects (Rukuni 1994). There was no effective implementation of the recommendations; there was a general election in 1995 and a presidential election in 1996.

In the early 1990s, Zimbabwe was reeling from a very weak fiscal position, a large and growing budget, and current account deficits, in part caused by loss-making parastatals (government-owned enterprises that often have some political power) in a controlled market environment. Many of these were also agricultural parastatals such as input companies (seed, fertiliser) and marketing boards for various commodities. Some reforms were carried out, particularly to agricultural commodity markets. Overall, the outcomes were less satisfactory. Economic hardship for the public continued and was growing.

With the growing hardship, civic organisations started to group and voice their discontent with Mugabe and ZANU-PF party policies; such as salary issues and the decline in the general health of the population. During the 1990s, there were frequent and growing demonstrations, protests, strikes, and riots.

The 'willing-buyer-willing-seller' land reform program brought limited changes to land ownership. By the late 1990s, the minority white Zimbabwean population of around 0.6% continued to hold 70% of the country's most fertile agricultural land. In 2000, the ZANU-PF government pressed ahead with its Fast Track Land Reform program, a policy involving compulsory land acquisition aimed at redistributing land from the minority white population to the majority black population.

Confiscations of white farmers' land did not result in improved agricultural productivity (Matondi and Munyuki-Hungwe 2006). Farming success of land-receiving farmers was limited. The smaller farming scale, coupled with continuous droughts and a serious drop in various farming supports, led to a sharp decline in agricultural output and subsequently agricultural exports, which were traditionally the country's leading export-producing sector (Rukuni 2006).

Food production suffered significantly. The output of most food crops experienced sharp decline. In Zimbabwe, rice production is minimal, and wheat and maize are the major cereal crops. Since the early 1960s, the country's output of cereals (wheat, maize and rice) showed an impressive rising trend, with net cereal exports in most of the years. From 2000, this trend ended. Zimbabwe became a net food importer and the amount of net imports was rising.

In addition to severe food shortages, many other problems in Zimbabwe had also reached crisis proportions by the late 2000s, one of which was sky-rocketing inflation. Mugabe continued in power, with authoritarian ruling. After he was re-elected president in the July 2013 Zimbabwean general election, allegedly due to massive fraud, the Mugabe ZANU-PF government re-instituted one party rule, leaving little chance for the country to correct the problems. Corruption was widespread. Violations of human rights were common.

It was once known as the 'Jewel of Africa' for its prosperity. This has not been the case since the late 1990s. The country's economy has been struggling, experiencing several crashes (World Bank 2018). In 2016, when Patrick Chinamasa, Zimbabwe's finance minister, was touring European capitals begging for money from donors, he told French radio, 'right now we literally have nothing' (The Economist 2016, p. 40).

There has been some expansion in the economy since 2009. However, it has not been sufficient to make up the contractions suffered in the previous years. In 1998, the country's total GDP was $32.84 billion (PPP, constant 2011 international $, the same hereafter). By 2008, it shrank to $17.47 billion. By 2016, it recovered to $30.36 billion, but still below the 1998 level. Due to population increase (from 12 million in 1998 to 16 million in 2016), per capita GDP had dropped from $2761 in 1998 to $1879 in 2016 (World Bank 2018).

In November 2017, the army led a coup d'état following the dismissal of Vice President Emmerson Mnangagwa, placing Mugabe under house arrest. On 21 November 2017, Mugabe tendered his resignation prior to impeachment proceedings being completed. By then, he had ruled the country for 37 years, leaving behind him a country in a situation that was far worse than when he started.

On 24 November 2017, Mnangagwa was sworn in as Zimbabwe's new president. He vowed to serve all citizens, revitalise the struggling economy, and reduce corruption, and he promised to 're-engage' with the world. However, he indicated that Mugabe's post-2000 land reform programs would be maintained, although white farmers would be compensated for their seized land (in the current budget of the Mnangagwa administration, provisions were made to compensate farmers who had been displaced during the land reform process. The compensation would be for improvements of the land only but not for the land itself).

By the end of 2018, one year after taking office, the situation in Zimbabwe was no better. In early 2019, there were protests against a sharp fuel price hike which was met with brutal crackdowns. It remains unlikely that the country will return to the recovery track.

Suffering from economic collapse, political suppression, and social disintegration, it is no wonder that the country has failed to improve its food security. Instead, its food security has become much worse. The FAO data (Table 11.7) show that food insecurity in Zimbabwe has become worse since the 1990s. In terms of the availability of all three macro nutrients (dietary energy, fat, and protein), the national average indicates that none of these is adequate. This has resulted in a very high prevalence of undernourishment; in most years since 1990, the prevalence was as high as 40% or even 45%.

It might be thought that population growth could have contributed to lower food availability. But this is not the case. Data from FAO show that during 1961–1981, total population grew at an annual rate of 3.40% but total cereal output grew at a much faster rate at 5.59%, resulting in continuous food supply improvement. The rising trend of cereal output prior to 1981 is shown in Figure 11.3. Since 1981, however, cereal output did not grow; instead it shrank by 3.97% annually. While cereal output declined, the population increased, at 1.97% per annum (FAO 2018).

Table 11.7 Key indicators of food security in Zimbabwe (five-year average)

	1991–1995	1996–2000	2001–2005	2006–2010	2011–2015
Dietary energy supply (DES) (kcal/capita/day)	1,953	1,997	2,028	2,123	2,183
Average dietary energy requirement (ADER) (kcal/capita/day)	2,195	2,228	2,246	2,241	2,249
Average dietary energy supply adequacy (ADESA) (%)	89	89	90	95	97
Average protein supply (g/capita/day)	48	47	48	52	na
Average fat supply (g/capita/day)	47	50	54	57	na
Prevalence of undernourishment (%)	45	44	43	37	34
Number of people undernourished (millions)	5.06	5.40	5.42	4.80	4.78
Political stability and absence of violence (index)	na	-0.71	-1.36	-1.12	-0.89
Domestic food price volatility (index)	na	na	na	na	na
Percentage of children under five years of age affected by wasting (%)	6.30	8.50	na	5.55	3.20
Percentage of children under five years of age who are stunted (%)	28.90	33.70	na	35.45	29.95
Percentage of children under five years of age who are underweight (%)	11.70	11.50	na	13.35	10.65
GDP per capita (in PPP) (constant 2011 international $)	2,440	2,597	2,213	1,505	1,658

kcal = kilocalorie, g = gram, GDP = gross domestic product, PPP = purchasing power parity, na = not available.
Source: based on FAO (2019).

The land confiscation movement that started in 2000 seems to have done even more damage to cereal production. Between 2000 and 2013, cereal output contracted by 7.71% every year. Consequently, the government decided to once again take control of the marketing of critical commodities such as wheat and maize, with the Grain Marketing Board as the sole buyer and the prices announced periodically by the government. By 2007, the prices of many life basics such as bread and mealie meal were also controlled. Supermarket shelves dried up.

Since 2000, Zimbabwe's major cereal output has never surpassed the level achieved in 1985 (3.035 mt) and has shown a steady declining trend (Panel A, Figure 11.3). By 2013, it was 0.793 mt, less than one third of the 1985 output. Domestic food supply became increasingly reliant upon imports and it went from being a net cereal exporter to being a net importer (Panel A, Figure 11.3). Its SSR dropped to around 50% but its IDR rose to around 50% (Panel B, Figure 11.3).

Panel A

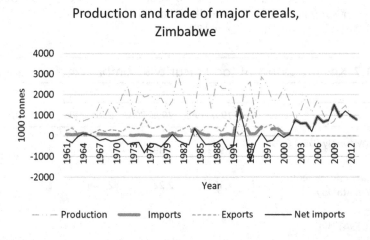

Panel B

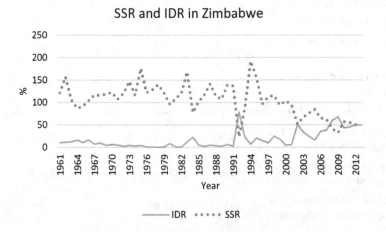

Figure 11.3 Cereal production and trade in Zimbabwe.
Source: based on FAO (2018), FAOSTAT database.

The GFSI compiled by the EIU does not include Zimbabwe. The other index, GHI by the IFPRI (2018), indicates the very insecure food status in Zimbabwe. Figure 11.4 shows that the hunger situation in Zimbabwe has been 'serious' and at times 'alarming'. The prevalence of undernourishment is very high. Since 2016, the situation has worsened.

The removal of Mugabe from office presented an opportunity for the country to correct the government failure. Unfortunately, the correction under Mnangagwa so far has been most disappointing. There continue to be large distortions in the economy which encourage 'rent seeking' and other bad behaviours. So far no policies supportive of the agricultural sector have been implemented. Even if there had been effective corrections, it would still, most likely, take some time for Zimbabwe's food security to significantly improve given the severe food shortage and the lack of funds for food imports, unless the international community is prepared to pour in a large amount of resources to help out.

It is imperative for Zimbabwe to quickly rebuild its collapsed economy and support the farming sector in restoring its ability to produce to its full extent. In the meantime, the country needs to restore law and order, ensure its judicial system is working properly, and reduce corruption to the minimum.

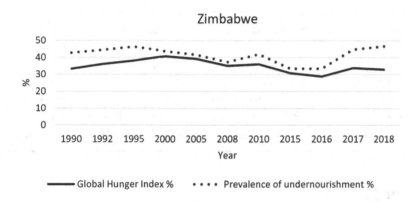

Figure 11.4 GHI and prevalence of undernourishment in Zimbabwe.

GHI: Global Hunger Index, ranks countries on a 100-point scale. Hunger is low if the HGI ≤ 9.9; moderate if between 10.0–19.9; serious if between 20.0–34.9; alarming if between 35.0–49.9 and extremely alarming if ≥ 50. Prevalence of undernourishment: the share of the population that is undernourished (that is, whose caloric intake is insufficient).

Source: based on IFPRI GHI publications from 2015 to 2018.

Review questions

1. What is your judgement about the status of food security in each of the countries examined?
2. What are the major forces that are responsible for shaping each of the countries' current food security status?
3. What is the most important issue for each of the countries to address to improve its food security?

4. Would it be sufficient to use the average availability of the three macronutrients (i.e., average dietary energy supply, average protein supply, and average fat supply) to evaluate a country's food security status? Why? Can you describe the likely merits and weaknesses from just using these three indicators?
5. If the country of your residence is a developing country and is food insecure, in addition to the average availability of the three macronutrients, what other indicators from the Suite of Food Security Indicators as developed by the FAO (see Table 1.1) should also be used for evaluating your country's food security? Briefly discuss why.

Discussion questions

1. Do you think there are any factors common to all the countries examined in this chapter that are responsible for their lower levels of food security? If so, what is the single most vital common factor that is applicable to all the six countries?
2. Both China and India have large populations. Is the size of population a likely key factor that crucially affects a country's food security level?
3. China has a very large population. Venezuela has a much smaller population. Currently, China has a much more comfortable food security status than Venezuela does. Why? Does your answer to Discussion Question 2 regarding the impact of population on food security support your answer to this question?

References

ACAPS (Assessment Capacities Project). (2015), 'Global emergency overview snapshot 17 Dec 2014–6 Jan 2015', http://reliefweb.int/report/world/global-emergency-overview-snapshot-17-dec-2014-6-jan-2015, accessed 20 March 2015.

Ah, H.Y. (2019), 'North Korea facing widespread farming problems', www.dailynk.com/english/north-korea-facing-widespread-farming-problems/, accessed 27 May 2019.

Ahluwalia, D. (1993). 'Public distribution of food in India: Coverage, targeting and leakages', *Food Policy*, Vol. 18, pp. 33–54.

Anido, R. and Daniel, J. (2015), 'Demand of food energy, food availability and nutrient intake in Venezuela: Main changes and their nutritional implications', Revista Espanola de Estudios Agrosociales y Pesqueros, Ministerio de Medio Ambiente, Rural y Marino (formerly Ministry of Agriculture), Issue No., 240, pp. 1–50. https://ageconsearch.umn.edu/record/249679?ln=en, accessed 1 February 2018.

Becker, J. (1996), *Hungry Ghosts: China's Secret Famine*, John Murray, London.

Carter, C. and Zhong, F.N. (1988), *China's Grain Production and Trade: An Economic Study*, Westview Press, Boulder, Colorado.

Commonwealth of Australia (Department of Climate Change and Energy Efficiency). (2011), 'Food security in the Pacific and East Timor and its vulnerability to climate change', Canberra, Australia.

DailyNK. (2017), 'Food insecurity riles North Korea's poorest provinces', www.dailynk.com/english/food-insecurity-riles-north-koreas/, accessed 27 May 2019.

Dikötter, F. (2010), *Mao's Great Famine: The History of China's Most Devastating Catastrophe, 1958–1962*, Walker, New York.

Ding, S. (1996), 'From the great leap forward to the great famine', www.cnd.org/HXWK/author/DING-Shu/zk9601a3-0.gb.html, Chinese News Digest, zk9601a1-3, accessed 15 October 1998.

FAO. (2012), 'Pacific Multi-Country CPF Document 2013–2017 for the cooperation and partnership between FAO and its 14 Pacific Island Members', www.fao.org/3/a-az134e.pdf, accessed 17 January 2019.

FAO. (2014), 'Crop prospects and food situation', No. 4, December 2014, FAO, Rome.

FAO. (2018), 'FAOSTAT database', www.fao.org/faostat/en/#data, accessed 6 January 2018.

FAO. (2019), 'FAOSTAT database: Suite of food security indicators', www.fao.org/faostat/en/#data/FS, accessed 24 January 2019.

FAO, International Fund for Agricultural Development (IFAD), and the World Food Programme (WFP). (2015), *The State of Food Insecurity in the World 2015: Meeting the 2015 International Hunger Targets: Taking Stock of Uneven Progress*, FAO, Rome.

Foraete, H.M. (2001), 'Food security strategies for the Republic of Fiji', Working Paper Series No. 55, The CGPRT Centre, https://ageconsearch.umn.edu/record/32704/files/wp010055.pdf, accessed 20 February 2018.

GOI. (1957), *Report of the Foodgrains Enquiry Committee*, Government of India, New Delhi.

GOI. (1995), *Economic Survey*, Government of India, New Delhi.

IFPRI. (2018), 'Global Hunger Index, 2018 and earlier issues', www.globalhungerindex.org/download/all.html, accessed 15 January 2019.

Makadho, J. (2006), 'Land redistribution experiences in Zimbabwe 1998–2004', in Rukuni, M., Tawonezvi, P., Eicher, C., Munyuki-Hungwe, M. and Matondi, P. (eds), *Zimbabwe's Agricultural Revolution Revisited*, University of Zimbabwe Publications, Harare, Zimbabwe, pp. 165–188.

Mallory, W.H. (1926), *China: Land of Famine*, American Geographical Society, New York.

Matondi, P. and Munyuki-Hungwe, M. (2006), 'The evolution of agricultural policy: 1990–2004', in Rukuni, M., Tawonezvi, P., Eicher, C., Munyuki-Hungwe, M. and Matondi, P. (eds), *Zimbabwe's Agricultural Revolution Revisited*, University of Zimbabwe Publications, Harare, Zimbabwe, pp. 63–97.

Moyo, S. (2006), 'The evolution of Zimbabwe's land acquisition', in Rukuni, M., Tawonezvi, P., Eicher, C., Munyuki-Hungwe, M. and Matondi, P. (eds), *Zimbabwe's Agricultural Revolution Revisited*, University of Zimbabwe Publications, Harare, Zimbabwe, pp. 143–163.

Pal, S., Bahl, D.K., and Mruthyunjaya. (1993), 'Government interventions in foodgrain markets: The case of India', *Food Policy*, Vol. 18, pp. 414–427.

Rukuni, M. (1994), *Commission of Inquiry into Appropriate Agricultural Land Tenure Systems*, The Commission, Harare, Zimbabwe.

Rukuni, M. (2006), 'Revisiting Zimbabwe's agricultural revolution', in Rukuni, M., Tawonezvi, P., Eicher, C., Munyuki-Hungwe, M. and Matondi, P. (eds), *Zimbabwe's Agricultural Revolution Revisited*, University of Zimbabwe Publications, Harare, Zimbabwe, pp. 1–21.

Sharma, K.L. (2006), 'Food security in the South Pacific Island Countries with special reference to the Fiji Islands', UNU-WIDER Research Paper No. 2006/68, www.wider.unu.

edu/publication/food-security-south-pacific-island-countries-special-reference-fiji-islands, accessed 20 February 2018.

Silberstein, B.K. (2017), 'Sanctions, and the weakness of North Korean food security', www.nkeconwatch.com/2017/10/18/sanctions-and-the-weakness-of-north-korean-food-security/, accessed 27 May 2019.

Silberstein, B.K. (2019), 'Famine, Amartya Sen, and the markets of North Korea', www. nkeconwatch.com/2019/05/20/famine-amartya-sen-and-the-markets-of-north-korea/, accessed 27 May 2019.

Song, J.H. and Kwon, T.J. (2017), 'Food security in the Republic of Korea and the Democratic People's Republic of Korea: Why the difference?', in Zhou, Z.Y. and Wan, G.H. (eds), *Food Insecurity in Asia: Why Institutions Matter*, ADB Institute, Tokyo, Chapter 6, pp. 139–191.

The Economist. (2016), 'Bailing out bandits; Zimbabwe's begging bowl', 9 July 2016, p. 40.

WFP. (2017), 'First-ever regional meeting on food security in disaster-prone Pacific Islands concludes in Fiji', www.wfp.org/news/news-release/first-ever-regional-meeting-food-security-disaster-prone-pacific-islands-concludes, accessed 20 February 2018.

World Bank. (2018), 'The World Bank data – Zimbabwe', https://data.worldbank.org/country/Zimbabwe, accessed 16 March 2018.

World Bank. (2019), 'World development indicators: Economy', http://datatopics.worldbank.org/world-development-indicators/themes/economy.html, accessed 16 January 2019.

Yang, J.S. (2008), *Tombstone: the Chinese Famine in the Sixties Documentary*, Cosmos Books, Hong Kong.

Zhao, F.S. and Qi, X.Q. (eds) (1988), *Grain in Contemporary China*, Chinese Social Sciences Press, Beijing.

Zhou, Z.Y. (1997), *Effects of Grain Marketing Systems on Grain Production: A Comparative Study of China and India*, The Haworth Press, New York.

Zhou, Z.Y. (2017), *Achieving Food Security in China: the Challenges Ahead*, Routledge, London.

Chapter 12

Country cases

High level of food security

Summary

Having examined the practices of countries that are less food secure in the previous chapter, we examine, in this chapter, the practices of countries with higher levels of food security. The countries to be examined are, Israel, Japan, the Netherlands, Singapore, and South Korea.

After studying this chapter, you should be able to:
- Form your own judgement about the status of food security in each of the countries examined.
- List and discuss major forces that are responsible for shaping each of the countries' current food security.
- Share your view on the most important thing that each of the countries has done that has helped it to attain a high level of food security.
- Share your view on the most important thing that each of them should do to ensure their country can sustain the same high level of food security.

12.1 Israel

Israel, officially the State of Israel, is a country in Western Asia, located on the south-eastern shore of the Mediterranean Sea and the northern shore of the Red Sea. It contains geographically diverse features within its relatively small area: from the Negev desert in the south to the inland fertile Jezreel Valley, the mountain ranges of the Galilee, Carmel, and towards the Golan in the north.

Israel became independent on 14 May 1948. Its landmass is 22,000 km². In 2017, its total population was about 8.7 million, with a per capita GDP of $38,262 (purchasing power parity, PPP, current international $) (World Bank 2019). Israel's Democracy Index (DI) was 77.9 in 2017 (EIU 2018). Its corruption level is about medium with the Corruption Perception Index (CPI) being 62 (Transparency International 2018). Israel has achieved a very high level of food security – in 2017 its GFSI (Global Food Security Index) was 79.2%, making it the third highest in Asia and the 19th highest in the world (EIU 2017).

At the time of independence, having adequate food to feed the population was a challenge in Israel. The problem was aggravated due to a large number of immigrants, many of whom were poor. In mid-1949, the Israeli government introduced food rationing (Yosef 1960). The rationing policy required taking measures against the spread of black markets, but success was limited. Over time, the food supply gradually improved and the rationing policy weakened. By 1959, food rationing was phased out.

Since the early 1960s, food supply in Israel has been more than adequate. In fact, by the mid-1960s, the supply of all three macronutrients – dietary energy, protein, and fat – had exceeded the normal requirements. By the mid-2010s, this excess has become larger.

More than half of the land in Israel is desert. Its natural resources are far from being favourable to agriculture and its climate is *a priori* not very conducive to agriculture. Yet, through food imports and boosting domestic production, Israel has managed to achieve a very comfortable food supply situation.

While food imports play an important role in ensuring a comfortable food supply, Israel's agriculture has played an even more important role in boosting food supply. Its agricultural sector is very productive and is able to produce 95% of the country's food requirements although the workforce in agriculture represents only 3.7% of the total labour force (Endeweld and Silber 2017). Major factors contributing to the high level of agricultural productivity are (1) investment in agricultural R&D and extension, (2) farmer education, and (3) cooperation in the agricultural communities.

12.1.1 Investment in agricultural R&D and extension

A generous amount of resources has been devoted to agricultural R&D and extension in Israel. Such investment enables R&D and extension activities to be carried out, which in turn significantly boosts productivity. Gelb and Kislev (1982) attribute 90% of the growth in Israel's farm output to growth in productivity.

The Israeli Ministry of Agriculture has played an important role in providing agricultural R&D and extension services. Its specialists give regular and often free help to farmers. Among the services that the Ministry of Agriculture provides, the most important ones are (1) instruction (providing updated agricultural knowledge to farmers), (2) training (providing farmers with concentrated professional knowledge allowing the adoption of new and advanced technologies), and (3) producing applied knowledge. The 'agricultural extension service' of the Ministry of Agriculture, in cooperation with regional R&D units and universities, conducts many experiments aimed at finding solutions to problems faced by farmers in the fields of water use (including water recycling), adoption of new technologies and automation, improvement of agricultural produce quality to meet international standards, and reduction in the use of pesticides.

As a result, Israeli farmers have been very successful in mechanising their production. They make intensive use of greenhouses and adopt very complex, profitable, and computerised irrigation systems. Investment in R&D and extension helped Israeli farmers to overcome the shortage of land and water and to boost farm output. The following are some illustrations of these technological advances in Israeli agriculture (Endeweld and Silber 2017):

1. The dairy industry is highly automated. Almost all dairy farms have become computerised. Every cow is connected to a sensor that transmits information to the computer on its health and the composition of its milk. Israel holds the world record in the yield of milk per cow.
2. The use of pierced irrigation pipes, an Israeli invention, has led to a considerable amount of water saving. These pipes are linked to a computer that allows control of the amount of water, fertilisers, and pesticides.
3. The intensive use of greenhouses allows computerised control of the temperature, humidity, light, and fertiliser amount, significantly boosting crop yields.
4. Fish farming in greenhouse pools allows the production of fish in desert areas by using salty water. These pools are often covered with plastic to lessen evaporation.
5. Biotechnological developments have enabled some varieties of vegetables and fruits to be transformed genetically so that they can be sold in new colours (e.g., peppers) or made more resistant to diseases. More recently, there has also been an increasing production of organic food.

12.1.2 Farmer education

Kibbutz and moshav members generally have a high level of education. Literacy has been almost universal among male Jews for more than 1,500 years (Endeweld and Silber 2017). Within the kibbutzim and moshavim, gender equality has been increasingly promoted. Hence, female members nowadays also have a very high level of education. Even in the 1950s and 1960s, kibbutz and moshav members had a level of education much higher than that observed among farmers in countries with a level of development similar to Israel. The high level of education may explain why kibbutz and moshav members have been quick to adopt new agricultural technologies.

12.1.3 Cooperation in agricultural communities

The widespread cooperation in the Israeli agricultural communities, through the kibbutz and the moshav, has also contributed significantly to agricultural productivity. Such cooperation allows the scale of production to increase. The cooperation among farmers in Israel is unique in that it is voluntary. Forced agricultural cooperation or collectivisation elsewhere has generally failed miserably; yet the voluntary cooperation in Israel has worked. In addition, cooperation in Israeli agricultural communities has also made investment in agriculture more effective.

Investment in R&D and extension, farmer education, and cooperation have greatly improved Israel's ability to produce a high portion of the country's needs (and it has also become increasingly export-oriented). Supplemented with food imports, Israel has attained a very high level of food security.

During the past six decades, the consumption of calories increased by 40%, from 2,610 kcal to 3,630 kcal per person per day. The data clearly show that even during the so-called austerity period in the early 1950s, the average per capita calorie intake was much higher than the minimum dietary energy requirement. In 2012, the amount of calories per person per day in Israel was among the highest in developed countries. Proteins consumed have undergone an increase of about 30% over the past 60 years. Most of the increase comes from food of animal origin, while the amount of proteins derived from grains and their products has declined. At the same time, fat intake has increased sharply (an increase of 90% during the same period).

Hence, in Israel, there is no problem of food availability at the national level. The country has in recent years increasingly paid more attention to the food security status at the household and individual levels, with a focus on the food security of people at the bottom of the income distribution ladder. In order to get a more detailed picture of food security at the micro level, Israel is one of the few developed countries that has conducted food security surveys of households and individuals (Endeweld and Silber 2017).

To improve the food security of low-income people, the Israeli government provides them with a safety net. The government also works together with more than 200 non-governmental organisations (NGOs) that distribute food to the poor. A number of NGOs such as Leket Israel and the United Children's Food Bank of Israel provide valuable support to those in need.

While food availability is not an issue in Israel, the country is nonetheless well prepared for emergencies. The 'emergency administration,' which is part of the Ministry of the Economy, is in charge of food emergency management in order to guarantee the delivery of goods and services to make sure the economy continues to function in such situations.

One of the departments of this 'emergency administration' is 'the supreme authority for food' whose duty is to ensure that essential food factories are ready to perform in emergency situations. This authority is also in charge of checking that food stocks are adequate and that the local authorities are prepared in case of mass disasters such as earthquakes, floods, epidemics, disastrous water pollution, and terrorist attacks.

The activities of this supreme authority for food include the requisition of manpower, vehicles, and equipment for those factories considered vital; the guidance and continuous training of the representatives of the 'emergency administration' in the vital factories and in local emergency committees; the regular tracking of additional factories whose activity may be vital in case of emergency; and the preparation (together with the civil defence institutions) of these vital factories for situations of emergency. About 200 factories in the food branch may find themselves under requisition in states of emergencies. Major foods covered by these factories include meat, rice, coffee, tea, canned food, and baby foods (Endeweld and Silber 2017).

The Ministry of the Economy also makes sure that there is always an adequate stock of basic food (e.g., for baby foods, the instructions are to have a stock that would last for one month). Although the implementation of such guidelines for cases of emergency is in principle at the level of local authorities, the army and civil defence institutions may also intervene if necessary.

12.2 Japan

Japan is an island country in East Asia. The Japanese archipelago has long been inhabited. Today's Japan is composed of over 6,800 islands, with a landmass of 365,000 km². About 73% of Japan is forested, mountainous, and unsuitable for agricultural, industrial, or residential use. Consequently, the habitable zones, mainly located in coastal areas, have extremely high population densities.

Japan's population in 2017 was about 126.4 million. Its total population peaked in the late 2000s at around 127.3 million. It is forecast that its total population will continue declining to about 100 m by 2050 and 50 m by 2100 (United Nations 2015). Its DI was 78.8 in 2017 (EIU 2018). The CPI for Japan in 2017 was 73% (Transparency International 2018). It is a high income country. Its per capita GDP was $43,279 in 2017 (PPP, current international $) (World Bank 2019). In 2017, its GFSI was 79.5%, being the second highest in Asia and the 18th highest in the world (EIU 2017).

Over Japan's long history, there have been many recorded food shortages and famines. The latest severe food crisis occurred in the late 1940s, immediately after its defeat in World War II. Prior to the end of World War II in 1945, food was already in shortage in Japan. A food control system was in place. The main components of this control system were the mandated delivery of rice (and other crops) from farmers to the government, a ration system, and price control. The crop failure in 1945 coupled with the malfunction of the 'rice delivery system' and food import disruptions resulted in a severe food crisis in 1946 (Hirasawa 2017a). Calorie intake in 1946 was the lowest in recent history, at 1,448 kilocalories (kcal) per capita per day.

The recovery was slow. A combination of measures were deployed, including rice delivery by force, raising official delivery prices (to reduce the gap between the official price and the black market price), a gradual expansion of imports, and to some extent, food aid (which ended in 1951). The initiatives taken by the Japanese government, which was under the control of the Allied Forces, were very instrumental. The government provided estimates of food shortages and early warnings of food crisis to the General Headquarters (GHQ) of the Allied Forces to gain permission to import more food to alleviate the crisis.

It took about ten years for the calorie intake in Japan to recover to the prewar level. During the ten-year period of 1945 to 1954, food availability remained seriously inadequate – hundreds of thousands of people died from tuberculosis and other infectious diseases caused by malnutrition, a decrease in resistance to illness. Nonetheless, Japan managed to avoid a major catastrophe, though narrowly. In 1955, per capita calorie intake reached 2,217 kcal, surpassing the level of 2,135 kcal achieved in 1938, which was the highest in the period 1930–1940.

From 1955 till 1960, per capita calorie intake was largely steady ranging between 2,200 and 2,300 kcal. From 1961, Japan entered into an era of high economic growth. Food intake also grew rapidly till 1973. From 1973, calorie intake continued increasing but at a slower pace. It peaked at 2,670 kcal per capita per day in 1996. From 1996 onwards, calorie intake has started to decline. It was 2,418 kcal per capita per day in 2015, almost as low as that in 1964.

The decline in calorie intake is not a reflection of a decline in food availability but due to other forces including: (1) reduced body energy consumption due to population aging, increasing automation both at home and at work, and improved public infrastructures (less demand for calories); and (2) shift to foods lower in calories but higher in other nutrients (due to consumer taste changes, including increased intake of processed foods and ready-made meals which generally contain less energy but more of other high-valued nutrients). Despite the decline in calorie intake, the level is still above the average dietary energy requirements (ADER). Fat and protein intake is also above bodily needs. Clearly, with a high GFSI in recent years, Japan has come a long way in improving its food security since the mid-1940s.

Important factors that have contributed to shape and sustain Japan's high level of food security are as follows.

The most important determinant is the government's will to provide an adequate amount of food for the citizens of the country. The Japanese government accepts that ensuring citizens have a secure food intake is its responsibility. This has been reflected in its efforts to feed the people during the years of severe food shortage after the War and to continuously improve the country's food security since the 1960s. Government officials, chiefly, those in the Ministry of Agriculture, are generally very conscious of the need to ensure a stable food supply in the country.

Clearly defined and long-term oriented food policy is another major contributing factor. As soon as the country's dietary energy intake reached a satisfactory level in the early 1960s, the Japanese government started to pay attention to long-term food supply strategies. An important strategic response was to coordinate the demand for limited resources between agricultural and non-agricultural sectors. The fast economic take-off meant that the comparative advantage of the agricultural sector was to decline. This in turn implies that maintaining a high level of food self-sufficiency was hardly possible. Japan would have to choose to produce some highly preferred foods, but import more of other foods. Consequently, the Agricultural Basic Act of 1961 directed the country to follow a 'Selective Expansion' strategy. That is, Japan's agriculture would take a major shift from land-extensive farming to relatively land-saving farming. It would produce less of most food crops, except rice. The gap between the demand and supply would be met by increased imports through more and more, but gradual, trade liberalisation. Figure 12.1 shows that by the mid-1960s, the self-sufficiency ratios (SSRs) for most food items were already low (MAFF 2018). Since then most of the SSRs have continued dropping and by 2015, many of them were very low, except for rice. By 2015, Japan's calorie SSR had fallen to 39%; it was 73% in 1965.

Raising farmer income through improving agricultural productivity has also played a part. One of the important purposes of the 1961 Agricultural Basic Act was to improve agricultural productivity so as to raise farmer income to be on par with that of other industries. This made it possible for some farmers to continue food production, especially the production of rice which is, in addition to being the staple food, of cultural and social significance to the Japanese people. Over the decades, while raising agricultural productivity

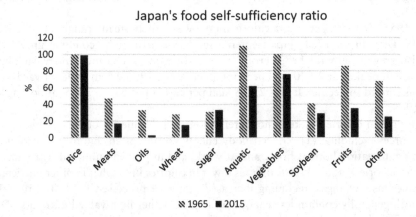

Figure 12.1 Changes in Japan's food self-sufficiency ratios.
Source: Based on MAFF (2018).

has helped improve farmer income, heavy government subsidies have also been important in maintaining high incomes for farmers.

Japan's food policy has been dynamic and responsive. Since the adoption of the 'Selective Expansion' strategy, Japan's food supply has become highly dependent upon imports. Any major disturbance to stable imports of food affects the stability of the domestic food supply. The then Ministry of Agriculture and Forestry reacted to the 1973 US soybean export ban by developing and maintaining a world food demand–supply model. This model has been used since 1973 to help forecast any major structural changes in global food demand and supply. Today, the Ministry of Agriculture, Forestry and Fishery (MAFF) monitors global food market developments on a daily basis (Dr Kabuta, GRIPS).

In response to the international food price hikes in 1996 and the expected huge expansion of food imports by China, in 1999, Japan developed the current Food, Agriculture and Rural Areas Basic Act to replace the Agricultural Basic Act of 1961. In formulating this new act, food security was one of the major considerations. The new act called for an increase in domestic agricultural production together with the use of imports and reserves. The new act has been implemented through the 'Basic Plan for Food, Agriculture and Rural Areas' which is renewed/updated every 5 years in principle. Under the new Basic Act and Basic Plans, an explicit food security policy has been in place since 1999.

Japan has also diversified sources of food imports and contributed to boosting the global food supply. When the 1973 US soybean export ban occurred, the US was the single most important source of imports. Realising that relying on limited sources for imports of key food items was not safe, Japan took measures to facilitate the imports of food from diverse sources, including: (1) sending delegates overseas to investigate potential sources; (2) acquiring land in other countries for production, with the intention of exporting back to Japan; and (3) helping exporting countries to trade food. The land acquisition approach has proven to be a failure (due to lack of farming expertise suitable to the environments of host countries and potential conflicts with locals). The trade facilitation approach has been a success. Host countries are generally happy to have Japanese companies help them trade their food. Another measure to ensure more diverse sources of imports, though more intangible and less spelt out, has been to maintain friendly relationship with food exporting countries.

Contributing to boosting global food supply has also benefited Japan. Japan assists other countries in developing their agriculture and increasing their food output. One large and successful agricultural development program with Japanese assistance is the development of the Brazilian Cerrado Region (1979–2001) into a major soybean producer and exporter. Brazil's ability to export more soybeans helped to meet China's fast growing demand. This in turn reduced the impact on Japan's large soybean imports. This is a great story of helping others in order to help oneself (www.jibtv.com/programs/cerrado2013/).

Japan adopts a preventive approach to deal with any potential food crises. Food availability has not been an issue since the early 1960s. What has been crucial for Japan is to attain a stable food supply through (1) domestic production, (2) imports, and (3) food reserves. Fluctuations in each of the three sources may occur, though to varying degrees. Consequently, Japan has been proactive in developing adequate preparatory and preventive measures to ensure that food supply is stable and that a high level of food security is sustained into the future. Worth particular mention is that when developing measures to deal with potential food emergencies, discrete measures have been devised for deployment according to severity (Table 12.1). This is most appropriate and is cost-effective.

Japan's attainment of a high level of food security shows that resource constraints and hence high dependence on imports do not necessarily detract from food security. Government

Table 12.1 Levels of food emergency and countermeasures in Japan

Level 0	Level 1	Level 2
• Collection, analysis and publicity of information on forecasted supplies of food • Utilisation of food stockpiles and securing food imports • Minimisation of food waste and distribution of substandard agricultural commodities • Monitoring and issuing administrative guidance on prices and distribution of food	• Increase in agricultural production through additional planting • Request to manufacturers to ensure the supplies of food production inputs • Instructions on food imports • Instructions on selling, transportation, and storage of food to balance regional food supply-demand and to rectify any panic buying and hoarding • Price inspections	• Production diversion to crops with higher calorie efficiency • Utilisation of lands other than existing farmlands for food crop production • Implementation of food rationing • Price control • Securing petroleum supplies for food production, and changing farming methods

Sources: based on Hirasawa (2017a; 2017b).

commitment to ensure citizens have secure food intake is fundamentally important. With such commitments, many other difficulties can be overcome. Japan's experience also indicates the importance of having clearly defined, long-term oriented and dynamic food policies, improving agricultural productivity and farmer income, contributing to global food supply, and preventing rather than reacting to food crises.

Looking into the future, increased attention needs to be directed to ensure food security at the household and individual levels among low-income people. After World War II, Japan has largely been an equitable society economically. Since the late 1980s, however, the stability of jobs, the level of salary, and the system of income redistribution have degraded gradually. Consequently, income disparity has increased. Hence, micro-level food insecurity may increasingly become a concern (Hirasawa 2017a). One other issue that requires attention is physical access to food by older people who choose to remain in familiar areas where local shops are disappearing due to population decline.

12.3 The Netherlands

The Netherlands is a country in Western Europe with a population of 17 million in 2017. 'Netherlands' literally means 'lower countries', in reference to its low land and flat geography, with only about 50% of its land exceeding one metre above sea level. Most of the areas below sea level are artificial. Since the late 16th century, large areas (polders) have been reclaimed from the sea and lakes, amounting to nearly 17% of the country's current land mass.

Since 1848 the country has been governed as a parliamentary democracy and a constitutional monarchy. It was one of the first countries in the world to have an elected parliament (although initially the proportion of the population who had the right to vote was very small and universal suffrage was adopted only in 1919). It has a market-based mixed economy, with the degree of its economic freedom being ranked the 17th out of 180 countries in 2018 according to the Index of Economic Freedom (The Heritage Foundation 2018).

People in the Netherlands have a very high quality of life. Per capita GDP was $52,503 in 2017 (PPP, current international $) (World Bank 2019). In 2018, the World Happiness Report by the United Nations Sustainable Development Solutions Network ranked the Netherlands as the sixth-happiest country in the world (Helliwell, Layard and Sachs 2018). It also ranks tenth in the Human Development Index (HDI) in 2017 (UNDP 2018).

Despite its small land mass, limited farming land, and high population density, the Netherlands' agricultural performance has been very impressive. Its agriculture is very highly developed: highly mechanised and intensive. The fertility of the soil and the mild climate also contribute to its very high agricultural productivity. It produces plenty of food, not only for domestic supply but also for exports. It ranks first in the European Union and second worldwide in value of agricultural exports, behind only the United States (Holland Trade and Invest 2018).

There was serious food shortage during the German occupation of the Netherlands in World War II. After the War, food supply quickly improved. Food availability has since never been an issue. FAO data show that in the early 1960s, the country's availability of macronutrients was well over daily requirements. A significant portion of the nutrients was obtained from foods of animal origin. In the case of protein, this share was already very high in 1961, being 57%. By the early 2010s, it had increased to 68%. Generally, protein of animal origin is regarded as being better quality. There has been a recent slight decrease in energy intake and esp., in fat. Because the intake of these nutrients by the Dutch has been well over daily requirements, this decrease must be due to health considerations.

Not only plentiful, food in the Netherlands is also ranked as the most nutritious and healthy, in a comparison of 125 countries (Oxfam 2014; Reaney 2014). The Global Food Security Index ranking also endorses the very high level of food security in the Netherlands. Since 2012, when the Index first became available, the ranking for the Netherlands has been steadily high, ranging between the fourth and the sixth highest among over 110 countries ranked. In 2018, its GFSI score was 84.7%, the fifth highest in the world.

Few people have problems in accessing food in the Netherlands. The country's low income inequality must have helped to achieve this. During 2010–2015, the Gini coefficient for the Netherlands was 28% (cf. Australia: 34.9%, the USA: 41.1%). The Gini coefficient measures the deviation of the distribution of income among individuals or households within a country from a perfectly equal distribution. A value of 0 represents absolute equality, a value of 100 absolute inequality. A value lower than 30 is considered low inequality. To reduce inequality, the Netherlands has a generous welfare system backed up by a strongly redistributive taxing system.

In addition to the low inequality, other social, economic and political attributes must have also helped the country to achieve a very high level of food security. The Netherlands has a long history of social tolerance and is generally regarded as a liberal country. The people are modest, independent, and self-reliant. They have an aversion to the non-essential and regard a lavish lifestyle as wasteful. Ostentatious behaviour is not welcome. Accumulating money is fine as long as people put it back into the system for the good of society. It is among the countries having low corruption (with a CPI being 82% in 2017), ranked the eighth least corrupt out of 180 countries. The governance of their country by an elected parliament provides important institutional support for the Dutch people to build their country as a modern society. In 2017, the DI for the Netherlands was 88.9, ranked the 11th highest in the world.

In highly food-secure countries like the Netherlands, consumers place even higher expectations on food safety. The Dutch government holds that consumers must be able to trust the safety of food. The Netherlands Food and Consumer Product Safety Authority (NVWA) is an independent agency in the Ministry of Agriculture, Nature, and Food Quality that monitors the safety of food. The NVWA ensures businesses comply with national and international laws and regulations. Its enforcement involves inspections, communication, and investigations, and aims to facilitate compliance. The NVWA also plays an important role in export inspections and the import of products to Europe. Its core values are transparency, reliability, independence, and leadership (NVWA 2018).

12.4 Singapore

Singapore is an island city-state off southern Malaysia. It is officially known as the Republic of Singapore. It came into being in 1965 after being separated from Malaysia, of which it was a part.

When it became a separate nation in 1965, there were many uncertainties. Issues that were threatening this new country's first steps were many, such as unemployment, lack of housing, a poor education system, and most worryingly the lack of natural resources and arable land. The new government aimed at building a 'Singaporean identity' as a multiracial and multilingual society. It made Malay, Chinese, Tamil, and English its official languages. Manufacturing was promoted as part of its economic strategies. The government intentionally prepared Singapore to become an international investment and financial hub. It also invested heavily in an education system that adopted English as the language of instruction and emphasised practical training to develop a competent workforce well suited to industry needs (Lepoer 1991).

After 50 years' endeavour, Singaporeans have transformed their country into a modern and highly developed society. In 2017, its per capita GDP was $93,905 (PPP, current international $) (World Bank 2019). With a population of 5.6 million, its population density is extremely high, at 7,916 persons per km^2, due to its very small land area. Corruption in this country is extremely low, with a CPI of 84% (Transparency International 2018). It was ranked the sixth least corrupt country in the world, and the first in Asia. Its DI in 2017 was 63.2%, better than the previous years (EIU 2018). Its GFSI was 84.0 in 2017, the highest in Asia and the fourth highest in the world (EIU 2017). In 2018, its GFSI was 85.9%, being the most food-secure country in the world (EIU 2018). Singapore has achieved such an enviably high level of food security despite having very limited natural resources.

Major factors that have contributed to Singapore's attainment of such a very high level of food security include:

- **A very low level of corruption:** Corruption is very low in Singapore. It is the 'cleanest' country in Asia. The very low level of corruption encourages more efficient allocation of resources (hence, benefiting its economic growth) and more equitable distribution of results from economic growth.
- **A lateral approach to managing food supply:** According to Teng (2013), Singapore resorts to three 'food taps' to manage its food supply: imports, self-production, and stockpiles, in that order of importance. Food imports account for about 90% of Singapore's food supply. If Singapore had insisted on having a high level of food self-sufficiency, it could have significantly disadvantaged itself economically and hence reduced its financial ability to import foods.
- **High vigilance in food security management:** Despite its very high level of food security status, Singapore has never been complacent. It has a designated agency to take care of the country's food security operations and strategies: the Singapore Food Agency (SFA). The country has recently developed its food security roadmap, which consists of

three strategies: 'core', 'supporting', and 'enabling'. 'Core' strategies place emphasis on diversification of sources of imports, investment abroad, industry development, optimised local production, and stockpiling. 'Supporting' strategies involve reduction of food wastage, strengthening of infrastructure, financial instruments, and affordability. Finally, 'enabling' strategies focus on cross-government coordination, emergency planning, communications, market monitoring, and fiscal, legal, and regulatory frameworks.

Since Singapore heavily relies on imports for its food supply, the major ongoing challenge is to tackle any import disruptions, both expected and unexpected. Import interruptions caused by widespread epidemics such as SARS, wars, and natural disasters are generally beyond Singapore's control and can be very devastating to its food supply. To mitigate food shortages caused by import disruptions, Singapore uses the following options (Teng 2013):

- Ensuring the supply of some essential foods from domestic production. According to Teng (2013), Singapore has set targets to domestically produce 15% of its total needs of finfish, 30% of eggs, and 10% of fresh vegetables. However, it recognises such supplies would be inadequate should supplies be disrupted for a prolonged period (Teng 2013).
- Diversifying sources of imports to reduce dependency on a single or a few exporting countries. This should be an easy and inexpensive option.
- Cooperating with others in the region. Being a member of the ASEAN Plus Three Emergency Rice Reserve (APTERR), Singapore can benefit from the regional 'reserve' when a disruption becomes lengthy. It is in Singapore's interest to play a significant role in promoting and contributing to this regional food security initiative (Teng and Escaler 2010; Kassim 2011).

As part of the strategy to handle import disruptions, Singapore has also started promoting the use of product substitutes, particularly liquid or powdered eggs and frozen meat cuts instead of fresh chilled meat. It has also started using contract farming through foreign investment and the creation of a designated 'food production and processing zone' situated in other countries (Kassim 2011).

Most food supply disruptions caused by epidemic or natural disasters tend to be localised. After initial shocks, a country is usually able to quickly find alternatives to handle food imports. However, if a large-scale war bursts out, the impact can be widespread and prolonged. In this regard, it will be most valuable for Singapore to play an active role in promoting and contributing to regional and global peace. Singapore is highly developed economically and also has high R&D capabilities. Coupled with its strategic location and friendly relationship with many other countries, Singapore can contribute to many worthwhile initiatives to ensure sustained peace in the region and globally. Singapore will be the ultimate beneficiary of a peaceful world as far as food security is concerned (Teng and Escaler 2010).

While food is abundant in Singapore, Singaporeans also demand high-quality food, especially poultry meat, seafood, vegetables, and fruits. As such, the Singaporean government is obliged to make sure that the available foods are safe to consume. However, as it imports over 90% of its food, it is vulnerable to food safety incidents in production countries.

Food wastage is another issue. Reducing food wastage is equivalent to having an increased food supply. The Singaporean government has made efforts to reduce food wastage by educating food manufacturers, retailers, food importers, food producers, and other stakeholders along the food supply chain on waste management. R&D in food waste reduction and recycling is also encouraged. Efforts have also been made to reduce food wastage through better post-harvest management and storage to prolong shelf life (Agri-food and Veterinary Authority of Singapore 2013/2014).

As in many other developed economies, excessive food energy intake or the intake of foods without balanced nutrition has also become an issue in Singapore. Coupled with lack of physical activity, the incidence of obesity is high. Avoiding excessive food intake and having a balanced nutrition intake will assist not only in preventing and controlling obesity and other health problems but also in making efficient use of foods and increasing the food supply in relative terms. The Singaporean government has seen the interest in paying attention to nutrition education (Gan and Pang 2012).

Overall, Singapore has very successfully managed its food security. It continues improving its strategies, seeking new opportunities and addressing risks, in an increasingly complex environment, in order to sustain its high level of food security. It has shown to the world that a high level of food security does not have to be achieved through having high self-sufficiency. Through effectively and equitably distributing food, diversifying food import sources, and having long-term and good partnerships, it is possible for a country with poor natural resource endowments to become highly food secure (Hong, Zhou and Wan 2017).

12.5 South Korea

Under Japanese colonial rule, the southern part of the Korean peninsula was largely an agricultural zone and the northern part an industrial zone. As a result, North Korea was economically more developed, and its per capita income was higher to start with after the division of the country. North Korea also had a larger land area with less population and thus was in a better position than South Korea in terms of food provision. However, after decades of separation, South Korea is food abundant and has become one of the developed economies of the world, while North Korea is still chronically short of food.

South Korea's land area is 97,500 km². In 2017, its per capita GDP was $38,335 (PPP, current international $) (World Bank 2019), with a population of 51.5 million. Corruption in the country is relatively low, with the CPI being 54% (Transparency International 2018). Moreover, in 2017 its DI of 80% is the highest in Asia (EIU 2018). Its GFSI was 74.7 in 2017 – the fourth highest in Asia (after Singapore, Japan and Israel) and the 24th highest in the world (EIU 2017).

Before South Korea achieved this high level of food security, it faced many challenges. At the time of its establishment in 1948, South Korea could not produce sufficient food to feed its people. The Korean War (1950–1953) worsened the food shortage problem due to loss of grain stocks, interruptions to farm production, and damage to fields and other production infrastructures. The influx of refugees from North Korea after the war sharply increased the population and thus the demand for food. The price of Koreans' staple food, rice, rose sharply (Song and Kwon 2017).

To cope with the severe food shortage and to stabilise the price of rice, the government revived the compulsory rice collection system from farmers, which was enforced during World War II by Japanese colonial ruling. The collected rice was then distributed to government employees, poor people, and military personnel. The procurement price for the rice was below the market price. This did not make farmers happy and did not contribute to boosting food production.

To increase domestic food production, the South Korean government developed two Food Production Expansion Five-Year Plans (1953–1957, 1958–1962). The most important measures were the expansion of cultivated land through land reclamation, increasing supply of fertilisers, developing high-yielding varieties, and appropriate application of pesticides and herbicides. In the early 1960s, a shift in food production took place: from producing many crops to a focus on rice. The government set a target to be self-sufficient in rice supply. In 1978, South Korea finally attained its rice self-sufficiency target. However, the production of other grain crops has shrunk continuously, and the deficit has been met through imports (Song and Kwon 2017).

Rice is Koreans' staple food and has always accounted for a significant portion of total food consumption. The South Korean government encouraged people to eat rice supplemented with barley and coarse grains to reduce the demand for rice at the times when rice was in short supply. In schools, teachers were asked to check whether mixed grains (rice and other grains) were used in students' lunch boxes. The government also monitored restaurants to ensure they were using mixed grains. In the meantime, imported wheat was processed into wheat flour and sold at a very low price to encourage consumers to substitute it for rice. Such measures helped South Korea mitigate the somewhat rigid demand for rice by consumers during those years of tight supply.

In more recent times, as income has grown, people have taken to consuming more meats and vegetables. This has helped reduce the intake of rice. Over the past decades, per capita consumption of rice has gradually declined from the peak of 136 kg in 1970 to 67.2 kg in 2013. Combined with lower per capita consumption of food grains, the relatively high level of the supply of rice from domestic production, through focused efforts, has enabled South Korea to be in a reasonably comfortable situation in terms of staple food supply, despite the increase in total population.

Nowadays, few South Koreans worry about the possibility of not having food to eat. The supply of energy has been way above the requirements, with an increasing portion coming from animal foods. Protein and fat supply has also become adequate. Poor people also seldom suffer from starvation thanks to various social safety-net programs. If there are any 'problems', they are those caused by 'too comfortable' food availability, such as obesity and food wastage.

What policy measures has the South Korean government used to transform the country from a situation of severe food shortage to a high level of food security? Which policies are more successful and which are less? Below are some major policy initiatives used by the government of South Korea (Song and Kwon 2017).

12.5.1 Compulsory rice collecting policies

In the 1950s, especially after the Korean War, food was seriously short and hyper-inflation prevailed. The government used a compulsory approach to collect rice. It did not help increase rice output. It was abolished in 1956. A new government procurement system was introduced: purchasing rice from farmers who wanted to sell rice at predetermined prices. However, the purchase price was lower than the production cost, not many farmers sold their rice to the government. The ratio of government purchases to total production remained very low at around 5% until 1960.

12.5.2 Price support

In the early 1960s, there were sharp drops in grain self-sufficiency, especially wheat and maize. To ensure a certain level of self-sufficiency was on the government's policy agenda. In the mid-1960s, price support for grain production was introduced. Grain procurement prices were increased substantially. A rise in total grain production followed. This resulted in large and increasing government expenditure. From the late 1960s, the government decided to limit price support to rice and barley to ensure a high level of self-sufficiency only for these two foods.

12.5.3 Public stockholding program

Many governments maintain public stockholdings or buffer stocks in their quest for better food security. South Korea also uses this approach to enhance its food security. It started a stockholding program in the 1950s. The volume of purchased rice gradually increased. Since 1975, the government has maintained the purchased volume at 16% of total rice produced.

12.5.4 Tariff protection

The high cost of producing agricultural products in South Korea implies low global competitiveness. Therefore, the South Korean government has tried to constrain imports by keeping tariffs high. Consequently, prices of most agricultural products in Korea are much higher than global prices. In 2015, South Korea's tariff rate for rice imports was 513%.

12.5.5 Establishment of organisations for better food security

South Korea has established various organisations to enhance food security. The Rural Development Administration (RDA), established in 1961, significantly contributed to boosting agricultural productivity by improving crop varieties, promoting machinery use in agriculture, and providing agricultural technology guidance and advice to farmers. The Agricultural Product Quality Management Service (APQMS) was established in 1998 by expanding and restructuring the Agricultural Product Inspection Service established in 1949. APQMS is in charge of certification of agricultural product quality, safety control of harmful substances including agricultural chemicals, and quality assurance. APQMS has contributed to enhancing consumer confidence in the safety and quality of agricultural products produced in South Korea. The Ministry of Food and Drug Safety is in charge of monitoring food safety including recalling harmful foods, promoting healthy living, and managing food-related regulations.

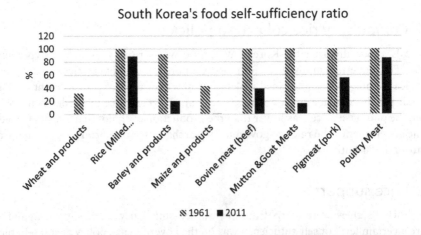

South Korea's food self-sufficiency ratio

♦ 1961   ■ 2011

Figure 12.2 Changes in food self-sufficiency ratios in South Korea.
Source: FAO (2018).

Despite the high level of food security, South Korea's food supply relies heavily on imports due to its limited agricultural resource endowment, which has resulted in low and declining self-sufficiency (Figure 12.2 (FAO 2018)). The only crop for which South Korea has managed to maintain a high rate of self-sufficiency is rice, the nation's staple food. It has also managed to maintain a high rate of self-sufficiency in poultry meat (Song and Kwon 2017).

A low self-sufficiency rate is not necessarily detrimental to food security, but it does disturb the minds of the public who have suffered bitterly in the past from insecure food provisions. This in turn bothers the politicians. For South Korea to maintain a high level of food security into the future, there are many challenges. The two major ones are: (1) maintaining a level of food self-sufficiency rate that is socially and politically acceptable and (2) coping with global food supply instability.

The potential for South Korea to produce more food domestically is not high. How stable the future global food market will be is also hard to foresee. Further, as a small player, South Korea can exert little influence over what is going to happen in the global food market. Hence, handling either of the challenges is not easy. Nonetheless, South Korea has taken actions or adopted various measures in a number of areas to pursue a sustained high level of food security into the future:

12.5.6 Global cooperation

Global cooperation can be an effective approach for import-dependent countries such as South Korea to ensure food security. South Korea joined the APTERR, an international emergency rice reserve initiative, in 2012. It is expected to continue its effort in promoting this and other available avenues of international cooperation.

12.5.7 Use of the direct payment program

The direct payment program for stabilising farmers' income contributes to enhancing stability of food production on a long-term basis. Earlier, direct payment in South Korea had focused mainly on rice. It has been extended to other field crops since 2014. The direct payment program was employed to compensate farmers for their income loss due to the withdrawal of protection (or increased opening up of the market). The program has been designed to operate in conformity with WTO rules in that the direct payment is decoupled from prices. The EU uses a similar policy approach.

12.5.8 Reducing and avoiding food waste

Reducing food wastage helps improve food supply. South Korea has made efforts to reduce food wastage. Koreans like to put a lot of food on their dining table, although they cannot eat all the food. This is especially the case when they entertain guests and friends. The food wastage in South Korea is close to 5 million tonnes every year, and the cost for treating the waste is approximately 808 billion won (approximately US$735 million). A volume-based food waste collecting fee system has been introduced in 2013 (Song and Kwon 2017).

Table 12.2 Food self-sufficiency targets in South Korea (%)

	2010 performance	2015 target Previous	2015 target New	2020 target
Total grain SSR	27.6	25.0	30.0	32
Food grain SSR	54.0	-	57	60
Calorie SSR	49.3	47	52	55

Source: MAFRA (2013)

12.5.9 Minimum food self-sufficiency targets

South Korea has established self-sufficiency targets for food grains and calories. The Basic Act on Agriculture and Rural Community enacted in 1999 regulates that 'the government shall establish and keep the target for the level of food self-sufficiency, and make an effort for ensuring a reasonable volume of food stock.' The act was amended in 2001 to 'include targets for reasonable food self-sufficiency in establishing the framework for developing agriculture and rural community.' In 2006, the self-sufficiency targets for total grain and calories were set for the country for the first time, at 25% and 47% respectively, to be met by 2015 (Table 12.2). In 2011, in view of the global food price crisis during 2006–2008, these targets were raised to be 30% and 52% for 2015. A new self-sufficiency target for food grain was also set for 2015 at 57%. At the same time, the targets for 2020 were also set, being 32% for all grains, 60% for food grains, and 55% for calories (MAFRA 2013).

A self-sufficiency rate of around 30% in total grains is very low. Even if it is achieved, its role in the likelihood of a prolonged serious global food shortage may be quite limited. On the other hand, the costs of pursuing it may be very high. However, taking into account the importance of food and the Korean public's suffering from food shortages in the past, such self-sufficiency targets may still be hugely valuable in the sense that these can act as an important psychological safety net among the public. In return, the government may win over their support for trade reforms in many other areas that could render greater benefits to South Korea.

Review questions

1. What is your judgement about the status of food security in each of the countries examined in this chapter?
2. What are the major forces that are responsible for shaping each of the countries' current food security status?
3. In your view, what is the most important thing that each of the countries has done to help them to achieve a high level of food security?
4. What is the most important thing each of them should do to sustain their high level of food security?

Discussion questions

1. Countries examined in this chapter all have high levels of food security. What do they have in common in pursuing such a status?
2. Choose one country that was examined in this chapter. Share your view on what else this country needs to do to further improve its food security.
3. Can the approaches used by countries in this chapter be applied to other countries that are keen to improve their food security? If so, what are some of the approaches that you believe should be adopted by countries that are less food secure?
4. Could it be the case that the approaches used by countries in this chapter are not applicable to countries with a low level of food security? If you think so, then, why?
5. Out of the approaches used by countries with a high level of food security, is there any particular one that impresses you the most? If so, what is it and why?

References

Agri-food and Veterinary Authority of Singapore (2013/2014), *AVA's Food Security Roadmap for Singapore, Food Security Special Feature* (pp. 1–8), Agri-food and Veterinary Authority of Singapore, Singapore.

EIU. (2017), 'Global food security index 2017', https://foodsecurityindex.eiu.com/Resources, accessed 12 October 2017.

EIU. (2018), 'Democracy index 2017', https://pages.eiu.com/rs/753-RIQ-438/images/Democracy_Index_2017.pdf, accessed 15 October 2018.

Endeweld, M. and Silber, J. (2017), 'On food security in Israel', in Zhou, Z.Y. and Wan, G.H. (eds), *Food Insecurity in Asia: Why Institutions Matter*, ADB Institute, Tokyo, Ch. 7, pp. 192–256.

FAO. (2018), 'Food balance sheet', www.fao.org/faostat/en/#data/FBS, accessed 2 March 2018.

Gan, G.L. and Pang, J. (2012), 'Obesity in Singapore, Prevention and Control', *The Singapore Family Physician*, Vol. 38, (issue 1): 8–13.

Gelb, E. and Kislev, Y. (1982), 'Farmers' financing of agricultural research in Israel', *Research Policy*, Vol. 11, pp. 321–327.

Helliwell, J.F., Layard, R., and Sachs, J.D. (eds) (2018), 'World happiness report 2018, The United Nations sustainable development solutions network', http://worldhappiness.report/ed/2018/, accessed 29 January 2019.

Hirasawa, A. (2017a), 'Food security measures in Japan since World War II', in Zhou, Z.Y. and Wan, G.H. (eds), *Food Insecurity in Asia: Why Institutions Matter*, ADB Institute, Tokyo, Ch. 5, pp. 89–138.

Hirasawa, A. (2017b), *Formation of Japan's Food Security Policy: Relations with Food Situation and Evolution of Agricultural Policies*, Norinchukin Research Institute, Tokyo.

Holland Trade and Invest. (2018), 'The Netherlands ranks second to US as worlds' top agricultural exporter', www.hollandtradeandinvest.com/latest/news/2018/january/24/the-netherlands-ranks-second-to-us-as-worlds%E2%80%99-top-agricultural-exporter, accessed 28 April 2018.

Hong, M.C., Zhou, Z.Y., and Wan, G.H. (2017), 'Food security in Pakistan, Bangladesh, Indonesia, and Singapore', in Zhou, Z.Y. and Wan, G.H. (eds), *Food Insecurity in Asia: Why Institutions Matter*, ADB Institute, Tokyo, Ch. 8, pp. 257–286.

Kassim, Y.R. (2011), Singapore's Growing Role in the Asian Food Security, www3.ntu.edu. sg/rsis/nts/resources/Media-reports/YR-0709-EAF.pdf, accessed 16 October 2015.

Lepoer, B.L. (1991), *Singapore: A Country Study, GPO for the Library of Congress*, Washington, D.C.

MAFF (Ministry of Agriculture, Forestry and Fisheries, Japan). (2018), 'Food self-sufficiency ratio', www.maff.go.jp/j/wpaper/w_maff/h28/h28_h/trend/part1/chap1/c1_1_01.html, accessed 25 October 2018.

MAFRA (Ministry of Agriculture, Food and Rural Affairs). (2013), *History of Grain Policy in Korea*, Ministry of Agriculture, Food and Rural Affairs, Seoul.

NVWA (The Netherlands Food and Consumer Product Safety Authority). (2018), *Food Safety Statement, Ministry of Agriculture, Nature and Food Quality*, Utrecht, The Netherlands.

Oxfam. (2014), 'Good enough to eat: Where in the world are the best and worst places to eat?' *Oxfam Media Briefing*, www.oxfamamerica.org/static/media/files/Good_Enough_ To_Eat_Media_brief_FINAL.pdf, accessed 27 March 2018.

Reaney, P. (2014), 'Netherlands is country with most plentiful, healthy food: Oxfam', www. reuters.com/article/us-food-countries/netherlands-is-country-with-most-plentiful-healthy-food-oxfam-idUSBREA0E01S20140115, accessed 27 March 2018.

Song, J.H. and Kwon, T.J. (2017), 'Food security in the Republic of Korea and the Democratic People's Republic of Korea: Why the difference?', in Zhou, Z.Y. and Wan, G.H. (eds), *Food Insecurity in Asia: Why Institutions Matter*, ADB Institute, Tokyo, Ch. 6, pp. 139–191.

Teng, P. (2013), *Food Security: What It Means for a Food Importing Country*, S. Rajaratnam School of International Studies, Nanyang Technological University, Singapore.

Teng, P. and Escaler, M. (2010), *The Case for Urban Food Security: A Singapore Perspective, NTS Perspective*, S. Rajaratnam School of International Studies, Nanyang Technological University, Singapore.

The Heritage Foundation. (2018), '2018 Index of economic freedom', www.heritage.org/ index/ranking, accessed 27 March 2018.

Transparency International. (2018), 'Corruption perceptions index', 2017, www.transparency. org/news/feature/corruption_perceptions_index_2017, accessed 15 October 2018.

UNDP (United Nations Development Programme). (2018), 'The human development report 2018', http://hdr.undp.org/en/2018-update/download, accessed 29 January 2019.

United Nations. (2015), *World Population Prospects: The 2015 Revision*, Department of Economic and Social Affairs, Population Division, https://esa.un.org/unpd/wpp/Download/ Standard/Population/, accessed 27 April 2017.

World Bank. (2019), GDP per capita, PPP (current international $), https://data.worldbank. org/indicator/NY.GDP.PCAP.PP.CD, accessed 29 January 2019.

Yosef, D. (1960), *Kirya Neemana – the Siege of Jerusalem 1948*, Shoken, Tel Aviv, pp. 234–240.

Chapter 13

Why countries' food security levels differ

Summary

Having examined the food security practices of diverse countries in the previous two chapters, this chapter looks into why some countries have succeeded but others have failed in achieving a high level of food security. In Section 13.1, major similarities and differences in food security practices and the associated experiences and lessons of those are highlighted. Based on the comparisons and analyses in Section 13.1, in Section 13.2, we demythicise some commonly made claims about what might be responsible for a country's persistent food insecurity. Finally, in Section 13.3, we pinpoint key factors that help improve or hinder a country's food security.

After studying this chapter, you should be able to:
- List and discuss what countries with high levels of food security have in common.
- List and discuss what food-insecure countries have in common.
- Discuss what countries with high levels of food security should do to sustain their food security.
- Prescribe what is important for food-insecure countries to do to improve their food security.

13.1 Similarities and differences, experiences and lessons

13.1.1 Levels of democracy and food security

Country experiences as examined in the previous two chapters suggest that a country's food security level is closely linked to its level of democracy (with some exceptions which we will address shortly). This is clearly reflected in the relationship between the Democracy Index (DI) and the other two indexes – Global Food Security Index (GFSI) and Global Hunger Index (GHI) – as shown in Table 13.1 (for countries with a high level of food security, GHI is not applicable). That is, for countries with higher DI, their food security level is also higher. In other words, if a country's DI is lower, its food security level is also lower.

Going beyond those selected countries as shown in Table 13.1, if we look at the relationships between the food security and democracy levels of many other countries included in the 'Food security and related variables' table, the same observation is borne out. When we plot GFSI against DI for all countries in a scatter diagram, there is a clear trend that the higher the level of democracy, the higher a country's food security (Figure 13.1). The correlation coefficient between these two variables is 0.69. There are a few countries that have reasonably high level of food security but with very low levels of democracy. These countries are oil-rich ones in the Middle East (such as Kuwait, Oman, Qatar, Saudi Arabia, and the United Arab Emirates). Very high income from oil could have enabled them to partially offset the negative impact of their low level of democracy on food security. Changes in their income from oil are likely to cause changes in their food security.

In democratic settings, it is most likely that governments are held 'accountable'. Politicians have to be accountable to the people who elected them. However, it must be pointed out that a higher level of democracy does not automatically guarantee a country a higher level of food security although it should facilitate improvement. For example, the level of democracy in India is higher than that in Singapore yet its food security level is much lower. India's institutional weaknesses such as the inefficient and ineffective judicial systems that indulge widespread corruption may have played a role in dragging down the level of food security.

Similarly, countries with a lower level of democracy such as Singapore may achieve high levels of food security. In Singapore, the level of corruption is low and its level of food security is very high (Table 13.1). Hence, apart from democracy, certain other institutional aspects also need to be strong to influence a country's food security. One of these is the presence of strong institutions that deter corruption.

13.1.2 Food security and levels of corruption

Countries with higher levels of corruption come lower levels of food security. Table 13.1 shows that food security has a strong inverse relationship with a country's corruption (Note that in Table 13.1, a higher index number for the Corruption Perception Index (CPI) means a lower level of corruption, and *vice versa*). In countries with low degrees of corruption, the levels of food security are higher, such as in Israel, Japan, Singapore, and the Netherlands. Otherwise, high degrees of corruption are associated with lower levels of food security, such as in North Korea, Venezuela, and Zimbabwe.

The correlation between corruption and food security (r = 0.831) is even stronger than that between democracy and food security (r = 0.686). Figure 13.2 shows that highly corrupt countries have lower levels of food security. Some exceptions are the few oil-rich countries, even though their food security has never been as high as those countries with low corruption.

Table 13.1 Food security and governance (score out of 100, 2017)

	Global Food Security Index (GFSI)	Global Hunger Index (GHI)	Democracy Index (DI)	Corruption Perception Index (CPI)
Low food security				
China	63.7	7.5	31.0	41
Fiji		8.1	58.5	
India	48.9	31.4	72.3	40
North Korea		28.2	10.8	17
Venezuela	50.2	13.0	38.7	18
Zimbabwe		33.8	31.6	22
High food security				
Israel	79.2	na	77.9	62
Japan	79.5	na	78.8	73
Netherlands	82.8	na	88.9	82
Singapore	84.0	na	63.2	84
South Korea	74.7	na	80.0	54

Source: IFPRI (2018).

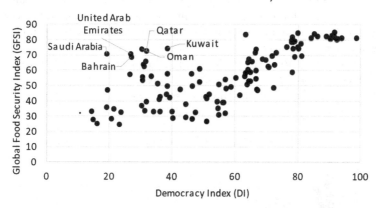

Correlation between GFSI and DI, r = 0.686

Figure 13.1 Relationship between democracy and food security.
Source: see the sources for "Food Security and Related Variables" table for the same indicators.

13.1.3 Poverty, inequality, and food security

A country's level of food security is inversely related to poverty incidence. Those countries with higher levels of food security such as Singapore and the Netherlands have very low levels of poverty. In countries with low levels of food security such as India and Zimbabwe, there are high levels of poverty.

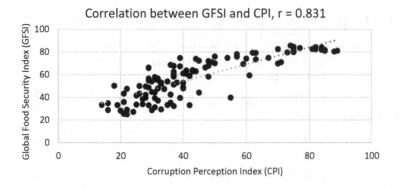

Figure 13.2 Relationship between corruption and food security.
Source: see the sources for "Food Security and Related Variables" table for the same indicators.

Globally, no countries with high poverty, as reflected by poverty headcount ratio in Figure 13.3, have achieved high levels of food security. Those countries that have achieved a high level of food security all have very low levels of poverty.

Inequality also has a negative impact on a country's food security. However, the negative impact tends to be weak as reflected by a much smaller negative correlation coefficient (-0.296, cf. -0.742 for poverty). Two countries (one rich and one poor) may have similar levels of income inequality, as measured by the Gini Index in the 'Food security and related variables' table. The income available to the poor in the two countries can be quite different. In the poor country, the poor may not have the economic means to buy food and thus have little access to it. In the rich country, the poor may have quite a reasonable income, due to protection rendered by the country's social security system. Such income protection enables them to have adequate access to food.

Poverty directly causes food insecurity among low-income groups, through the lack of economic access to food. Inequality can further reinforce poverty, especially in poorer countries. Poverty and inequality are sources of social unrest. When a country suffers from social instability, food security is also undermined.

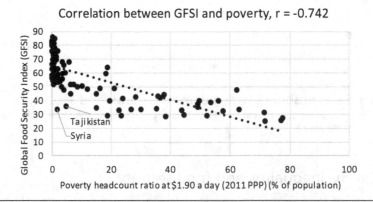

Figure 13.3 Relationship between poverty and food security.
Source: see the sources for "Food Security and Related Variables" table for the same indicators.

It must be pointed out that although on the surface food insecurity is closely related to poverty, poverty itself, however, is not the fundamental cause of food insecurity. The fundamental causes are serious inequality, corruption, and the lack of democracy. The poor have continuously been taken advantage of by those with power and been marginalised by corrupt systems.

13.1.4 Resource endowment and food security

Resource endowment alone does not determine a country's level of food security. Countries like Israel, Japan, Singapore, and the Netherlands all have a very low per capita natural resource endowment. Table 13.2 shows that in none of the countries with high food security is the amount of arable land per capita greater than that of those with low food security. Yet, they all enjoy a very high level of food security. In the case of South Korea, its per capita water and arable land resources are one half or one third of those of North Korea. Yet, South Korea's food security level is much higher than that in North Korea.

Similarly, countries such as Venezuela and Zimbabwe all have comparatively high per capita resource endowments, yet all are now suffering from low levels of food security. Clearly, lower resource endowment does not prevent a country from achieving a higher level of food security; higher endowment does not guarantee a country a higher level of food security. Globally, none of the resource endowment indicators show a high correlation with food security. For example, the correlation coefficient between per capita arable land and food security is 0.093 while that between per capita total actual renewable water resources (TARWR) and food security is 0.144.

13.1.5 Population size and food security

Population size also does not determine a country's level of food security. China's experience provides most convincing evidence to support this point. In 1974, China's total population was 909 million. By 2014, its population had reached 1,364 million, 455 million more people than in 1974. Yet, China's food security level in the 2010s is much higher than it was before the 1980s. It is a fact that since the early 1980s China's food security level has steadily improved while its population has increased. Today in China, people can buy whatever food they want as long as they can afford it. Before the 1980s, China had a lower population but people were unable to buy the food they wanted even if they had money.

The correlation coefficient between population size and food security of all countries around the globe tells the same tale: they are hardly related. The coefficient is only -0.003.

13.1.6 Income level and food security

Higher per capita income is generally associated with higher levels of food security. As can be seen from country cases in Chapter 12, countries with higher levels of food security all have higher per capita incomes. Countries with lower levels of food security as those studied in Chapter 11 all have lower incomes.

Indonesia is another case in point. Its economy suffered a major setback due to the 1997 Asian financial crisis, leading to lower consumer income. This in turn had a significant negative impact on its food security (Figure 13.4 (World Bank 2019)). With sustained economic recovery over the past two decades, however, consumer income has gradually improved and its food security has again started improving (Hong, Zhou and Wan 2017).

The correlation between the income indicator (per capita GDP) and food security is high. The coefficient is 0.808; being slightly lower than that between corruption and food security, which is 0.831.

Table 13.2 Food security and resource endowment

Country	Global Food Security Index (GFSI) (2017)	Global Hunger Index (GHI) (2017)	TARWR per inhabitant (2011)	Total land area (2016)	Share of arable land (2015)	Per capita arable land (2015)	Population density (2017)
	Score	Score	m^3	1000 km^2	% of total land area	ha	Persons per km^2
Low food security							
China	63.7	7.5	2060	9388.2	12.7	0.09	148
Fiji		8.1	32892	18.3	9.0	0.18	50
India	48.9	31.4	1539	2973.2	52.6	0.12	450
North Korea		28.2	3155	120.4	19.5	0.09	212
Venezuela	50.2	13.0	41886	882.1	3.1	0.09	36
Zimbabwe		33.8	1568	386.9	10.3	0.25	43
High food security							
Israel	79.2	na	235	21.6	13.7	0.04	403
Japan	79.5	na	3399	364.6	11.5	0.03	348
Netherlands	82.8	na	5461	33.7	30.7	0.06	509
Singapore	84.0	na	116	0.7	0.8	0.00	7916
South Korea	74.7	na	1440	97.5	15.0	0.03	528

TARWR: total actual renewable water resources.
Sources: see the sources for the 'Food security and related variables' table for the same indicators. GHI: IFPRI (2018).

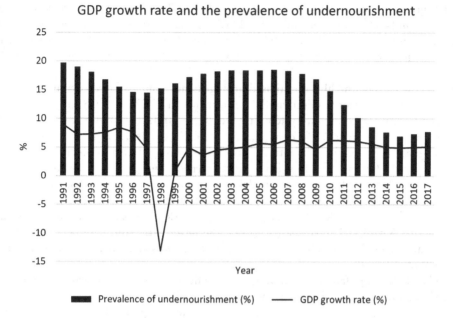

Figure 13.4 GDP growth and the prevalence of undernourishment in Indonesia.
Source: World Bank (2019).

13.1.7 Investment in agricultural R&D and food security

Countries with higher levels of investment in agriculture, such as Israel, Japan, the Netherlands, and South Korea, have higher levels of food security. And the opposite is also true, with countries such as North Korea and Zimbabwe. Adequate investment in agriculture in general and in research and development (R&D) in particular is crucial in improving a country's food supply and thus promoting food security. In the case of Israel, investment in agricultural R&D is claimed to be the major factor in achieving a high level of food security (Endeweld and Silber 2017).

China and India's practices provide further support. China has increased its investment in agricultural infrastructure and R&D since the 1990s. This has helped improve its agricultural total factor productivity (TFP), which in turn helped achieve high grain output. India also increased its investment in agriculture but at a lower level compared to China's. Consequently, its TFP was also lower, so was output level. Between 1990 and 2010, total agricultural production grew 4.5% in China but only 2.9% in India (ABARES 2014).

13.1.8 Farm production models and food security

How food production is organised has a significant impact on food security. Since the end of World War II, countries have tried different farm production models. These models have had different, sometimes drastically different, impacts on food security:

● **Producing through cooperatives:** Some countries use cooperatives to help boost agricultural output. For example, in Israel, cooperatives are widely used. Farmers join or exit agricultural cooperatives on a voluntary basis. These cooperatives are practical and effective in Israel (Endeweld and Silber 2017). China also used agricultural cooperatives, which proved effective during 1954–1956 when farmers could join the cooperatives voluntarily (these cooperatives were soon, however, transformed into involuntarily collectives) (Zhou 2017).

- **Producing through highly collectivised arrangements**: China started coercing farmers to produce through more collectivised arrangements in 1957. In 1958, all farmers were forced to join the commune system in which farm production and many aspects of life were highly collectivised. The consequences were disastrous, resulting in vastly declining or stagnant food output. The return to traditional family-based production in the early 1980s saved China as far as food supply is concerned (Zhou 2017). North Korea also uses a highly collectivised production model. Consequently, the country has been suffering from serious food shortages over the past decades. It has made efforts to move away from such a highly collectivised model, but the process is slow and sometimes slips backwards (Song and Kwon 2017). (In North Korea, the term 'agricultural cooperatives' is used, but it actually refers to highly collectivised working units and not cooperatives like those practised in Israel.)

- **Producing through family-based units**: The model of family-based farming units, either small or large in scale, has been most widely used. It has also proven to be the most effective in many societies. Not all countries adopting family-based farming have achieved a high level of food security (such as India and Zimbabwe) but all countries with a high level of food security (with the exception of Israel) use the family-based farming model.

13.1.9 Role of market and food security

The market has an important role to play in achieving food security. When the market is not allowed to function (partially or fully), food shortage problems emerge, persist or even became further aggravated (such as in China (before the 1980s) and North Korea, and recently in Venezuela and Zimbabwe). When the market functions with greater freedom, it helps a country to achieve higher levels of food security (such as in China since the 1980s and in the Netherlands, Japan, and South Korea).

One extreme approach that has been used to intervene in the market has been for the state to monopolise food trade; this means that food is exclusively procured from producers and then distributed to consumers by the state, as has been practised in both China and North Korea. This approach has always been a failure. The negative impacts on food production are similar in both countries. While China has abandoned this approach, North Korea is still practising it (Zhou 2017; Song and Kwon 2017).

State-controlled procurement and distribution may be justified during times of food emergency. When food was in short supply after World War II, both Japan and South Korea forced their farmers to deliver to the government, often at low prices. Both failed to gain cooperation from farmers. Nonetheless, they stopped using this method as soon as their food supply started to improve (Hirasawa 2017; Song and Kwon 2017). Food rationing was also used for a short time in Israel (Endeweld and Silber 2017).

In Table 13.3, the Index of Economic Freedom (IEF) and its components are provided next to food security indicators of selected countries. Countries with higher food security levels have higher economic freedom indexes; and *vice versa*. The Index is based on 12 quantitative and qualitative factors (see Box 13.1). Business freedom most closely represents how freely

Table 13.3 Food security and economic freedom (the Index of Economic Freedom and its components, 2017, scores, out of 100)

	Global Food Security Index (GFSI)	Global Hunger Index (GHI)	The Index of Economic Freedom	Rule of law			Government size			Regulatory efficiency			Open Markets		
				Property rights	Judicial effectiveness	Government integrity	Tax burden	Government spending	Fiscal health	Business freedom	Labour freedom	Monetary freedom	Trade freedom	Investment Freedom	Financial Freedom
Low food security															
China	63.7	7.5	57.4 (111)	48.3	60.7	41.6	70.0	73.0	92.5	53.9	63.4	71.8	73.6	20	20
Fiji		8.1	63.4 (71)	67.7	41.9	32.7	80.7	72.5	84.1	61.3	70.5	75.5	68.8	55	50
India	48.9	31.4	52.6 (143)	55.4	44.4	44.3	77.2	77.4	11.0	52.8	41.6	75.0	72.6	40	40
North Korea		28.2	4.9 (180)	32.4	5.0	11.6	0.0	0.0	0.0	5.0	5.0	0.0	0.0	0	0
Venezuela	50.2	13.0	27.0 (179)	6.8	10.3	11.6	72.5	51.5	15.2	39.7	28.5	16.8	60.7	0	10
Zimbabwe		33.8	44.0 (175)	27.3	26.1	14.7	61.1	75.2	90.6	36.2	33.1	76.5	52.8	25	10
High food security															
Israel	79.2	na	69.7 (36)	71.9	82.0	47.6	61.0	50.5	71.8	69.9	64.3	84.9	88.0	75	70
Japan	79.5	na	69.6 (40)	89.4	73.8	86.1	68.5	52.3	9.5	82.3	77.5	83.0	82.6	70	60
Netherlands	82.8	na	75.8 (15)	87.4	69.9	85.7	53.2	37.0	83.0	80.2	70.5	85.8	87.0	90	80
Singapore	84.0	na	88.6 (2)	97.1	91.5	87.9	90.5	90.1	80.7	95.1	90.8	84.3	90.0	85	80
South Korea	74.7	na	74.3 (23)	77.8	59.9	67.3	73.7	68.9	97.4	90.6	57.0	84.0	79.5	65	70

Note: The number in brackets is the world rank out of 186.

Sources: GFSI: see the sources for the 'Food security and related variables' table for the same indicators. GHI: IFPRI (2018). The Index of Economic Freedom: www.heritage.org/index/download#, accessed 13 February 2019.

BOX 13.1

The Index of Economic Freedom

Economic freedom is the fundamental right of every human to control his or her own labour and property. In economically free societies, individuals are free to work, produce, consume, and invest in any way they please. Governments allow labour, capital, and goods to move freely, and refrain from coercion or constraint of liberty beyond the extent necessary to protect and maintain liberty itself.

Economic freedom brings greater prosperity. Economic freedom is strongly associated with healthier societies, cleaner environments, greater per capita wealth, human development, democracy, and poverty elimination. Unfortunately, in many parts of the world, many individuals have lacked economic freedom and opportunity, condemning them to poverty and deprivation.

The Index of Economic Freedom is compiled and published by The Heritage Foundation, based in Washington, DC, to help track advancement in economic freedom in 186 countries. It is an annual publication. The 2019 Index is its 25th edition.

The Index measures economic freedom based on 12 quantitative and qualitative factors, grouped into four broad categories of economic freedom:

1. Rule of law (property rights, government integrity, judicial effectiveness)
2. Government size (government spending, tax burden, fiscal health)
3. Regulatory efficiency (business freedom, labour freedom, monetary freedom)
4. Open markets (trade freedom, investment freedom, financial freedom)

Each of the twelve economic freedoms within these categories is graded on a scale of 0 to 100. A country's overall score is derived by averaging these twelve economic freedoms, with equal weight being given to each. Based on the score, countries are placed into one of the following five categories: free: 100–80; mostly free: 79.9–70; moderately free: 69.9–60; mostly unfree: 59.9–50; and repressed: 49.9–40. In the 2019 Index, six countries achieved the 'free' status.

The Index can be accessed at: www.heritage.org/index/. Countries or regions with highest and lowest economic freedom according to the 2019 Index are shown in Table 13.4.

Table 13.4 Countries or regions with highest and lowest Index of Economic Freedom (2019 score)

Highest Index	Score	Lowest Index	Score
Hong Kong	90.2	Algeria	46.2
Singapore	89.4	Timor-Leste	44.2
New Zealand	84.4	Bolivia	42.3
Switzerland	81.9	Equatorial Guinea	41.0
Australia	80.9	Zimbabwe	40.4

(continued)

Table 13.4 (cont.)

Highest Index	Score	Lowest Index	Score
Ireland	80.5	Congo, Republic of	39.7
United Kingdom	78.9	Eritrea	38.9
Canada	77.7	Cuba	27.8
United Arab Emirates	77.6	Venezuela	25.9
Taiwan	77.3	Korea, North	5.9

Source: The Heritage Foundation (2019), '2019 Index of Economic Freedom', www.heritage.org/index/ranking, accessed 22 April 2019.

the market is allowed to operate, supplemented by a few other indicators such as property rights, judicial effectiveness, and investment freedom. The difference in these indicators between high and low food security countries is notable.

13.1.10 Role of international trade

Trade is indispensable for countries to achieve a high level of food security but in particular for those countries whose own food production is not self-sufficient. The cases in the previous two chapters show that without food trade, some of those countries would have suffered badly from insecure food supplies. Trade has made it possible for all those countries included in Chapters 11 and 12 to attain a higher level of food security.

For food-insecure countries such as Zimbabwe, food trade has in recent years helped enormously to mitigate the consequences of severe food shortages. Without food imports, its very limited domestic output would have made things much worse.

In the case of China, without trade it would be unable to achieve the current level of food security. Its current annual soybean imports are in the order of 80–90 million tonnes. If the soybeans had to be produced domestically, it would have taken a large amount of resources, making the production of other essential foods difficult.

Countries that have low food security but engage less in food trade also tend to sustain low food security. India and North Korea are two examples.

As shown in Table 13.3, the three indicators in the 'open markets' category all have higher scores for higher food security countries. This lends further support to the role of international trade in improving food security.

13.1.11 Handling food emergencies

Countries have handled food emergencies differently. After World War II, when there were serious and devastating food shortages, Japan and South Korea resorted to imports to avoid catastrophic consequences. During China's 1958–1962 famine and during North Korea's mid-1990s famine, these countries did not import an adequate amount of food, leaving people to die (Song and Kwon 2017; Zhou 2017).

Since its independence, India has experienced several food emergencies. Each time, the Indian union government and the state governments worked together and acted quickly to bring the situation under control to minimise severe casualties. The public were also able to voice their demands to the government to help those in need (Drèze and Sen 1989).

The Great Famine in China during the period 1958–1962 was nationwide. During the famine, assistance from the government to help those in need was limited. The lack of action saw the famine last for several years. Similarly, in North Korea, during famines action to help those in need was lacking. Residents, especially those in rural areas, often had few alternatives to resort to for survival.

During emergencies, many countries have controlled food distribution, e.g., through food rationing, especially in urban areas. Japan and South Korea both resorted to rationing during food shortages but lifted the rationing soon after food supply improved. In Israel, during the 'austerity period,' food rationing was also used.

China and North Korea also used food rationing in the early 1950s to handle shortages. However, this became part of their food management policy (as the other side of the compulsory food procurement) for decades. In China, the 'unified sale system' did not get abolished until 1993. In North Korea, this practice still exists.

13.1.12 Handling food crisis information

Countries have also used different approaches to handling food crisis information. In some countries, news of occurrences of famine was not allowed to be publicised. During the 1958–1962 Great Famine in China, the media was not allowed to publicise the food crisis. Local cadres did not allow hungry people under their jurisdiction to travel to other areas to beg to prevent the news spreading (Yang 2008; Zhang 2013). The Chinese government also tried to hide the news from the international community (Yang 2008). In Indonesia, famines occurred frequently during the 1950s and 1960s. However, these famines were not reported in the local media because local authorities feared being blamed for poor administration (Van der Eng 2012). Similarly, in North Korea, the media were not allowed to report famines.

In contrast, famines have been well publicised in India. During several severe food crises, the public was informed of the scope and depth of the famines. The public made use of such news to put pressure on the governments to do more to assist those in need, even resorting to public protests. Drèze and Sen noted that many accounts of popular protests were reported in the columns of India's influential *Economic and Political Weekly* (Drèze and Sen 1989).

13.1.13 Food crisis prevention

Food-secure countries make great efforts to prevent food crises from happening. One key similarity is that the governments take responsibility for ensuring food security, and the right to food of each and every individual is protected under law. Under this approach, their governments have also innovatively implemented measures to sustain their high level of food security. In these countries, there is generally a designated government agency that is in charge of the maintenance of the country's food security.

Japan's preventive approaches are worth mentioning again. Since the 1970s, the Japanese government has been exercising a high level of diligence and a high degree of innovation in devising preventive measures to ensure the country's food security:

(i) **Helping foreign agricultural development to help Japan's own food imports**: Brazil's increased capacity to produce and export soybeans due to the assistance of the Japan International Cooperation Agency (JICA) notably increased global supply. This in turn significantly eased the upward pressure on the price of soybean imports to Japan due to China's increasing imports of soybeans.

(ii) **Inventing models to better understand global food demand–supply conditions**: Understanding and being able to forecast possible changes in global food demand and supply is important when a country has to use imports to manage its food supply and food security. As a consequence of the food crisis in the early 1970s, Japan devoted resources to developing a world food supply–demand model for the first time (MAFF 2009).

(iii) **Categorising food security emergencies**: Food security emergencies are of different severity. Handling emergencies without distinguishing the level of severity can be costly and less effective. Japan's categorisation of a food security emergency according to the extent of the severity is sensible and is most valuable for other countries to look into and follow.

In India, famine prevention policies have been put into place since its independence. The deployment of such policy measures has gone a long way in terms of reducing mortalities during various famines. The zero death rate in the 1972 Maharashtra Drought is well known for the successful utilisation of famine prevention policies. After the People's Republic of China was founded, there were no famine prevention measures in place. When the 1958–1962 Great Famine occurred, there were no measures to deploy. Progress has been made in China since the 1980s in terms of the preparedness for food emergencies, such as the building up of buffer stocks.

13.1.14 Attention to food security during normal times

When examining the food security practices of different countries, one puzzling phenomenon observed is their different approaches to food security during normal times. In more food-secure countries, people pay attention to food security all the time, no matter whether there are food-related events or not. In less food-secure countries, people pay a great deal of attention to food security issues when there are food-related events (such as when there are price hikes or supply shortages). However, when the events are over, attention to food security tends to wane.

13.2 Food insecurity: commonly believed myths

There have been myths about why lower levels of food security are persistent in some countries. For example, my country is poor in the natural resources needed to produce food; it is difficult to have a high level of food security because my country has too large a land mass and has too many people; my country is financially too poor; or, perhaps, there are social and cultural differences between my country and other countries.

The vast differences in food security status achieved by countries as presented in the previous chapters can be explained by none of such claims. Hence, all such claims must be dismissed.

13.2.1 Resource endowments

The argument and evidence presented in the previous section has already made it clear that being resource rich or poor cannot be held responsible for a country's high or low level of food security. Singapore has few resources to produce food. If resource endowment is held responsible, people in Singapore would have starved to death many times. Similarly, Israel and the Netherlands also have very limited resources. Yet, none of these countries suffer from food insecurity. Indeed, their level of food security is very high. In contrast, both Venezuela and Zimbabwe have great resource endowment, but many people in these countries are suffering from food shortage.

Another convincing example refers to China. Before the 1980s, the world's most populous nation suffered from serious food shortages. Yet, today food is abundant everywhere in China. Compared with the years before 1980, the country's resource endowment has not increased, rather, it has decreased notably due to encroachment as a result of industrialisation and urbanisation. On a per capita basis, the resource availability is much lower due to population increase.

13.2.2 Country and population size

The size of population or land mass is not a determining factor of a country's level of food security. China is the most populous country in the world. Before the 1980s, China had a smaller population size, but it suffered from chronic food shortages. Today, China's population has increased by a large margin compared to what it was before the 1980s (956 m in 1978 and 1395 m in 2018), yet its food security has dramatically improved.

Similarly, a country's lower level of food security cannot be attributed to the fact that it has a large population with limited land mass (thus higher population density). In Israel, much of the land mass is desert; hardly suitable for dwelling and farming. Population density is much higher if the desert is not counted. Yet, Israeli agricultural productivity is high and its food security level is high.

It is noted that while population does not determine food security status, by no means does this suggest that unchecked population growth is not an issue. Indeed, *ceteris paribus*, the greater the population, the greater the challenge for food security. This is especially so for those countries that are currently struggling to raise their level of food security.

Indeed, the correlation coefficient between population and GFSI is very small, being -0.003, which says that there is virtually no relationship between the two. Similarly, the correlation between a country's land mass and GFSI also has a very weak relationship, being only 0.141.

13.2.3 Economic conditions

A country's past economic conditions do not determine its level of food security. When Korea was divided in 1945, both countries had similar economic conditions (with North Korea being even better, Song and Kwon (2017)). Since then, North Korea has been struggling to feed its people, while South Korea quickly improved its food supply and has remained at a high level of food security. Similarly, by the end of the 1970s, China's economy was close to collapse. Yet, today China's food security level has much improved.

Experiences of other countries also confirm that poor economic conditions do not keep a country's food security level low and that good economic conditions do not guarantee a country a high level of food security forever. In 1965, when Singapore left Malaysia to become a separate nation, the country faced many uncertainties and was economically poor. In 2018, its GFSI was 85.9, the highest in the world (EIU 2015). Both Venezuela (which once was the wealthiest nation in Latin America) and Zimbabwe (which once was regarded as jewel of Africa) had high per capita incomes in the 1970s (Venezuela) and in the 1980s (Zimbabwe). Today both countries suffer from low and deteriorating food security.

Adequate institutions must be present that help transform a country's poor economy into a status of affluence and that are able to sustain a country's economic prosperity.

13.2.4 Cultural or social differences

Cultural traditions and social settings can affect food security to some extent; however, again, they are not determining factors. Before the separation in 1945, North Korea and South Korea were part of the same country, with the same cultural traditions and social settings. Today, while food availability is no longer an issue in South Korea, the number of undernourished people in North Korea is still large. China is another example where people, culture, and society remain the same, but the food security status has changed enormously. Before the 1980s, tens of millions of people died of hunger or suffered from chronic undernourishment. That is no longer the case today.

The above arguments strongly suggest that finding excuses for persistent low level of food security is not the way for a country to improve its food security. If a country wants to improve its food security, it can. The responsibility rests on the government of the country as we have earlier argued. A government is inept if it is unable to supply adequate food to its citizens.

Countries can learn from and help each other. Food-insecure countries can learn from the many successful practices used in food-secure countries. Many food-secure countries can, and actually are very willing to, help food-insecure countries. When food-insecure countries struggle to improve their food security, fundamental causes must be found elsewhere but not in the myths above. We believe that weak institutions and high levels of corruption are the most fundamental causes for the lack of, or persistent low levels of food security – a subject that will be further discussed in Chapter 14. In the section below, we summarise key factors that facilitate or retard food security.

13.3 Food security or insecurity: key influential factors

Examining and comparing country practices helped to reveal that (1) some factors contribute to improving a country's food security, (2) some deter the achievement of food security, and (3) some do not have an important influence.

Factors that facilitate a higher level of food security:

- Responsible governments with their officials accountable, operations efficient, and policy processes transparent.
- The presence of strong institutional arrangements that promote sustained economic development and equitable income distribution and redistribution.
- The presence of strong institutions that deter corruption.
- Laws and regulations that enable markets to function well.
- Adequate levels of investment in agricultural key infrastructure, agricultural research, development, extension, and education.

Factors that retard a country's food security:

- Forced collective farming.
- Compulsory delivery of foods from farmers to the government.
- No markets or heavily controlled markets.
- High incidence of poverty and severe income inequalities.
- Inadequate use of trade by a country.
- Disharmonious international trade institutions that disturb trade.

Factors that do not have determining influences on food security include:

- The size of a country's population and land mass.
- The availability of food production resources.
- Cultural traditions.
- Weather and climate conditions (e.g., Israel, desert climate).

A country can be expected to achieve a higher level of food security if:

- The government of the country is held accountable to its people.
- The government accepts that ensuring the food security of its citizens is its responsibility.
- Government operations are transparent and efficient.
- Corruption is seriously curbed.
- Markets are allowed to function more freely.
- Food producers are rendered financial rewards that are comparable to people working in other industries.

Review questions

1. What do countries with high levels of food security have in common?
2. What do food-insecure countries have in common?
3. Choose one country with a high level of food security as an example and highlight what you believe are most important things this country has done to sustain its high level of food security.
4. Choose one country with a very low level of food security and highlight what are most important things for this country to do to improve its food security.

Discussion questions

1. What did you used to think were the most important determinants of a country's food security? Did the study of Chapters 11–13 result in any modifications to your previous thoughts? Explain.
2. Having studied the previous chapters, do you still believe food-insecure countries have any excuses for not being able to achieve a higher level of food security? Why?
3. If your answer to Discussion Question 2 is no, and if your country of residence is food insecure, what do you think your country should do to improve its food security and to make it food secure for all citizens? Explain.
4. If your country of residence is very food secure, what is the biggest threat that may undermine your country's future food security? Why?

References

ABARES (Australian Bureau of Agricultural and Resource Economics and Sciences). (2014), *What India Wants: Analysis of India's Food Demand to 2050*, Australian Government, Canberra.

Drèze, J. and Sen, A. (1989), *Hunger and Public Action*, Clarendon Press, Oxford, UK.

EIU. (2015), *Democracy Index 2014: Democracy and Its Discontents*, EIU, London.

EIU (2018), Global Food Security Index 2018, https://foodsecurityindex.eiu.com/Resources, accessed 25 January 2019.

Endeweld, M. and Silber, J. (2017), 'On food security in Israel', in Zhou, Z.Y. and Wan, G.H. (eds), *Food Insecurity in Asia: Why Institutions Matter*, ADB Institute, Tokyo, Ch. 7, pp. 192–256.

Hirasawa, A. (2017), 'Food security measures in Japan since World War II', in Zhou, Z.Y. and Wan, G.H. (eds), *Food Insecurity in Asia: Why Institutions Matter*, ADB Institute, Tokyo, Ch. 5, pp. 89–138.

Hong, M.C., Zhou, Z.Y., and Wan, G.H. (2017), 'Food security in Pakistan, Bangladesh, Indonesia, and Singapore', in Zhou, Z.Y. and Wan, G.H. (eds), *Food Insecurity in Asia: Why Institutions Matter*, ADB Institute, Tokyo, Ch. 8, pp. 257–286.

IFPRI. (2018), 'Global Hunger Index, 2018 and earlier issues', www.globalhungerindex.org/download/all.html, accessed 15 January 2019.

Ministry of Agriculture, Forestry and Fishery (MAFF). (2009), *Points of Outlook for World Supply and Demand of Food in 2018*, MAFF, Tokyo.

Song, J.H. and Kwon, T.J. (2017), 'Food security in the Republic of Korea and the Democratic People's Republic of Korea: Why the difference?', in Zhou, Z.Y. and Wan, G.H. (eds), *Food Insecurity in Asia: Why Institutions Matter*, ADB Institute, Tokyo, Ch. 6, pp. 139–191.

Van der Eng, P. (2012), *All Lies? Famines in Sukarno's Indonesia, 1950s–1960s*, College of Asia and the Pacific, Australian National University, Tokyo, https://crawford.anu.edu.au/pdf/events/2012/20120916-Famine-in-Indonesia-1950s-60s.pdf (accessed 5 October 2015).

World Bank. (2019), 'World Bank data (GDP growth (annual %))', https://data.worldbank.org/indicator/NY.GDP.MKTP.KD.ZG?locations=ID&view=chart, accessed 14 March 2019.

Yang, J.S. (2008), *Tombstone: the Chinese Famine in the Sixties Documentary*, Cosmos Books, Hong Kong.

Zhang, D.J. (2013), 'Men eat men, dogs eat dogs, hungry rats chew bricks: My mother's personal experiences in the great famine in Xinyang, Henan Province', in *Those Years When Humans Turned to Cannibalism*, Laogai Research Foundation, Washington, DC. pp. 231–237.

Zhou, Z.Y. (2017), 'From food scarcity to food abundance: The people's Republic of China's quest for food security', in Zhou, Z.Y. and Wan, G.H. (eds), *Food Insecurity in Asia: Why Institutions Matter*, ADB Institute, Tokyo, Ch. 4, pp. 41–88.

Part 6

Achieving food security

What ultimately matters

Contents

Discussions in the previous chapters helped us to understand important factors that affect a country's food demand–supply balance and its food security. In particular, the country case studies in Part 5 enabled us to focus our attention on some of the more important factors that contribute positively and negatively to a country's food security. However, whether these factors are present and significant depends on the institutions of a country and their strength. In this final part of the book, we expand our discussion about the importance of institutions to a country's food security.

Chapter 14

Achieving food security

The importance of institutions

Summary

In earlier chapters, we have remarked that a country's institutions are very important to its food security. In this final chapter of the book, we provide further arguments to support our view. In Section 14.1, we first explain what we mean by institutions. In Section 14.2, we show how a nation's institutions may promote or curtail the forces that either contribute to or retard food security. Finally, in Section 14.3, we emphasise that, of all institutions, the most crucial one is a nation's political or governmental institutions; the one that significantly influences other institutions.

After studying this chapter, you should be able to:
- Form your own view as to which institution is the most important in determining a country's food security.
- Explain how, and through what kinds of channels, a country's food security is ultimately affected by this most important determinant.
- Develop a list of key do's and don'ts for a food-insecure country to improve its food security.

14.1 What are institutions?

'Institutions are systems of established and embedded social rules that structure social interactions' (Hodgson 2006). Ferrante (2006, p. 13) defines institution as 'a relatively stable and predictable arrangement among people that has emerged over time with the purpose of coordinating human interaction and behavior in ways that meet some social need'. There are other definitions; e.g., Landis (1998, p. 234) and Brinkerhoff et al. (2008, p. 77). The essence remains similar.

It is widely held that the following five primary institutions are found among all human groups (Landis 1998; Ferrante 2006; Brinkerhoff et al. 2008):

(1) *Family institutions*: determining kinship.
(2) *Political or governmental institutions*: providing for the legitimate use of power.
(3) *Economic institutions*: regulating the distribution of goods and services.
(4) *Educational institutions*: transmitting knowledge.
(5) *Religious institutions*: regulating our relation to the supernatural.

There have been extensive writings that emphasise the importance of institutions and thus the subsequent governance of societies on food security (e.g., Gibson 2012, Chapter 22; Anderson 2017). All the above five primary institutions can affect the food security of a country. However, we hold that two of them, political and economic institutions, are more important; subsequently, in the rest of the discussion, we will pay most attention to these two. In addition, we will also discuss the influence of educational institutions on a country's food security. Each of the five primary institutions is complex. Our discussion focuses on aspects that are most relevant to food security.

14.2 Institutions and food security

14.2.1 Political institutions

Political institutions (or governmental institutions) are the sets of rules and norms within which governments operate, including the right to vote, responsible government, and accountability. Governments create, enforce, and apply laws; mediate conflicts; and make policies on the economy and social systems. In a very general sense, political institutions include all those institutions concerned with the social structure of power.

Among all the political institutions, the most prominent one is the state. The state is the social structure that successfully claims a monopoly on the legitimate use of coercion and physical force within a territory (Brinkerhoff et al. 2008, p. 303). A variety of social structures can be devised to fulfil the functions of the state. Most basically, states are categorised into two basic political forms: authoritarian systems and democracies (Brinkerhoff et al. 2008, p. 304).

Authoritarian systems are political systems in which the leadership is not selected by the people and legally cannot be changed by the people. These political systems vary in the extent to which they attempt to control people's lives, the extent to which they use terror and coercion to maintain power, and the purposes for which they exercise control. Other names for authoritarian governments include, for example, dictatorships, military juntas, despotisms, monarchies, and theocracies. Some authoritarian governments, such as monarchies and theocracies, govern through traditional authority; others have no legitimate authority and rest their power almost exclusively on coercion.

Democracies can be direct or indirect. Direct democracy (or pure democracy) is a form of democracy in which people decide on policy initiatives directly. In an indirect democracy (or representative democracy), people vote for representatives who then enact policy initiatives.

Currently, most established democracies are representative democracies. Representative democracy also has different forms. All representative democracies, however, share two characteristics; (1) there are regular, constitutional procedures for changing government leaders, and (2) these leadership changes reflect the will of the majority.

In reality, government types adopted by countries are very complex. As a result, the proportion of power retained by the state and being bestowed on the people differs dramatically. At one extreme where the people have more power, majority rules prevail (government decisions are based on the will of the majority), there are free elections (to ensure public officials listen to the will of the people), individuals enjoy liberty (everyone has equal opportunity and has the freedom to act as he or she wishes as long as it does no harm to others), and multiple political parties are allowed to compete (by offering choices). At the other extreme where the people have no power at all, they have little ability to control many aspects of their life and they have little influence on the decisions about how their countries are run.

The country cases presented in Chapters 11 and 12 suggest that a country is likely to have a higher level of food security, and *vice versa*, when:

- A government is elected by the people following constitutional procedures.
- Public officials are held accountable to the people.
- Opposition parties are allowed to compete for government.
- Groups are allowed to exist.
- Individuals have the freedom to control their own life and are able to influence the decisions about how their countries are run.

Countries with the above traits are generally those with higher levels of democracy. Countries without are those with low levels of democracy.

If we examine a country's democracy index and its food security level compiled by The Economist Intelligence Unit (EIU) in greater depth, the relations between them are further reinforced: that is, democratic political systems are associated with higher food security and authoritarian political systems with lower food security. Based on democracy index (DI) values, the EIU place countries within one of the following four types of regime (EIU 2018):

(1) **Full democracies** (scores greater than 80): Countries in which not only basic political freedoms and civil liberties are respected, but which also tend to be underpinned by a political culture conducive to the flourishing of democracy. The functioning of government is satisfactory. Media are independent and diverse. There is an effective system of checks and balances. The judiciary is independent and judicial decisions are enforced. There are only limited problems in the functioning of democracies.

(2) **Flawed democracies** (scores greater than 60, and less than or equal to 80): These countries also have free and fair elections and, even if there are problems (such as infringements on media freedom), basic civil liberties are respected. However, there are significant weaknesses in other aspects of democracy, including problems in governance, an underdeveloped political culture and low levels of political participation.

(3) **Hybrid regimes** (scores greater than 40, and less than or equal to 60): Elections have substantial irregularities that often prevent them from being both free and fair. Government pressure on opposition parties and candidates may be common. Serious weaknesses are more prevalent than in flawed democracies – in political culture, functioning of

government, and political participation. Corruption tends to be widespread and the rule of law is weak. Civil society is weak. Typically, there is harassment of and pressure on journalists, and the judiciary is not independent.

(4) **Authoritarian regimes** (scores less than or equal to 40): In these states, state political pluralism is absent or heavily circumscribed. Many countries in this category are outright dictatorships. Some formal institutions of democracy may exist, but these have little substance. Elections, if they do occur, are not free and fair. There is disregard for abuses and infringements of civil liberties. Media are typically state-owned or controlled by groups connected to the ruling regime. There is repression of criticism of the government and pervasive censorship. There is no independent judiciary.

Based on the characteristics of each of the four types of regime and following the categorisation of two basic political forms (i.e., authoritarian systems and democracies (Brinkerhoff et al. 2008, p. 304)), 'authoritarian regimes' and 'hybrid regimes' can be regarded as authoritarian systems and 'flawed democracies' and 'full democracies' as democratic systems. The average of the Global Food Security Index (GFSI) by the EIU for all countries adopting authoritarian systems is 45.6 while that for all countries adopting democracies is 70.0. The latter is 24 points higher than the former (Table 14.1).

When the average is calculated for each of the four types of regime, it also trends upwards when the level of democracy increases. Fully democratic countries have an average of 80.7, 15.3 points higher than that of flawed democracies (65.4). The average GFSI of flawed democracies is in turn 23.8 points higher than that of hybrid regimes (41.6). There is an exception. The average of authoritarian regimes (48.6) is higher than that of hybrid regimes (41.6). Several oil-rich countries with low levels of democracy fall into the authoritarian regime category, raising its average. China (with a DI 31) and Russia (with a DI 31.7) also contributed to this skewedness.

At the two extremes, the average GFSI of countries with a DI in the top percentile (90–100, 9 countries) is 82 and that of countries with a DI in the bottom percentile (>10 to 20, 7 countries which includes an oil-rich country, Saudi Arabia) is 40.1 (the lowest DI is 14.3 which is Syria). The GFSI in the former (82) is more than double that (40.1) in the latter countries.

In countries where democratic political systems are adopted, their judicial systems tend to be more effective. This generally results in lower levels of corruption. In Table 14.2, the

Table 14.1 Relationships between food security and political systems (average GFSI under different political systems)

Political system	Authoritarian systems		Democracies	
Level of democracy	DI ≤ 60		DI > 60	
Average GFSI	45.6		70.0	
Types of regime	Authoritarian regimes	Hybrid regimes	Flawed democracies	Full democracies
Level of democracy	DI ≤ 40	40 < DI ≤ 60	60 < DI ≤ 80	DI > 80
Average GFSI	48.6	41.6	65.4	80.7

The calculation is based on the data contained in the 'Food security and related variables' table.

Table 14.2 Relationships between political systems, judicial effectiveness, and the level of corruption (average judicial effectiveness and the level of corruption under different political systems)

Political system	Authoritarian systems		Democracies	
Level of democracy	DI ≤ 60		DI > 60	
Judicial effectiveness	36.4		57.9	
Level of corruption	31.6		57.1	
Types of regime	Authoritarian regimes	Hybrid regimes	Flawed democracies	Full democracies
Level of democracy	DI ≤ 40	40 < DI ≤ 60	60 < DI ≤ 80	DI > 80
Judicial effectiveness	39.6	32.1	49.9	78.7
Level of corruption	31.8	31.4	48.5	79.7

Data for democracy index (DI) and the level of corruption (Corruption Perception Index, CPI) are from the 'Food security and related variables' table. For CPI, the higher the index, the lower the corruption. Data for judicial effectiveness are obtained from the Index of Economic Freedom. See Box 13.1 for details.

average score for judicial effectiveness for democratic political systems is 57.9 whereas it is 36.4 for authoritarian systems, a difference of 21.5 points. In terms of the level of corruption, it is much lower in democratic countries (57.1) but much higher in authoritarian countries (31.6), a difference of 25.5 points. These observations about judicial effectiveness and the level of corruption hold across the four types of regime (Table 14.2).

Recall that in Chapter 13, we argued that the level of a country's corruption has extremely important bearings on its food security. Among all the correlation coefficients between GFSI and other variables as presented in the 'Food security and related variables' table, the highest is between GFSI and corruption.

Corruption hurts food security in various ways. For example, when there is a lack of or no enforcement of food quality and safety regulations and legislation, low quality and unsafe food become widespread in the market (such as in China and India). Damage to the environment not only compromises the existing level of food security but also that of the future (such as in China, India and North Korea). Corruption leads to leaks and waste in the operation of public food distribution systems (as in India) and to mismanagement of buffer reserves that undermines a country's food security in case of emergency (as in China). The poor suffer the most from the reduced level of food security due to corruption. In corrupt systems, inequality and discrimination against the poor are common, trapping the poor in a vicious circle of poverty and chronic lack of economic access to food.

The lower the corruption, the higher the food security in a country. Compared to authoritarian systems, democratic political systems tend to have more effective judicial systems which help to curtail corruption and subsequently result in higher food security.

14.2.2 Economic institutions

Economic institutions are the sets of rules and norms that govern the production and distribution of goods and services, e.g., laws governing property rights and commercial transactions, court systems, and policy organisations such as regulatory agencies. In today's modern world, two broad types of economic institutions can be identified: capitalism and socialism.

Capitalism is an economic institution in which most wealth (land, capital, and labour) is private property and is used by its owners to maximise their own gain. It is based on competition. As an ideal, socialism is an economic institution in which most wealth is owned and managed by the workers and used for the collective good.

Generally, a capitalist economy is very productive. However, it has a major drawback concerning distribution. Thus, any capitalist systems must have some means of equitable distribution other than just relying on the market. Theoretically, socialism has a major advantage over capitalism in equitable distribution (though more often than not this has not been the case). However, it is generally accepted that socialism is less productive.

In reality, very few countries practise pure capitalism or socialism for two important reasons: (1) the need to balance production efficiency and equitable distribution and (2) the need to adapt to different political and natural environments. Hence, most countries adopt some kind of mixture of both capitalist and socialist economic structures. Most western developed economies are examples of mixed economies. Some typical socialist economies, such as China and Vietnam, have also become mixed economies. The major difference is the extent to which markets are allowed to operate freely. Compared to most western societies, there are relatively more constraints on market operations in previously socialist economies.

As a result, it makes sense to discuss the impact of economic institutions on a country's food security in terms of the extent to which markets are allowed to operate rather than in terms of whether a country's economic system is capitalism or socialism. This is the approach we adopt in the rest of our discussion.

The experiences from country case studies indicate that all those countries with high levels of food security allow markets to operate freely (e.g., Singapore and the Netherlands). Some countries' food security has notably improved when they loosened control over their food market (e.g., China and North Korea); and some countries' food security notably deteriorated when they introduced more controls over their food market (e.g., Venezuela and Zimbabwe).

Markets help society allocate scarce resources to meet the needs and desires of consumers. Human history so far has demonstrated that no other mechanisms other than markets can efficiently signal fluctuations in scarcity or abundance of resources and products. With regard to food security, markets are most efficient in coordinating resource allocation for food production and in balancing food supply and demand. To ensure the markets to work to their best, attention must be given to the following three aspects.

14.2.2.1 Ensuring comparable returns for workers in farming and non-farming industries

Those who produce food must be treated as equitably as those working in other industries so that food producers have adequate incentives to farm. It is not excusable to depress the returns of food producers so that consumers can 'afford' to buy food. As noted earlier, ensuring everyone, including those that farm, to have adequate access to food is the responsibility of the government. Farmers are workers like others in society and they should not be obliged to help the government to help others to buy 'cheaper' food. Japan and South Korea started to help their farmers to improve income soon after their economies took off.

14.2.2.2 Having institutions to protect private traders

The private sector plays a significant role in distributing food across regions and stabilising prices in the market through their arbitrage. Their participation in food trade eases the demand for public resources enormously. To help them to work to their best, private food traders must be treated the same as any other traders. Adequate institutions need to exist to protect their interests. Similarly, their misconduct must be penalised to deter further occurrences.

14.2.2.3 Trading responsibly and dealing amicably with other nations

Food trade is often essential when there are domestic shortages or surpluses. It is crucial that all countries contribute to the maintenance of a stable and harmonious international trade regime so that all nations can trade in peace and confidence. Using food trade as a weapon should not be contemplated. Whether importing or exporting, countries should be friendly towards each other. Without importers, food-exporting countries have no place to export; similarly, without exporters, food-importing countries cannot buy more food. Countries that have perpetual food surpluses or shortages should negotiate longer-term cooperation between themselves. This benefits not only them but also other countries that can better plan their trade in the world market.

It must be noted, however, markets may fail at tasks that society regards as important. One failure is its inability to take care of the less fortunate in society. Other major failures include neglect of the environment and lack of provision of public goods, which have negative impacts on a country's food security. Thus, governments have to intervene. In particular, it is the government's responsibility to ensure food supplies are readily and reliably available and accessible to the less fortunate in society.

Another concern about the market is related to the likely conduct of the private sector during food emergencies. It is often argued that during food emergencies, the private sector may not perform the way as the government would wish. This is possible. Hence, should food emergencies emerge, greater control over the markets may be justified (ADB 2017). Nonetheless, it can still be beneficial to allow the private sector to operate if food emergencies occur during peacetime. This is because the private sector can be much more efficient in moving food around, hence helping to reduce or avoid hunger-related casualties.

14.2.3 Educational institutions

Educational institutions are a central component of a society's cultural heritage and have profound effects on a society and its individuals. Their role is the systematic transmission of knowledge, skills, and values from one individual or group to another and from one generation to the next. In most societies there is little concern about how *knowledge and skills* are transferred. But, the role of educational institutions in transmitting values is sometimes problematic.

Those countries with higher levels of food security are societies in which people demonstrate a greater sense of fairness, justice and equality. People also care more about their environment. The opposite is also largely true in countries with lower levels of food security. In some of these countries, the upholding of fairness, justice, and equality by individuals is not always encouraged or promoted. Sometimes those who choose to uphold such values are harshly treated.

It may be argued that people in more food-secure countries behave the way they do due to their higher levels of food security. Whether better food security leads to greater fairness, justice, and equality, or the other way around, is certainly beyond the scope of the discussion here. However, what is certain is that a society with great fairness, justice, and equality will achieve better food security. As such, fostering the development of a sense of fairness, justice, and equality in citizens should be useful.

When the public is educated to have a greater sense of fairness, justice, and equality, individuals will more likely play a role in improving a society's food security in ways such as:

- Reducing or avoiding food waste.
- Reducing or avoiding pollution to the environment.
- Consuming responsibly to protect rare species.

- Eating healthily.
- Producing safe foods.
- Assisting the needy in society.

When everyone behaves in ways that contribute to better food security, many problems that negatively affect food security are mitigated. The behaviour of individuals can be affected by other people in society. That is why educational institutions matter. In societies where fairness, justice, and equality are not commonly practised, some reforms to their educational institutions should be useful. For example:

- Starting to teach school children to understand, accept, and practise the value of humanity through formal educational institutions.
- Upholding the value of humanity in wider society to influence individuals through informal institutions.
- Through both formal and informal educational institutions, fostering individuals' understanding of and desire for democracy. Encouraging individuals to demand personal rights and protect their own rights.

Some societies in today's world still do not encourage, but on the contrary, punish, people who practise fairness, justice, and equality. Governments in these societies refuse to educate their citizens to develop a sense of democracy. Some even choose to keep their citizens unaware of their rights or to scare them from exercising their rights. If you are reading this book and it happens that you live in that kind of society, would you think you are obliged to make your contribution to induce good changes in your society, no matter if what you do is big or small?

Are we born equal and endowed with basic human rights? The answer is yes. The following famous 55 words from the Declaration of Independence of the United States of America have enlightened and encouraged many people around the globe:

> We hold these Truths to be self-evident, that all Men are created equal, that they are endowed by their Creator with certain unalienable Rights, that among these are Life, Liberty, and the Pursuit of Happiness – That to secure these Rights, Governments are instituted among Men, deriving their just Powers from the Consent of the Governed, ...

'Unalienable Rights' are rights that we are unable to give up, even if we want to (Center for Civic Education 2019). However, it is a fact that many governments today still try desperately to deprive their citizens of such 'unalienable Rights'.

Without basic rights, societies can become dangerous. In such societies, truths are often hidden from the public. Individuals are brainwashed, fooled, or manipulated by their governments in order to protect the interests of the elite few. The lack of individual rights and the lack of courage to defend their basic rights also lead many of the public to know little or care little about, let alone support, fairness, justice, and equality. Societies of such individuals pose less threats to their ruling regimes. However, food security in such societies can hardly be ensured.

Taking China as an example. Over its thousands of years of history, some value systems have promoted the welfare of the people and some have promoted the welfare of elites. Since the late 1940s, many values reflecting the common humanity of the people have been abandoned due to numerous political campaigns under the communist government (Xin

1999, pp. 557–603; Yang 2008, Chapter 26; Dikötter 2013; Yang 2016). Consequently, the Great Famine started in late 1958, a very good crop year, and lasted for five years. The 1958–1962 Great Famine is the largest man-made catastrophe in the human history (Becker 1996; Yang 2008; Dikötter 2010). Today, the lack of fairness, justice and equality continues causing serious problems to society. Bad behaviours in the form of widespread corruption, adulteration of food, and pollution of the environment are persistent. In turn this has severely affected the country's food safety and security. Many of the public do not have safe food to eat. Reforms to its educational institutions would be necessary to encourage the re-emergence of a value system that recognises common humanity, equality, justice, fairness, and compassion.

14.3 The ultimate determinant of food security: governmental institutions

All of the five institutions as listed in Section 14.1 may mutually influence each other. While such mutual influence occurs easily in more democratic systems, as described above, it may be impossible in many authoritarian systems. In authoritarian systems, especially in dictatorship countries, governmental, or political institutions impose strict constraints on the operations of other institutions. The public have often been told what they are allowed or not allowed to do with little right to make their choices. Subsequently, the influence from other institutions on governmental or political institutions is often minimal or none. One example is that the communist government in China insists that it should have a say over the appointment of Catholic bishops, for which the Vatican made unusual compromises while China gave almost nothing (Bodeen 2018; Horowitz and Johnson 2018; Zen 2018).

As such, it is hard not to conclude that the ultimate determinant of a country's food security is its governmental institutions. Given that democratic political systems tend to provide stronger institutional guarantees for higher food security and that authoritarian systems are more often associated with lower food security, authoritarian societies need to endeavour to transform their governmental institutions to be more democratic.

It may be argued that democracy has many flaws and is not perfect. True. But:

> Many forms of Government have been tried, and will be tried in this world of sin and woe. No one pretends that democracy is perfect or all-wise. Indeed it has been said that democracy is the worst form of Government except for all those other forms that have been tried from time to time.
>
> (Churchill, House of Commons, 11 November 1947, in Churchill 2008, p. 574)

Hence, for the sake of achieving and sustaining a high level of food security:

- Countries around the globe where democracy is not strong need to transform their governmental institutions to be more democratic and bestow more power to the people.
- Countries that are more democratic should make continued efforts to sustain and make further improvements to their high level of democracy.
- Highly democratic countries have an obligation to assist other countries to become more democratic – this is the approach that is fundamental to improve global food security and to foster a more peaceful world!

> ## Review questions
>
> 1. Write down your own view as to which institution is the most important in determining a country's food security and elaborate why.
> 2. Write a 1000 word essay to explain how, and through what kinds of channels, a country's food security is ultimately affected by this most important determinant (as determined by you for Review Question 1).
> 3. For a food-insecure country to improve its food security, it may be the case that many changes need to be made. Choose a food-insecure country that you are familiar with. Develop a list of 10 actions that you believe the country should undertake. Discuss how each of the actions can help the country to improve its food security and rank the 10 actions in terms of urgency and importance.

References

ADB. (2017), *At a Glance: Food Insecurity in Asia, Why Institutions Matter*, Asian Development Bank Institute, Tokyo.

Anderson, J.R. (2017), 'Toward achieving food security in Asia: What can Asia learn from the global experience?', in Zhou, Z.Y. and Wan, G.H. (eds), *Food Insecurity in Asia: Why Institutions Matter*, ADB Institute, Tokyo, Ch. 11, pp. 345–366.

Becker, J. (1996), *Hungry Ghosts: China's Secret Famine*, John Murray, London.

Bodeen, C. (2018), 'Vatican agreement with China draws concerns amid crackdown', www.apnews.com/5b17e841053e4f46943bc30a9f24099e, accessed 19 April 2019.

Brinkerhoff, D.B., Whit, L.K., Ortega, S.T., and Weitz, R. (2008), *Essentials of Sociology*, 7th edn, Thomson Wadsworth, Belmont, CA.

Center for Civic Education. (2019), 'Terms to know', www.civiced.org/resources/curriculum/911-and-the-constitution/terms-to-know, accessed 17 April 2019.

Churchill, W. (2008), *Churchill by Himself: The Definitive Collection of Quotations*, by Winston Churchill (Author), Richard Langworth (Editor), PublicAffairs, New York.

Dikötter, F. (2010), *Mao's Great Famine: The History of China's Most Devastating Catastrophe, 1958–1962*, Walker, New York.

Dikötter, F. (2013), *The Tragedy of Liberation*, Bloomsbury Press, New York.

EIU (2018), Global Food Security Index 2018, https://foodsecurityindex.eiu.com/Resources, accessed 25 January 2019.

Ferrante, J. (2006), *Sociology: A Global Perspective*, 6th edn, Thomson Wadsworth, Belmont, CA.

Gibson, M. (2012), *The Feeding of Nations: Redefining Food Security for the 21st Century*, CRC Press, Boca Raton, FL.

Hodgson, G.M. (2006), 'What are institutions', *Journal of Economic Issues*, Vol. 40, pp. 1–25.

Horowitz, J. and Johnson, I. (2018), 'China and Vatican reach deal on appointment of bishops', www.nytimes.com/2018/09/22/world/asia/china-vatican-bishops.html, accessed 19 April 2019.

Landis, J.R. (1998), *Sociology: Concepts and Characteristics*, Wadsworth Publishing Company, Belmont, CA.

Xin, H.N. (1999), *Which Is the New China: Distinguishing between Right and Wrong in Modern Chinese History*, Blue Sky Publishing House, New York.

Yang, J.S. (2008), *Tombstone: The Chinese Famine in the Sixties Documentary*, Cosmos Books, Hong Kong.

Yang, J.S. (2016), *The Upside Down: The History of the Chinese Cultural Revolution*, Cosmos Books, Hong Kong.

Zen, J.Z.K. (2018), 'The Pope doesn't understand China', www.nytimes.com/2018/10/24/opinion/pope-china-vatican-church-catholics-bishops.html, accessed 19 April 2019.

Index

Page numbers in **bold** refer to information in tables; those in *italics* refer to figures; and page numbers which are underlined refer to information in boxes.

Printed in the United States
by Baker & Taylor Publisher Services